"Morrill deftly relates the Church's liturgical tradition and its revised liturgies for sickness, dying, and death to the paschal mystery of Christ and the biblical tradition of Jesus as Healer, as well as to contemporary perceptions of illness and death. With a solid theological foundation, the book is useful for pastoral ministers, lay and ordained, who wish to see how these liturgies relate to human life, personal and social, in [today's] world."

David N. Power, OMI
Professor Emeritus
The Catholic University of America

"Few theologians writing today can match the rare combination of Bruce Morrill's encyclopedic understanding of contemporary biblical and theological currents and his graceful writing style. Morrill's new book offers a compelling case for the importance of Christian worship for the healing of broken persons, a wounded church, and a world wracked by violence and despair. To read and ponder this volume is to wonder how Christianity ever got to the bizarre situation, so evident today, in which the ministry of healing is seen as an occasional element of the church's mission rather than the very heart of the good news it preaches."

Richard R. Gaillardetz
Murray/Bacik Professor of Catholic Studies
University of Toledo

"With all the gifts of a well-trained theologian, the skills of an experienced liturgist, and the heart of a pastor, Bruce Morrill has crafted a unique and compelling resource for ministers, medical professionals, and all concerned with the pastoral and ritual care of the sick and dying. Eschewing mechanistic and biomedical approaches to sickness, Morrill offers a holistic vision of healing rooted in an evocative vision of Jesus the healer in dialogue with the fully contextualized faith community. . . . This mind-expanding work is a must read for all those committed to the care and nourishment of the sick and dying."

Edward Foley, Capuchin
Director, Ecumenical Doctor of Ministry Program
Professor of Liturgy and Music
Catholic Theological Union

"Bruce Morrill's wide-ranging study . . . invites us to see healing as a helpful postmodern lens by which we can revisit liturgical renewal, eschatology, and, above all, salvation. The book is about the rites for the sick and the dying and the dead, but it is much more than that. In new and fresh ways, Morrill draws us into [realizing] that . . . the more the fullness of well-done symbolic ritual is experienced, the more people will be able to enter into and be transformed by their participation in the eucharist . . . and indeed, all the ecclesial actions which create and express our faith in the Triune God."

Dr. Lizette Larson-Miller
Graduate Theological Union
Berkeley, California

Bruce T. Morrill

Divine Worship and Human Healing

Liturgical Theology
at the Margins of Life and Death

A PUEBLO BOOK

Liturgical Press   Collegeville, Minnesota

www.litpress.org

A Pueblo Book published by Liturgical Press

Cover design by David Manahan, OSB. Illustration: *Christ Healing the Woman with an Issue of Blood*, 4th-century fresco, Catacomb of St. Marcellinus and St. Peter, Rome. Image from Scala/Art Resource, New York.

Library of Congress Cataloging-in-Publication Data

Morrill, Bruce T.
    Divine worship and human healing : liturgical theology at the margins of life and death.
        p.   cm.
    "A Pueblo book."
    Includes index.
    ISBN 978-0-8146-6217-5 (pbk.)
    1. Catholic Church—Liturgy.   2. Worship.   3. Healing—Religious aspects—Catholic church.   I. Title.

BX1970.M674   2009
264'.0208—dc22   2009019128

Contents

Preface

In this book I have attempted a systematic (biblical, historical, philosophical, social-scientific) study of current Roman Catholic sacramental rites of healing, specifically those serving the seriously ill, aged, and dying, as found in the *Pastoral Care of the Sick,* and the dead and bereaved, in the *Order of Christian Funerals.* Investigation of those rites comprises the book's third part, building upon an opening pair of chapters proposing a theology of liturgy and definition of healing (part 1), followed by part 2's chapters treating Scripture and tradition as fundamental sources for theologizing about these rites. Originally I had also envisioned a chapter on the Rite of Penance, cognizant of its fascinating history and the current impasse in its pastoral-theological interpretation and practice in late-modern American Catholicism. The naiveté with which I conceived the scope of this project in the early 2000s, however, gradually gave way to the realization that in the complex endeavor of writing academic theology attentive to pastoral practice (just as in teaching such matter), less is more. Surely, an exhaustive treatment of the sacraments and healing, drawing on early and medieval Christian sources, would entail equally close attention to baptism and the Eucharist. One need only consider the stellar example of Aquinas, whose medicinal concept of Christian sacrament built upon Augustine and other patristic authorities.

The present era of post–Vatican II liturgical reform has brought predominant, if not in many places nearly exclusive, concentration on the celebration of the Mass, a pattern in theology and practice that may be buckling under its own weight. Meanwhile, as regular Sunday Mass attendance continues to slide, many of the faithful voice discontent over their inability to find a connection between liturgy and life. Reasons for this malaise are numerous and complex, encompassing the social conditions of late-modernity and problems in church order. In the course of these present chapters I shall touch on many of these challenges, but with a shift of focus to individual and corporate experiences at the margins of life, situations of human need so urgent and real as to render the "liturgy and life" question obvious.

Over many years of pastoral ministry I have seen for myself how beautifully the reformed rites for the sick, dying, and deceased can serve the people of God in moments when life gets most real. I have, however, also experienced clerical and lay resistance—conscious and unconscious, informed and ignorant—to the symbolic and ritual dimensions of these sacraments, squandering the treasures of a tradition that discloses divine mystery as saving (healing) word written on human bodies of faith. My hope is that the following pages will serve as a scholarly ministry to word and sacrament through a greater pastoral proliferation of these rites and a more adequate academic theology of liturgy as the source and summit of the church's life.

Acknowledgments

Since beginning studies in college thirty years ago I have often read book prefaces in which the author admits (if not laments) how long it took to write a book and how supportive various persons were in the process. That certainly is the case here. On reflection I think the complexity of liturgy as a social, personal, and ecclesial reality requires time to organize and argue if the author wishes to avoid ending up an irrelevant textual positivist or the dreaded liturgical terrorist. I hope readers find the maturing of my thought over several years fruitful and the published result helpful. Encouragement that such might be the case has come from numerous opportunities afforded me to present and explore the topics comprising this book.

In my early years at Boston College the then-director of the Institute for Religious Education and Pastoral Ministry Claire Lowery and the Institute's associate director for academics Bud Horrel promoted my developing and teaching a new course I titled "Divine Worship and Human Healing." I learned so much in working on the history, theology, and practice of these rites with scores of committed, often insightful, students during the 1999, 2000, and 2003 offerings of the course. In 2002 I likewise enjoyed a year-long fellowship in the Center for Religion, Ethics, and Culture at the College of the Holy Cross, which included my teaching a course on suffering and healing. Boston College granted me a sabbatical in 2003–2004, during which I was able to make much headway on the research. In 2006 the university awarded an Undergraduate Research Fellowship for Mireille Azzi to compile and summarize helpful data on American perceptions of healing, health, and resurrection. My thanks to Mireille for doing a fine job. Seattle University's School of Ministry invited me to teach the course "Ritual and Healing" to an ecumenical student body in 2007.

I am grateful for having been afforded opportunities to present papers on this material at the annual meetings of the North American Academy of Liturgy, Catholic Theological Society of America, and Societas Liturgica, as well as plenary addresses at the 2007 conference of the Pappas Patristic Institute in Brookline, Massachusetts, and the 2008 congress of the Societas Oecumenica in Leuven, Belgium. I also benefitted from sharing various aspects of my biblical, anthropological, and liturgical research on healing at faculty colloquia at the Milltown Institute of Philosophy and Theology (Dublin, Ireland, where I enjoyed a semester-long research fellowship in 2006) and Seattle University (where a visiting professorship afforded me ample time for writing in 2007), as well as in a public lecture at the Institut Catholique de Paris in 2006. In that same year I gave a day-long workshop on the entire scope of these rites under the sponsorship of Creighton University at the Saint Joseph Educational Center, Des Moines, Iowa. I am likewise thankful to the board of directors of Forum 104, who invited me to give a lecture on Christ as healer at that Marist-sponsored pastoral center in Paris, France, in 2004. Most recently I enjoyed the invitation to present an evening on the rites for the sick, dying, and deceased in the 200 2009 Liturgy Lectures series at St. Ignatius Church in Chestnut Hill, Massachusetts. And in July 2009, I offered a two-day colloquium on this material at Jesuit Theological College, Melbourne, Australia.

Along the way portions of my research and writing have appeared as articles in the journals *Worship*, *Transversalités*, *Liturgical Ministry*, *Studia Liturgica*, and *Liturgy* (for which the Liturgical Conference holds the rights). Small portions of this book's second and third chapters are taken from Bruce T. Morrill, "Challenges and Resources for a Liturgical Theology of Healing: Roman Catholic Practice and Postmodern Theory" (in *Liturgy* 22, no. 3 [July, 2007)]: 13–20, © 2007). I wish to thank E. Byron (Ron) Anderson, president of the Liturgical Conference, for permission to reprint that material as well as for the opportunity to serve as guest editor for that thematic issue of *Liturgy*, titled "Healing and Anointing." I learned much from the several colleagues who contributed masterfully (and punctually) to an ecumenically broad treatment of the subject.

I extend thanks to colleagues, former students, and friends who read portions of this manuscript, providing helpful feedback and suggestions: Patricia Hayes; Denise Morency Gannon; Suzanne Dwinell; Vincent Miller; Lisa Cahill; Thomas Massaro, SJ; Mark Burke, SJ; William

Stempsey, SJ; Judith Kubicki, CSSF; Geza Pakot, SJ; Cindy Dobrzynski; Joe Duggan; Joshua Allen; and Ron Anderson. Any shortcomings in the text, of course, are fully my responsibility. Finally, a word of thanks to Peter Dwyer, Hans Christoffersen, and all the good staff at Liturgical Press.

Part 1

Liturgy and Healing

Chapter 1

Divine Worship: A Theology of the Liturgy

LITURGY AND HEALING?

At the outset of this project, a few years ago, when describing to various folks its basic scope, namely, a theological book on worship (or liturgy) and healing, I repeatedly found that the very eliding of the two terms would strike fellow believers as intriguing, if not provocative. People seemed ready to sense something promising, perhaps life-giving, in the association of Christian liturgical worship with healing, even as many were likewise quick to say that they had never thought of putting the two concepts together. One friend, a seminarian in his early thirties, pondering the working title of my book, was able to articulate why he found the combination of liturgy and healing baffling. Everything about his formation as a Catholic, he explained, seemed to convey that liturgical worship is a matter of celebration, not of healing. His statement strikes me as carrying two significantly telling implications: first, that the church's worship is a unidirectional action, something an assembly of believers does *for* or offers *to* God; and, second, that the positive nature of such celebration, as an expression of praise and thanksgiving, runs counter to the negative or distressful nature of a situation in which healing is needed. Pressing his reflections even a bit further, I found that the words "worship" and "liturgy" bear for him the narrow connotation of Eucharist or the Mass.[1]

The rites proposed here for theological inquiry—the Pastoral Care of the Sick: Rites of Anointing and Viaticum, and the Order of Christian Funerals—often do not come to fellow Catholics' minds in reference to the notion of liturgy. They tend, rather, to connote the ministration

[1] While my hope is that this book might be of service to Christians of all churches and communions, I write from my particular context of Roman Catholicism. I do this not for exclusivist, let alone triumphalistic, reasons; rather, the theory and practice of my theology, while ecumenically informed and committed, is situated in the Roman tradition.

of a certain sacrament *by* a priest *for* the benefit of an individual (and perhaps, in the case of the Order of Christian Funerals, not only for the deceased but also the loved ones). Would many Catholics think of "going to confession" as an act of worshiping God? Likewise, would they consider the "last rites" a celebration of liturgy? On the other hand, what does it mean for the church to say that healing occurs in anointing the sick or administering Viaticum to the dying? An elderly priest and veteran of decades of service in parishes, when occasionally inquiring about the progress of my project, has used these occasions to ascertain, "You are, of course, talking about *inner* healing, right?" This question-cum-statement points to what would generally be called the spiritual dimension of human existence. But it can also imply a problematic view of salvation (from the perspective of Christian anthropology), one in which the sacred element of human being is immaterial and set apart from the bodily. God is concerned about saving the soul. This tendency toward a rigid bifurcation of the "inner" and "outer" aspects of reality has riddled theological reflection on sacramental liturgy from early centuries onward. If the physical sign of a sacrament only functions to make believers think of a more real spiritual dimension, then why bother doing the sign at all, why not just *talk* about what is spiritually real? Such theory has also supported symbolically minimalist, clerically instrumentalist, and narrowly juridical practices of the sacraments—approaches to the rites that are utterly antithetical to their fundamentally liturgical (and thus, pastoral) nature.

My wager is that putting these two terms, "liturgy" and "healing," together affords an opportunity to pose good questions and arrive at theological and pastoral insights into Christian worship as an ecclesial activity both human and divine. A sense of wholeness is intrinsic to both divine worship and human healing, as will hopefully become clear in this first part of the book. An authentic and fruitful celebration of Christian liturgy (no matter which sacramental rite) is an encounter with the divine origin and final end of all creation, a real and nourishing foretaste of the fullness of life in the divine presence. An adequate grasp of what human healing entails is likewise holistic, a matter of arriving at a much-desired comprehensive sense of meaning that transforms a disorienting, alienating, and often life-threatening situation. This is one of the reasons the notion of healing is so attractive in our contemporary social (including religious) context. It bears relief and deliverance, the promise that pain, fragmentation, and indeed, judgment have passed. One of the primary Christian metaphors for what God has done for humanity in the person and mission of Jesus of Nazareth is salvation, a medicinal concept sharing the same Latin root, *salus* (health), with salve, a healing ointment.[2] This points to the profound conjunction of divine worship with human healing in the content and practice of Christian faith.[3]

These introductory remarks invite several questions about the nature of Christian liturgy, rite, and celebration, about the role of word and sacrament, about liturgy's symbolic and official dimensions in the context of the entire life of the church and its members. I will address such questions at different points, and in some cases repeatedly, over the course of the following chapters. Again, my hope is that attention to one thematic dimension of Christian faith and human experience, namely, healing, will prove an opportune angle for shedding light on the wider theology of the church's liturgy. Toward that end, an exposition of what is meant by Christian worship is necessary at the outset, one constructed already with a view toward the notion of healing (chapter 1). This will usher in a subsequent investigation into the connotations of healing in contemporary Catholic discourse (chapter 2).

THE NECESSITY OF LITURGY FOR CHRISTIAN FAITH

An adequate understanding of Christian liturgy, as part of the broader activity of divine worship, fundamentally depends on recognizing what God it entails. The content, shape, and scope of Christian worship is a function of the God who is both its subject and object, namely, the God of biblical revelation, the God of Jesus, the triune God revealed through his life, death, and resurrection.[4] This apparently innocent, if not seemingly tautological, statement is a stick of theological

---

[2] See Susan K. Wood, "The Paschal Mystery: The Intersection of Ecclesiology and Sacramental Theology in the Care of the Sick," in *Recovering the Riches of Anointing: A Study of the Sacrament of the Sick*, ed. Genevieve Glen, 5–7 (Collegeville, MN: Liturgical Press, 2002).

[3] The tradition's roots lie in what Daniel Harrington describes as "the New Testament vocabulary of salvation," which includes words and phrases that translate into English as "get well" and "restored to health." *The Gospel According to Matthew*, New Testament, vol. 1, Collegeville Bible Commentary, ed. Robert Karris (Collegeville, MN: Liturgical Press, 1983), 43.

[4] See Louis-Marie Chauvet, *The Sacraments: The Word of God at the Mercy of the Body* (Collegeville, MN: Liturgical Press, 2001), 155–61.

dynamite that, when ignited by the gift of faith in the Gospel, explodes conventional notions of divine worship, breaking down the barriers narrowly confining it to cultic activity, that is, to religious ritual. Put simply, worship of God is the entire Christian life, and thus the entire mission of the church in the world. Liturgy is the symbolic, ritual activity of the assembled church. It gives believers an explicit sense, a tangible presence, of the God hidden in their daily lives, as well as something of the specific content, through proclaiming and responding to Sacred Scripture, of what this ongoing human encounter with the divine is like. In the church's liturgy believers glorify God by participating more deeply in God's vision for the world and their place in it through word and sacrament.

Thus Christians have an irreducible need for the liturgy, the *ritual* worship they celebrate, even as those sacramental rites do not in themselves comprise the total practice of the faith, the single locus for knowing the one true God and his Son Jesus Christ. The Second Vatican Council's Constitution on the Liturgy articulates this dynamic of Christian ecclesial life by stating: "the liturgy is the summit toward which the activity of the Church is directed; at the same time it is the font from which all her power flows."[5] To speak in terms of source and summit indicates that liturgy is not the sole work of the church and its members but, rather, what guides and nourishes all the activity of their lives, creating the possibility of encountering God therein. Christian faith is a praxis in the world. Guided by the ever-beckoning summit revealed in the church's sacramental worship, believers traverse a terrain experienced as the *creation* in which God delights in granting them active roles and, moreover, gives them the living water (John 4:14), the bread of life (John 6:35), to sustain them in this co-creative, salvific process. To join in Holy Wisdom's ongoing work in the history of suffering and the promise of ultimate triumph for all Her creatures is to worship God.[6]

---

[5] *Sacrosanctum Concilium* (Constitution on the Sacred Liturgy), no. 10. *Vatican Council II: The Basic Sixteen Documents*, ed. Austin Flannery, OP, rev. ed. (Northport, NY: Costello Publications, 1996), 122.

[6] See Elizabeth A. Johnson, *She Who Is: The Mystery of God in Feminist Theological Discourse* (New York: Crossroad, 1992); and Jill Y. Crainshaw, *Wise and Discerning Hearts: An Introduction to Wisdom Liturgical Theology* (Collegeville, MN: Liturgical Press, 2001).

Over the past century and a half, theological scholarship and official church leadership have adopted the term "liturgy," based on the ancient Greek concept *leitourgia*, meaning "work of the people," to recover the proper, fundamental sense of worship found in Scripture and most ancient tradition.[7] In contrast to such terminology as going to (or hearing) Mass or assisting at Divine Offices or receiving a sacrament, the rhetoric of liturgy revitalizes a sense of the church's sacramental rites as the symbolic and, in the power of the Holy Spirit, very real participation of all the faithful in the divine-human *mystery* of creation and redemption.

THE MYSTERY OF FAITH:
GOD'S GLORY IN HUMANITY'S SALVATION

At the origins of Christianity, mystery was not about esoteric cults or secret rituals but rather the revelation that in the person and mission of the Jewish eschatological prophet Jesus of Nazareth, crucified by sin but raised to life by the Spirit, God's purpose for creation has been fulfilled. In Jesus, whom faith acclaims the Christ, God's boundless and merciful love for the suffering and the guilty *in the very context of human lives in history* has been definitively manifested. The mystery of Jesus' death and resurrection reveals that his words and actions, his total person and personal history, gave glory to God by saving and sanctifying people. In the Gospel of Luke, heavenly messengers proclaim at its outset the meaning of the entire life of Jesus that will follow:

"Glory to God in the highest,
and on earth peace to those on
    whom his favor rests." (2:14, NAB)[8]

As the Christian tradition developed over the next few centuries, this inseparable relationship of divine glorification and human salvation would pervade the sermons, catechetical instructions, and letters of the fathers of the church. By the close of the twentieth century, the

---

[7] Irénée Henri Dalmais and others, *Principles of the Liturgy*, ed. Aimé Georges Martimort, trans. Matthew O'Connell, The Church at Prayer, vol. 1 (Collegeville, MN: Liturgical Press, 1987), 7–9, 229–34.

[8] See Paul S. Minear, *To Heal and To Reveal* (New York: The Seabury Press, 1976), 50.

theologically and pastorally revitalizing potential of this recovery of ancient tradition became evident in the widespread quoting and paraphrasing of the words of St. Ireneaus, a second-century bishop of Lyons: "'For the glory of God is a living man, and the life of man consists in beholding God,' in the Spirit and through the Son, who is 'the visible of the Father.'"[9]

It is in this broader soteriological perspective that the meaning and purpose of Christian worship resides. The significance of the church's liturgical form of worship does not lie in its cultic personages, objects, actions, and locations in themselves but rather in their symbolic function in relation to the biblical narratives that have revealed the entire cosmos and human history as the arena of God's creative and redemptive activity. What Christian liturgy is about is entirely a function of the specific God it worships—not the distant, mechanistic God of modern deism, nor the idealistic Transcendent in our personal experiences and feelings, nor the divine One "up there" who only appears in certain sacred places "down here"—but the God who covenants, that is, the God who has committed himself in love to the deliverance of humanity in history. This covenantal origin and basis of biblical faith is the reason worship is not a unidirectional ritual action done by believers for God but rather a full-life response to the gracious love (*hesed*) and trustworthy faithfulness (*ʿemet*) God has shown the people,[10] compelling them to behave in kind:

> Hear, O Israel: The LORD is our God, the LORD alone. You shall love the LORD your God with all your heart, and with all your soul, and with all your might. (Deut 6:4-5; cf. Matt 22:37)

> This is the greatest and first commandment. And a second is like it: "You shall love your neighbor as yourself." (Matt 22:38-39; cf. Lev 19:18)

The Christian Church reads the Jewish biblical texts, the First (or Old) Testament, as a covenant history, focused on the climactic events of the Exodus and Mount Sinai but founded in the promises to Abraham

---

[9] *Against Heresies* 4.20.7. Quoted in Douglas Farrow, *Ascension and Ecclesia: On the Significance of the Doctrine of the Ascension for Ecclesiology and Christian Cosmology* (Grand Rapids, MI: W. B. Eerdmans , 1999), 66.

[10] See Edward Schillebeeckx, *Christ: The Experience of Jesus as Lord*, trans. John Bowden (New York: Crossroad, 1981), 93–100.

and the patriarchs and revitalized in the symbolic words and deeds of Isaiah, Jeremiah, and the other prophets. God chose Israel to be the recipients of this covenantal heritage, receiving through it the mission to be light to the nations (Isa 42:6; 49:3, 6). The content of the covenant and the character of the God it reveals comprise the reason that sacred feasts and sacrifices are only pleasing if offered by a people actively striving for justice, mercy, and peace (Amos 5:21-24; Mic 6:6-8).[11] The need for such justice and peace, nonetheless, points to their absence and thus to the evil and suffering with which human history is riddled in the presence of the all-powerful and all-loving, but thereby totally Other, God.

THE PASCHAL MYSTERY PERSONIFIED: COVENANTAL LIFE IN CHRIST JESUS

The testament of the first believers in Jesus as the Christ is that God's covenantal promise of deliverance to Israel was taken up and transformed in the person, mission, and message of Jesus, with his death and resurrection constituting the climactic moment of covenant history. The gospels present Jesus as an eschatological prophet who claimed that Israel's longed-for, final deliverance from exile, the reign of God, was coming about through his words and actions.[12] The entire New Testament witnesses to the unexpected shape that God's faithfulness to Jesus took, raising him bodily from death into a new form of life, revealing his singular divine origin and end as the firstborn of a new creation that will one day be realized for all. This is the mystery revealed at the heart of Christian faith, the revelation that the strength of death is past and that the promised covenant of love written on human hearts is underway. Jesus enacted this greatest of his parabolic actions[13] at the most important point in the Jewish cycle of sacrificial worship, the Passover, the memorial of deliverance from slavery and oppression that bore the promise that God would yet redeem his people definitively. In his mission and death Jesus took on both the

[11] See Frederick C. Holmgren, "Priests and Prophets: Spirituality and Social Conscience," *Worship* 79, no. 4 (July 2005): 304–16.

[12] My thought here has been greatly shaped by N. T. Wright's series, Christian Origins and the Question of God, vols. 2 and 3: *Jesus and the Victory of God* (Minneapolis: Fortress Press, 1996), and *The Resurrection of the Son of God* (Minneapolis: Fortress Press, 2003), respectively.

[13] See Minear, *To Heal and To Reveal*, 24.

nation's plight and the form their obedience to the covenant needed to take. In raising Jesus to life after he lay dead, God revealed a new, unexpected outcome for his Passover, the first installment of the resurrection for all humanity.

The mystery of Christian faith, then, is paschal (that is, pertaining to Passover and more specifically to Jesus himself as the definitive sacrifice[14]). The specific content of this paschal mystery needs to be repeatedly expounded through word and sacrament lest we lose sight of what God we are worshiping: the God who is for humanity, for the happiness and peace of all people; the God who is known in those who join in that activity; the God whose images are not sought in static objects but in actions. Liturgical theology, then, seeks to comprehend the vision and practice of Christian faith not in religious terms of sacred versus profane but rather of mystery disclosed in history: "In doing [the liturgy], the Church pursues its most essential purpose, which is to ensure the active presence of divine realities under the conditions of our present life—and that is what 'mystery' means."[15] The paschal mystery likewise bears the pain of that which it does not disclose, the inexplicable wisdom in God's still waiting to deliver all the suffering into "a new heavens and a new earth" (2 Pet 3:13; Rev 21:1).[16]

In Jesus the categories of sacred and profane break down. Christian liturgy is not a matter of taking believers out of the world for a moment but rather of immersing them more deeply in the mystery of God's paradoxical purpose for it over time.[17] Sin is not what happens in the profane world, while perfection can be found in some sacred, separate precinct. Rather than the religious division of sacred and profane, the categories shaping Christianity are past, present,

[14] See Robert J. Daly, "Sacrifice Unveiled and Sacrifice Revisited: Trinitarian and Liturgical Perspectives," *Theological Studies* 64 (2003): 24–42.

[15] Dalmais, *Principles of the Liturgy*, 266.

[16] In contrast to what he describes as Christian theology's long trivialization of suffering as an eschatological question, along with its pursuit of "too many clever answers to such questions as Who is God? And Where is God?" Johann Baptist Metz argues compellingly for a turn "to the primordial biblical question, What is God waiting for?" *A Passion for God: The Mystical-Political Dimension of Christianity*, ed. and trans. J. Matthew Ashley (New York: Paulist Press, 1998), 58; see also 84.

[17] See Gustavo Gutiérrez, *The Power of the Poor in History*, trans. Robert R. Barr (Maryknoll, NY: Orbis Press, 1983), 31–33.

and future.[18] The key to Christian faith, and thus the meaning and purpose of its liturgy, is time. The mutually informing ritual activity of word and sacrament draws those present in the church's liturgical assembly into the memory of God's actions and promises of human redemption, transforming them, through the power of the Holy Spirit, into a foretaste of their promised fulfillment, when God will be all in all (see 1 Cor 15:28). We live in an utterly paradoxical time between the definitive inauguration of God's reign in the person of Jesus and the final realization of the whole creation's peaceful, just, and loving existence in God's presence. The two primary sacramental rites of the church, baptism and Eucharist, reveal this paradoxical divine world-view, initiating and sustaining believers' participation or communion (*koinonia*) therein. The church celebrates the paschal mystery of Christ liturgically so that this mystery might be writ large across our lives, embracing the "joys and hopes, the grief and anguish of the people of our time, especially of those who are poor or afflicted."[19]

CHRISTIAN BAPTISM:
ENTRY INTO THE PRACTICAL LOVE OF GOD

Perhaps the most prominent metaphor for our entrance into the life of faith is St. Paul's description of baptism as our being buried with Christ in death, "so that, just as Christ was raised from the dead by the glory of the Father, so we too might walk in newness of life" (Rom 6:4, NRSV). Having no sooner made this indicative proclamation of our death to sin in Christ, Paul immediately goes on to exhort believers

---

[18] See Alexander Schmemann, *Introduction to Liturgical Theology*, trans. Asheleigh Moorhouse (Crestwood, NY: St. Vladimir's Seminary Press, 1966, 1986), 70–81, 183–84; and Bruce T. Morrill, *Anamnesis as Dangerous Memory: Political and Liturgical Theology in Dialogue* (Collegeville, MN: Liturgical Press, 2000), 87–115.

[19] *Gaudium et Spes* (Pastoral Constitution on the Church in the Modern World), no. 1. Flannery, *Vatican Council II*, 163. Building on Paul's proclamation of a new social order in Galatians 3:28 and the Gospel's eschatological vision of the reign of God, Bernard Cooke argues: "Such a global sharing of the Spirit of God will not be a specifically religious phenomenon but something as broad as human life worldwide. If and when it occurs, it will make clear that Christianity was not meant to be a religion in any narrow sense of the word but rather the catalyst for a whole new way of being human." *Power and the Spirit of God: Toward an Experience-Based Pneumatology* (New York: Oxford University Press, 2004), 27.

not to allow sin to have any power over us (6:14). This is but one way of describing the mystery that *is* the Christian life of faith, a life patterned on Christ's God-given mission of redemptive solidarity with a suffering world. Paul's reference to baptism is part of the larger argument he mounts in the first eight chapters of Romans, his effort to explain Christian life as a passing over from law to freedom, sin to Spirit, Adam to Christ—all of this so that humanity might walk (a biblical metaphor for ethical action) in a new way, a way through this world toward what awaits all in the final resurrection.

Likewise, although written in an obviously different mystical vein, the Johannine discourse on being born from above, or born again (John 3:3), is nonetheless about giving glory to God in the medium of human history. To look upon the one who was "lifted up" (on the cross) and to see in him the Son of Man (3:14) is to recognize in the torture, trial, and execution of Jesus the ultimate revelation of who God is, namely, the Creator so in love with the world that he gives his only son so that all might live (3:16). The First Letter of John teaches that living out such love now in community is the medium for glorifying God, a matter of "walk[ing] in the light as he himself is in the light" (1 John 1:7), that is, a matter of mutual service and charity. Through such ecclesial fellowship (*koinonia*), believers share in the very fellowship of the Father and his Son (1:3). Such is the life of those born of water and Spirit (John 3:5).

Jean-Marie-Roger Tillard finds in the First Letter of Peter one of the most important New Testament expositions of daily life in the Christian community as the practical form of communion that renders praise to God. Crucial for Tillard is this letter's rhetoric of God's people as the "priestly community of the king," "living stones . . . built into a spiritual house," a "holy priestly community worthy of offering through Jesus Christ spiritual sacrifices pleasing to God," who "proclaim the mighty acts of the one who called [them] out of darkness into God's marvelous light" (1 Pet 2:9-10[20]). Given the letter's teaching that mutual love and service are the fruits of the baptismal seed (1:23), glorifying God through Christ Jesus (4:10-11), Tillard explains the sense in which spiritual sacrifices (*pneumatikai thusiai*) worship God:

---

[20] The translation of 1 Peter 2 is Tillard's own. See Jean-Marie-Roger Tillard, *Flesh of the Church, Flesh of Christ: At the Source of the Ecclesiology of Communion*, trans. Madeleine Beaumont (Collegeville, MN: Liturgical Press, 2001), 22n25.

The context indicates that these sacrifices are not primarily liturgical cultic actions but the existential acts of the holy life of this community. Its communion comes fundamentally from the Spirit, and it serves God in the daily actions of its members. . . . To become holy 'in all [one's] conduct' (1:15) means to place oneself, with faith and courage, within the network of relationships based on baptism which together make of the community, not a collection of persons seeking their own sanctification, but the unique and indivisible 'royal priesthood,' the 'priestly community of the king,' the 'spiritual house' of God. In the holiness of all those whom the gospel has engendered 'anew' (1:23; see 2:2), individual and community cannot be separated . . . the individual is a living stone of the 'spiritual house' (2:5) only by remaining bonded to others and acting with the awareness of this bond.[21]

In an inversion of the sacred-profane dichotomy, spiritual sacrifice is primarily about ethical, existential living.[22] Spiritual sacrifice is a practical love shared not only among believers but also extended to non-Christians, giving them a sense of God's love and even assuring them that, in the end, they too will "glorify God when he comes to judge" (1 Pet 2:12).

THE EUCHARIST: SUSTAINING COMMUNION IN THE SELF-GIVING LIFE OF GOD

The Eucharist is what both reveals and sustains such interpersonal and social love as a communion in the very life of God. The eucharistic assembly's celebration of word and sacrament reveals the nature of these actions and the human bonds they form as coming from God through the Spirit of Jesus while also gathering them up in a (ritual) sacrifice of praise and thanksgiving to God. In the liturgical sacrifice believers enjoy a multifold presence of Christ,[23] symbolically made real

---

[21] Ibid., 22–23.

[22] Louis-Marie Chauvet has captured the upshot of this sacramental worldview: "Faithful to its biblical roots, ecclesial tradition has attempted to discern what is most 'spiritual' in God on the basis of what is most 'corporeal' in us. This is especially the case in the liturgy. But it is more widely the case in the whole of *Church Life*." *Symbol and Sacrament: A Sacramental Reinterpretation of Christian Existence*, trans. Patrick Madigan and Madeleine Beaumont (Collegeville, MN: Liturgical Press, 1995), 523.

[23] See *Sacrosanctum Concilium*, no. 7; Peter Fink, *Worship: Praying the Sacraments* (Washington, DC: Pastoral Press, 1991), 81–93; and Bernard Cooke, *Sacraments and Sacramentality*, rev. ed. (Mystic, CT: Twenty-Third Publications, 1994), 94–107.

through the power of the Holy Spirit, that nourishes their spirits and bodies. Gathering to remember with wonder the depth of God's love for all creation revealed in the life mission, death, resurrection, and ascension of Jesus, the assembly's doxological response of thanksgiving constitutes "a distinctive element of Christian identity."[24] As remembrance (*anamnesis*) of the executed and risen Jesus, the Eucharist is not only a ritual but also a prophetic action, for the event it commemorates, Jesus' supper on the eve of his death, was forward-looking. What Jesus did with the bread and cup found its meaning proleptically in the total gift of himself he would offer the next day but also in the sacramental (real symbolic) presence of himself it would give to his followers thereafter. This sustains them as they carry on his mission and ensures their future sharing in the ultimate banquet of the kingdom.

Xavier Léon-Dufour perceives the intermediate time between the "night when he was betrayed" (1 Cor 11:23) and the promised day of the kingdom's fulfillment (see Luke 22:14) as the period of the church's sacramental meal:

> What Jesus does [at the Last Supper], then, he does in anticipation: not only his 'dying' (which he anticipates in order to bring out its meaning and to express his free consent to it), but also the giving of his presence in symbols. Through the commemoration which the disciples will make of him, this 'real' presence of Jesus will light up, from within, the night of the passion that lasts through the centuries in countless sufferings of human beings and their real 'dying.' The liturgical action will enable believers to express ever anew their confidence that love has conquered death.[25]

The mystical activity of the Eucharist is essential to the life of the church, for it reveals over and again the presence of God, seen in the light of Christ, in the situations of life that would seem to be the most godless, the places where God is experienced as absent, the darkness of suffering and death. The Eucharist not only consoles believers with the promise of Christ's presence but also compels them to discover him in the practical, ethical activity of their lives, wherein they embrace his mission and know something of the paschal mystery that

[24] Tillard, *Flesh of the Church, Flesh of Christ*, 117.

[25] Xavier Léon-Dufour, *Sharing the Eucharistic Bread: The Witness of the New Testament*, trans. Matthew O'Connell (New York: Paulist Press, 1987), 72. See also Morrill, *Anamnesis as Dangerous Memory*, 180–86.

is still painfully yet positively passing through time. By proclaiming and responding to the merciful loving presence and trustworthy faithfulness of God, members of the church abide in a joy founded in their participation in the kenotic (self-emptying) life of God. As Léon-Dufour intimates, moreover, the company of those participating in this great divine-human mystery is not confined to the sum total of those who liturgically celebrate the Eucharist nor, as Tillard demonstrates through Scripture and tradition, is the body of the church merely the sum total of its members.[26] The reality of the church in the larger paschal mystery of the world's suffering and salvation is itself a mystical communion with the God whose cause is the ultimate happiness and peace (wholeness) of all humanity. Christians know something of that salvation, that healing and wholeness, as they help one another to shape their lives by this mystery.[27]

SACRAMENTAL LITURGY: MAKING KNOWN THE CHRIST HIDDEN YET PRESENT IN OUR LIVES

To use the now classic language made famous by the early work of Edward Schillebeeckx, we can say that Christ, church, and sacramental liturgy constitute encounters with God in the bodily, historical medium of human lives.[28] The Jesus who revealed through his entire mission of teaching and healing unto death the very presence of God in his person-body has ascended to God's right hand and thus we can see him no longer. To say that the church, through the mission of the Holy Spirit, is now the sacrament of Jesus—the bodily presence of this divine-human person in history—is really an affirmation that every member of that body, every living stone bonded into that temple, is also a sacrament of Christ.

Is it too bold to assert that, in the end, it is the people who are the sacraments? Given the paradoxical, in-between state of believers' existence—having been freed from death (and its instrument, sin) in baptism yet needing still to struggle, despite repeated failure, against sin's influence—this may well seem an overstatement. If we focus on any given individual and the story of his or her life, the history of his or her decisions and actions, an unqualified manifestation of divinity

---

[26] See Tillard, *Flesh of the Church, Flesh of Christ*, 50–51, 58–61.

[27] See Schillebeeckx, *Christ: The Experience of Jesus as Lord*, 631–44.

[28] See Edward Schillebeeckx, *Christ the Sacrament of the Encounter with God* (New York: Sheed and Ward, 1963).

is certainly doubtful. At precisely this point the importance, indeed the necessity, of the third element in Schillebeeckx's formula, namely, the church's liturgical sacraments, becomes evident.[29] For when the church assembles under the leadership of an ordained minister in celebration of word and sacrament, that assembly becomes something far greater than the sum of the individuals; but also in their sacramental participation in the paschal mystery, each member comes to know something of his or her own self as the bodily locus, the living parable, of God's love for the world. The ritual action of believers together in liturgy, that is, their engagement of powerful symbols of evangelical faith, makes possible an experiential knowledge of themselves and our world as God sees us.

While baptism initiates people into life in the Spirit of Christ and then the Eucharist nourishes them throughout that journey of life toward the fullness of the kingdom,[30] a complement of other official sacramental rites reveal the presence and action of the Spirit of Christ in particular believers at specific moments in the story of their faith lives. It is not overstating the case to say that, for example, *in the celebration* of the sacrament of anointing, the sick person himself or herself

---

[29] Bernard Cooke has made a singular American appropriation of and contribution to this crucial trajectory in theology: "[A] fundamental principle of sacramental liturgy, particularly eucharistic liturgies [is this]: The most important sacramental symbol, the most significant reality, in any liturgy is the people who perform the action." *Sacraments and Sacramentality*, 102. Elsewhere, Cooke elaborates on the significance of this tenet for liturgical worship: "Apart from bodiliness we could not communicate with one another and so form community, either as humans or as Christians. Rituals capable of expressing and shaping our faith identity as body of Christ would be impossible, for the fundamental sacramental symbol in all Christian rituals is the observable assembly." In *Bodies of Worship: Explorations in Theory and Practice*, ed. Bruce T. Morrill, 48 (Collegeville, MN: Liturgical Press, 1999).

[30] My own position on the theologically and pastorally troubled sacrament of confirmation is that it functions as the sacramental-liturgical bridge leading the fledgling Christian from the font of baptism to the table of the Eucharist. The explicit, symbolically real invocation of the Spirit of Christ upon the baptized person is an act of epiclesis that initiates him or her for participation in the eucharistic prayer, making him or her an eligible recipient of the Spirit each time it is invoked upon *the assembled members of the church*, along with the bread and wine they will share as Christ's Body and Blood. See Bruce T. Morrill, "The Meaning of Confirmation: Searching with the Bishop, the Liturgy and the Holy Spirit," *Liturgical Ministry* 9 (2000): 49–62.

becomes a special sacramental presence to that community of faith. Raised up amidst the assembly in the context of proclaiming and responding to the word of God, the person who is the subject of the sacramental anointing becomes in that event the tangible, bodily-human manifestation of God's merciful love and steadfast faithfulness. For this to happen, however, the rite must be approached not as an instrumental ministration of some quantifiable thing (the unfortunate, long-regnant view of sacramental grace), as if Christ through his vicars were dispensing something of utilitarian value that can "get results" (in this case, the cure of a disease). As Chauvet has so beautifully argued, what happens in the divine-human encounter of Christian liturgy is rather more a matter of a gift exchange, wherein the value of the person, the worth of his or her being as a further gift to the community, is primarily what is being celebrated and thus built up.[31] Sacramental celebration is not so much about *having* something at the conclusion that one did not have before but rather about *being* more deeply aware of oneself and others as the very site of the loving faithfulness and gracious mercy of God, in whatever condition we find ourselves.

All of this, of course, can only be so if the sacramental ritual in question is approached as paschal celebration, as liturgy. "Paschal" indicates that in liturgy we seek a deeper affective knowledge of ourselves as part of the history of the God revealed in Jesus. The ultimate revelation of this God who is for humanity in the death and resurrection of Jesus requires awareness of at least two key factors about the life of faith: first, that it is founded upon a paradoxical story, the inexplicable revelation of God as Father, Son, and Spirit *through* the events of the life, death, and glorification of Jesus; and therefore, second, the irreducibly narrative structure of this revelation.[32] The scandal of the Gospel, of the crucified God it reveals, can never be worked into a total systematic theory or a complete metaphysical explanation. This

---

[31] See Chauvet, *The Sacraments*, 117–27; *Symbol and Sacrament*, 99–124, 266–89.

[32] "By [paschal mystery] the church has intended to focus on the paradox of God's disclosure and hiddenness in Christ and, likewise, the hiddenness of human lives with Christ in God. . . . Here is mystery that requires form: word and act patterned after the witness to what Jesus said and did. The mystery is not a puzzle to be solved, but a liberating power of life to be received." Don E. Saliers, *Worship as Theology: Foretaste of Glory Divine* (Nashville: Abingdon Press, 1994), 193.

is why Sacred Scripture is so fundamental to the content and practice of Christian faith, why tradition, including sacramental liturgy, always proceeds on the basis of and in obedience to the biblical word of God.[33] Thus is the liturgy of the church essentially a matter of word and sacrament, of myth (formative, revelatory story) and symbolic ritual, which draws people into the creative world of God's redemptive imagination, requiring that they, as participants, put to work the range of symbolic capabilities (narrative, art, architectural design, music, oratory, choreographed movement) with which God has endowed them. This is why ritual celebration is an essential, not an auxiliary, dimension of the church's sacraments.

THE LITURGICAL-THEOLOGICAL PROBLEM AND NEED FOR REFORM

Perhaps the import of this argument for sacramental liturgy as essentially paschal celebration can become more evident by expounding what it seeks to correct. Despite the risk of reducing the complexities of history and social (ecclesial) constructions to caricatures, one can nonetheless observe the sorts of theological and pastoral problems that both necessitated the Second Vatican Council's mandate for liturgical reform and renewal, and remain daunting challenges forty years later. These are intricately intertwined and therefore not easily ordered in terms of causal priorities among them.[34] Still, one might perceive the primary poles of hobbled Catholic sacramental practice to be an extremely, if not exclusively, metaphysical explanation of their purpose and function and an excessive clericalism in the understanding of their ministration—all to the detriment of their pastoral, humanly beneficial efficacy.

[33] See Gordon Lathrop, *Holy Ground: A Liturgical Cosmology* (Minneapolis: Fortress Press, 2003), 25–50. See also, *Lectionary for Mass: Introduction* (1997), no. 3; and *Sacrosanctum Concilium*, nos. 24, 35, 51.

[34] One helpful historical-theoretical template for studying this problem is Bernard J. Cooke's argument that beginning in the fourth century the originally powerful symbolic immediacy of God's personal presence in sacramental liturgy became increasingly eviscerated by developments in philosophical theology, hierarchical structures of authority, and the adoption of imperial ritual forms. Those three problems, according to Cooke, remain the challenge for contemporary liturgical renewal. See *The Distancing of God: The Ambiguity of Symbol in History and Theology* (Minneapolis: Fortress Press, 1990), 37–56.

The scholastic turn to metaphysics to explain the supernatural reality of the Eucharist and other sacraments of the church in the Middle Ages cannot but be appreciated as one attempt to understand what might be called the grace dimension of salvation, the divine presence and action in human lives that exceeds all human phenomena *and* effort. The historical problem, however, has been that, whereas the various medieval theologians had applied the abstract categories of matter and form, cause and effect, substance and accident, to the concrete sacramental practices of their day, the subsequent manual (schoolbook) theology of the sacraments ultimately reversed the relationship between (pastoral) practice and (theological) theory. The latter came to shape the former. Such formulas as instrumental cause and principal effect came to reduce each of the seven official sacraments to narrowly defined objectives and results focused upon the minimum of material and formulary needed to assure, canonically, that the imperceptible dispensation of grace had indeed occurred.

Crucial to the orchestration of the matter and form of a sacrament, moreover, was the authority of the priest, whose ecclesially invested power assured the transmission of grace. The sacramental order of ministry is of great value and indeed necessity for the continuance of apostolic tradition in the church through history. The problem, however, became (and far too often remains) the all but exclusive identity of the church with the priest to the neglect of Christ's liturgical presence in the active participation of all the faithful assembled.[35] The historical result, to this day, has been a persistent dualism in the church's sacramental practice. What really matters about a sacrament in any given case is that a priest use the officially sanctioned materials and words that guarantee the dispensation of grace, which the (canonically eligible) faithful receive. That constitutes the sacred, the really holy, content and purpose of the sacrament. All the rest of the ceremonial (music, environment, perhaps even the proclamation of the Word) is ancillary, a question of what might prove secondarily beneficial to people's experience of the rite.

---

[35] Thus has the Second Vatican Council's identification of the full, conscious, active participation of all as the key priority in the restoration and promotion of the liturgy remained the guiding principle for a great deal of the ensuing theological scholarship and pastoral development of the liturgy. See *Sacrosanctum Concilium*, no. 14.

This marginalization of both the fundamentally symbolic-ritual effectiveness of liturgy and the distinct roles of various nonclerical members of a given assembly has been sustained by an operative metaphysical view of the sacraments that cannot but cut off the divine presence and action from human bodily participation. As Chauvet and other leading sacramental theologians have astutely argued, any metaphysics of causality always fails to address the gap between the supernatural order of grace and the natural medium of human life and experience. Sacraments come to be seen as things that answer ideas, as means to supernatural ends, and thus the focus is on the supernatural agent (the priest) while the biblical *content* of the words and materials he uses become of minimal concern to their recipients. A sacrament is a supernatural instrument delivering a guaranteed product rather than a revelatory sign engaging the participants in a way that changes their perception of themselves and their world.[36]

The resulting symbolic minimalism, clerical instrumentalism, and narrow juridicism characterizing modern Roman Catholic sacramental practice, let alone much of the theory and ideology surrounding it, have all contributed—along, of course, with other social, economic, political, and religious factors—to ever-increasing numbers of the faithful drifting away from regular participation in the rites. These just do not matter so much in the regular rhythms (if there is such a thing in postmodern society) of people's lives. As punitive images of God and church authority have diminished in the increasingly postmodern worldviews of the middle and younger generations of Roman Catholics in the West, fear of ultimate (eternal) consequences for not assisting at Sunday Mass or confessing grave sins or marrying in the church has collapsed as a motivation for seeking out these and other rites. Furthermore, if sacramental liturgy effectively remains, in people's thought and imagination, predominantly a matter of metaphysical changes (even if the vast majority of folks would not utilize such a term) and canonic obligations executed by a priest for people, then their practical irrelevance can only, unfortunately, increase. In my experience as an ordained pastoral minister and religious educator, I find that people either bemoan or shrug off what they themselves describe as the utter disconnection between liturgy and life. It is not, to my observation, that people lack respect for priests or the sacramental rites. On the contrary,

[36] See Chauvet, *Symbol and Sacrament*, 7–45, 128–40.

they often hold them in great but problematic respect as sacred realities at an awesome distance from the profane commerce of life.

People may well be consoled in the church's providing a menu of what effectively serve as rites of passage across the life cycle, but if left at that, the genuine evangelical power of sacramental liturgy can only be missed, the pastoral treasure of the reformed rites of the church, squandered. Such liturgies as the Order of Christian Funerals or the sacrament of confirmation or the Rite of Marriage become, at best, genuinely sincere *expressions* of what people *already* think and know about themselves, each other, the world, and God. What the liturgy adds to such expressive experience is its divine endorsement in the person of the ordained priest, the sacramental objects, and the sacred space of the church. The clergy's own understanding and execution of the rites by means of the very same mindset only exacerbates the problem. Without exaggerating I would say that this is tragic, for I am convinced of the far greater pastoral-theological potential of the reformed rites, of the glory they can give God through their transformative impact on (their sanctification of) people's lives. Here one brief example of the problem, a situation concerning the sacrament of anointing the sick, may help to demonstrate the types of understanding that remain at odds with the healing potential of the rites.

A PASTORAL-LITURGICAL EXAMPLE

The scenario I will briefly describe and analyze here entails the contrast between perceiving the sacrament of anointing as (1) an instrumental action a priest does in order to signal and spiritually allay the immanence of death and (2) a liturgical celebration deepening a sick person's, as well as the assembled community's, awareness of his or her evolving participation in the paschal mystery. A few years ago I became involved in a pastoral initiative at a Catholic college, an original effort to celebrate the sacrament of anointing as part of the larger complex of rites comprising the Pastoral Care of the Sick. An institution whose administration, faculty, staff, and students all expound highly vocal pride in its strong sense of community, this relatively small residential campus seemed an environment well disposed to exploring a new way of supporting some of its members who might be struggling with chronic or acute health conditions. Having consulted chaplains and student-life administrators, I led a group of students in launching a three-point pastoral-liturgical initiative to evangelize, catechize, and finally, celebrate a communal rite of anointing the sick during Mass.

The project met widespread indifference and even resistance. I realize that multiple factors contribute to the attractiveness or irrelevance of a pastoral initiative in a particular community. The notable, recurrent feedback I received on or around the scheduled first catechetical gatherings, nonetheless, included people's strong perception of the sacrament as relevant only to the deathbed, despite all efforts we had made to educate to the contrary. People were not receptive to the written quotations from the reformed rite with its clear articulation of the sacrament as being for the benefit of those suffering from chronic or recurring illnesses or conditions, nor to its encouragement for communal celebrations.[37] My conversations with a staff member in her forties and a student in his early twenties were almost identical: "Father, for people this sacrament is what the priest does to somebody who is dying. It's the last rites. And that's it." Likewise, more than one of my fellow clergy on campus told me how bemused they were at my "trying to do something" with "extreme unction" (one priest's words) or "the last rites" (another's). The consistent language of the instructions and ritual texts of the rite bespeak healing and strengthening, comfort and pardon through the ministration of Christ as healer, savior, messiah, and physician.[38] The people with whom I spoke, on the contrary, seemed adamant in perceiving the sacrament only as providing a final forgiveness of sins at the last possible moment of earthly life.[39]

What difference does it make, this obstinacy of clerics and laity, young and old, toward a reformed understanding of, if not participation in, the sacrament of anointing? Well, a lot it would seem, given

[37] See International Commission on English in the Liturgy, *Pastoral Care of the Sick: Rites of Anointing and Viaticum* (Collegeville, MN: Liturgical Press, 1983), nos. 8, 13, 97, 99, 108.

[38] Ibid., nos. 5, 6, 91, 125, 145.

[39] Summarizing discussions at an international symposium on the sacrament of anointing the sick held in 2001, Genevieve Glen reports Catholics' resistance to its reform and renewal: "Both by its layout and by its content, *Pastoral Care of the Sick* makes clear the distinction between the rite of anointing as the sacrament that sustains us through sickness and the rite of viaticum as the sacrament that prepares us more immediately for death. . . . Yet a great deal of the formal and informal conversation in this gathering has reflected the tacit presupposition, often quite unrecognized, that anointing is the sacrament normally given to those on the point of death." *Recovering the Riches of Anointing: A Study of the Sacrament of the Sick*, ed. Genevieve Glen (Collegeville, MN: Liturgical Press, 2002), 119.

the highly positive experience we shared in our catechetical process (a series of weekly sessions modeled on the RCIA principles of gathering in an atmosphere of prayer, Scripture reading, psalmody and song, faith sharing, instruction, intercessions, and blessing), as well as the actual Mass with Anointing (celebrated almost entirely in song and with the help of professional liturgical dancers). Among the dozen people anointed during that liturgy, for example, was a woman in her twenties who several months later died from complications following surgery. She was the type of person who would not have seen much sense in being anointed alone in a hospital bed. Indeed, I learned she was not anointed again, that is to say, after that Mass, prior to her surgery. She did see the value, however, in being part of a communal assembly celebrating word and sacrament with music and processions and gestures. She was not alone, and that mattered greatly. Another participant in her sixties was suffering from cancer that had for several years been in remission. Her life had recently become extremely stressful, causing tangible diminishment in health. She needed to be anointed again, she discerned. She was able to describe to me the great benefit the liturgy afforded her at that time. That Mass with Anointing became a personal resource as the subsequent year became a time for her to make the decision to retire from her job in the college. Having negotiated changes in locations and commitments, she continues in her life to contribute to and receive from the lives of others as well as in her prayerful relationship with God.

Nor were those anointed the only clear beneficiaries of the celebration of the sacrament in the context of that Mass and the wider pastoral initiative (for which we had done much publicity). Among the students anointed was a young man in his first year of college, struggling not only with new complications from a severely debilitating congenital condition but also with the stressful knowledge that the mother he had left back home was failing quickly to a cancer that had emerged from several years' remission. She (by then significantly weakened and in a wheelchair) and the young man's father traveled to campus to assist at our Mass with Anointing. They came not for the mother's anointing, for she had suitably been anointed at various turning points in her own illness, but rather to participate in the sacramental celebration of a crucial moment in their son's life. The mother died less than two weeks later. Many of our catechetical (by that point, mystagogical) group went to the wake. As I met the young man and his father, the latter immediately told me, "Father, I cannot thank you enough for that Mass during which you anointed our son. The moment after my wife and I watched you anoint him, she turned to me and said, 'Now I know he is going to be okay.'" I was left speechless, marveling at how the anointing her son had received gave this dying mother the assurance that she could let go of him in peace. That assurance had in turn become a consolation to her now grieving husband and child.

Finally, a quite different indication of the benefit of our work with the Pastoral Care of the Sick and the sacrament of anointing was given me by the director of the college's campus ministry, who told me that although not a large number of students had taken part in the sacramental process, still the very public steps of the initiative (from the initial evangelization by student presentations at weekend Masses and a broad-ranging written and personal information campaign through the final Mass) had generated a significant measure of discussion on campus about health issues as part of the larger picture of individual and communal life. The director told me that I should not doubt the number of counseling sessions that had taken place between students and chaplains and other professionals, as well as dialogues among friends, peers, and resident assistants concerning personal health issues.

All these positive pastoral outcomes, nevertheless, stand in contrast to those who resisted the project from start to finish, and they were many. To them the sacrament of anointing the sick remains a privatized affair at the deathbed, a moment to seal the imminent end of earthly life, a chance to ascertain that God blesses them. Up to that point, however, people struggle along as best they can, utilizing counselors and therapists, social workers and healthcare providers, even as we read repeated plaints over the absence of effective rituals in our late-modern contexts. That is what is at stake.

People really do, of course, desire wholeness, a sense of their world that answers their ongoing search for meaning. The broad indifference to our initiative in that Catholic college community, let alone the overt rejection I encountered by some, left me questioning finally just what these people do mean by healing. I gradually became sensitive to the extent the word is used in our contemporary context. It clearly is highly charged symbolically. The next chapter, therefore, studies what seems to be going on when people engage the rhetoric of healing, what is the scope of the experiences being addressed, as well as the ways they go about addressing various of these.

Chapter 2

Human Healing:
Observations and Analyses with a View to Liturgy

INTRODUCTION

While many mainstream Catholics today might not readily associate liturgy with healing, there certainly is no lack of healing imagery and rhetoric evident in the wider ecclesial and social context. Attention to recent mass-media reporting on religion yields at least two types of situations wherein the principal actors speak of healing. One category tends to pull from the margins of the church: the realm of paranormal or miraculous events. We will consider this locus for contemporary experiences of healing briefly toward the end of this chapter. The other situation occasioning discourse of healing has erupted at the very center of the institution of the church, but only after a long struggle to be heard from the margins: the clergy sex abuse scandal and ensuing crisis of authority. An investigation into this contemporary experience can provide some clues to the seemingly widespread disassociation of sacramental ritual from healing but, even more so, numerous insights into the conditions and expectations that characterize people's invocation of healing as an at once human yet somehow transcendent phenomenon. Having achieved those observations, the chapter will continue by enlisting interdisciplinary scholarship on the perception of health, illness, and death in postmodern culture. The goal of this contemporary overview is to arrive at a set of categories for comparing and contrasting our world of suffering and deliverance with that of Jesus and the first believers in the New Testament (our work in chapter 3). That is a vital connection we must make, for our practice of tradition necessarily depends first and always on our encounter with the Word in Scripture.

DESCRIPTION: HEALING AND
THE SEXUAL ABUSE SCANDAL IN THE CHURCH

During the very months I was encountering fellow Catholics' resistance—clergy and laity—to our pastoral-liturgical initiative with the sacrament of anointing the sick,[1] I gradually became aware of the nearly constant use of the word "healing" by bishops, priests, lay faithful, healthcare professionals, and social workers embroiled in the clergy sexual abuse crisis that had exploded in the Catholic dioceses of New England. Whereas I found people resisting the notion of God, through the church, healing afflicted people in the rites of the Pastoral Care of the Sick, all manner of parties readily invoked the rhetoric of healing as shocking waves of alleged abuse and cover-ups rolled through parishes and school campuses, across television screens and newspaper pages.

In the fall of 2002, for example, a group of parishioners in the suburban church where I'd helped for many years on weekends formed a "response group" to the archdiocesan sexual abuse crisis. They inaugurated a letter-writing campaign to the archbishop, calling for fair treatment of alleged victims and abusers as well as the wider faithful. The group exhorted their fellow parishioners to "remain united in our faith and in our prayers . . . to resolve this crisis," and articulated this objective: "By taking this action, of writing a letter, it becomes a part of our healing process and hopefully it can make a difference." Meanwhile, the provincial superior of the New England Jesuits (of which I am a member) wrote his own series of letters in light of the crisis: "I believe we [Jesuits] need to enter into solidarity with victims not only as members of a Eucharistic community who wish to be healers, but also as men in need of healing ourselves." He described healing as a "long journey" in which victims tell their stories in safe environments; shame, fear, and isolation are replaced by hope and confidence; and the possibility of forgiveness can at least be dreamed. Healing, he instructed, comes through "graced relationships" replacing the tendency to persevere through loss alone, which often results in bitterness and despair. The alternative, he argued, is to join Jesus' call "to make the windings [sic] straight and the rough ways smooth (Luke 3:5)."[2]

Reporting on the semiannual meeting of the U.S. Conference of Catholic Bishops the following June, the front pages of both the *Boston Globe* and the *New York Times* carried headlines describing the bishops as healers. The *Globe* piece entitled "Bishop urges fast conclusion to Boston suits: Conference head seeks 'healing,'" reported Conference

[1] See the concluding section of chap. 1, pp. 21–24.

[2] Robert J. Levens, SJ, to the Society of Jesus of New England, Province Memorandum 2002/02, 16 September 2002.

president Bishop Wilton Gregory telling the press that "to bring healing" to the church nationwide, the Boston archdiocese needed to settle
its hundreds of cases quickly, while also receiving a new archbishop.
Those two actions Gregory identified as "the healing process" for
that local church.[3] Meanwhile, the front-page article in the *Times* read,
"Small Band of Healer Bishops For Troubled U.S. Churches," with
the bulk of the piece appearing in the National section under "Healer
Bishops Are Sent to Ease Pain of a Troubled Church." The qualities
needed in a healer-bishop, according to the report, could be either dynamic forcefulness or gracious humility. The work of healing a diocese
entailed these activities: "reaching out to victims and their families,
comforting parishioners, disciplining bad priests and reassuring good
ones, negotiating with prosecutors and lawyers, raising money to pay
off settlements."[4] The article described an entire diocese as being in
pain, and a veteran "fixer" bishop as having healed it. Other healing
activities mentioned included regaining people's trust "through small
gestures," acknowledging the pain of victims who had been snubbed
by bishops or diocesan officials, and helping to pay for therapeutic or
medical treatment.[5] The category of pain is important to note. It is, as
we shall see further below, a significant health concern in late-modern
American society. The notion of pain carries an indefinite sense, and
that is part of its power over people in its thrall. The culturally conditioned desire for immediate relief from pain could arguably have
contributed to the "quick fix" mentality so prevalent in the newspaper
reports of that semiannual meeting of the U.S. Conference of Catholic
Bishops.

Some months later, another metaphor that emerged for the crisis
was that of a wound or scar, an image bespeaking a more patient,
gradual view of healing. Under the headline, "O'Malley vows to
help heal those scarred by sex abuse," a *Boston Globe* article quoted
the recently appointed archbishop of Boston, Sean O'Malley, as telling a conference of mental health professionals, "The wound which
was left by the abuse was not only to one's psyche, but also to their
spiritual life and identity, because their Catholic identity had been so

[3] Michael Paulson, "Bishop urges fast conclusion to Boston suits: Conference head seeks 'healing,'" *Boston Globe*, 22 June 2003, A1.
[4] Laurie Goodstein, "Small Band of Healer Bishops For Troubled U.S.
Churches," *New York Times*, 22 June 2003, front sec., 1, 16.
[5] Ibid., 16.

important and so central in their existence, and now that had been seriously damaged."[6] One of the goals of the conference was to encourage research into the "spiritual suffering" of and "spiritual care" for the clergy abuse victims. Psychiatric professionals described a long list of mental health, substance abuse, and interpersonal problems experienced by the sexually abused,[7] but they also held "spiritual suffering" as a further category in the case of clergy abuse. Still, one might wonder whether the separation, however analytically necessary, is so pronounced in the experience of these victims, many of whom were described as suffering physical reactions to certain places or symbols. The "healing" for this spiritual and psychological damage has entailed therapy, financial support for therapy, meetings of various church officials—especially the archbishop—with victims, prayer, and the formation of communities of abuse survivors, their friends, and supporters. Victims' and professionals' quotes clearly indicated their perception of their suffering as having a distinctive spiritual dimension, the desired healing as "spiritual wholeness."

In the ongoing crisis, sacramental ritual, specifically the Mass, has proven another Catholic practice both clergy and laity identify as healing. A summer 2005 *Washington Post* article reported a range of methods and timeframes employed in outreach to clergy sexual abuse victims. One man victimized in Washington described, yet again, the local hierarchy's efforts at rapid resolution: "It's not a matter of sitting down with a bishop for five minutes and him apologizing and [me] being able to move on—it's more than that."[8] Such perfunctory acts had "not quite closed his wound." Joining in this critique of clericalism, while also employing the metaphor of physical wound, was a canon lawyer who countered that "human connection," including bishops visiting victims at their homes, was needed in conjunction with other such healing remedies as therapy, support groups, and financial aid. He further averred that such gestures were needed

[6] Michael Paulson, "O'Malley vows to help heal those scarred by sex abuse," *Boston Globe*, 15 January 2004.

[7] "[S]tudies have shown that childhood sexual abuse can lead to depression, sleep problems, anger, sexual dysfunction, substance abuse, and interpersonal problems, and that many victims develop post-traumatic stress disorder." Ibid.

[8] Caryle Murphy, "Outreach to victims differs by format, frequency: Clergy atonement checked by audit," *Boston Globe*, 7 August 2005.

to restore the hierarchy's credibility, thus indicating that lost identity (reputation) was also afflicting the bishops. Baltimore Cardinal William Keeler's pastoral response to both groups' needs to recover holistic identity was a liturgical one: a "healing Mass" with some one hundred people, wherein he performed "an act of public atonement to victims" by kneeling before them and reciting the *Confiteor*. That symbolic gesture of "healing and reconciliation" drew this reaction from one woman: "You have no idea of the healing that came out of that for me."[9] Keeler earned further praise in the article for having invited victims to help plan the liturgy, in contrast to many diocesan efforts that merely foisted such "healing Masses" on victims, causing them to feel passive and thus, further personally and spiritually alienated.

Lay refusal of passivity and assertion of their own ability to activate ecclesial healing characterized an op-ed piece wherein two leaders of the group Voice of the Faithful-Boston explained their rationale for organizing "A Mass of healing on Boston Common." John Hynes and Sheila Connors Grove identified three reasons for celebrating a liturgy in the city's central public park: "to spotlight the pain of [the more than sixty-five] parishes slated to close in the Archdiocese of Boston . . . to address the false hope of the assertion that the clergy sexual abuse crisis is history . . . [and] in our nature as Catholics to gather together for healing and growth, to address our pain, and to celebrate the gifts we have been given."[10] Most notable about that list is the association of Catholic identity with gathering for celebration, as well as the explicit conviction that the liturgically assembled church can affect healing. The authors, moreover, articulated what healing (negatively) corrects and (positively) advances: "pain" and "growth," respectively. The healing needed is a matter of life and death for this once religiously and socially powerful local church, which the authors asserted is now "dying in an arduously long and painful process." The lay-sponsored Mass "represents the first step" in the healing process by placing a "spotlight" on the all-encompassing pain, inspiring the faithful to action, and empowering them "to reclaim our rituals, our traditions, and our faith."[11] What I am noting here is how the imagination and reasoning of these committed American Catholics function, how

[9] Ibid.

[10] John Hynes and Sheila Connors Grove, "A Mass of healing on Boston Common," *Boston Globe*, 14 August 2004, A14.

[11] Ibid.

steeped in images of sharing in the Eucharist and deliverance from death. The story, however, also indicates the people's dependence upon the clergy for the celebration of the sacramental rites, how inextricable in the Catholic Church is the practice of the liturgy from the authority of the hierarchy. To the extent that the clergy do not perceive and lead the people in the liturgy as a corporate action of the assembled faithful open to the consoling yet challenging Word that comes to life in sacrament, they exercise a crippling grip on the genuine pastoral power inherent in the rites.

The historical fact is that the Mass did not draw overwhelming numbers, that those who did participate were, as is the continued problem for Voice of the Faithful, largely older middle-aged and elderly Catholics, and that active membership in Boston parishes has continued to decline steadily. That the performative language of healing, faith, tradition, and (liturgical) celebration remains evocatively powerful and inspiring for American Catholics seems clear. That the ability of these performed symbols to have an effective impact on the church's membership and mission depends on a range of contested societal, cultural, and political factors also seems quite evident. Not unlike the term "community," "healing" would seem to be widely employed for its sense of personal wholeness and communal unity. The practices healing entails, however, can be broad and evasive, with multiple claimants to power in peoples' individual and corporate lives—wealth, fame, law, office, nature, creativity, love[12]—influencing their images of wholeness and thus healing. For Christians that list of human power factors plays out not only through their participation in their social milieu but also in their practices of the faith, including the extent of their engagement in communal or institutional religion and encounter with the Gospel.[13] Faith and culture interact in people's construction of what healing means to them.

ANALYSIS:
THE HEALING DISCOURSE OF A CHURCH IN PAIN

The above scenarios betray a wealth of popular wisdom among contemporary believers, both lay and ordained, that can assist theological efforts to realize more fully the personal, pastoral, and ecclesial benefits of the church's reformed rites for the alienated, sick, dying,

[12] See Bernard Cooke, *Power and the Spirit of God: Toward an Experience-Based Pneumatology* (New York: Oxford University Press, 2004), 45–119, 159–77.
[13] See ibid., 123–55.

dead, bereaved, and those who accompany them. Just as the powerfully symbolic term "healing" pervades the instructions and prayers of
all those sacramental rituals,[14] so too does it pervade the popular discourse that has developed in a church that describes itself as wounded
and in pain. Healing among these committed, practicing Catholics
connotes a social process entailing: (1) a crisis, including physical
and/or psychological violence, a breech in community coherence and
power relations, a condition of feeling injured or enduring pain, and
a serious "spiritual" questioning of ultimate meaning; and (2) subsequent efforts to transform the situation, that is, for people to change
how they perceive themselves individually and collectively so as to
recover a sense of wholeness, rightness, or even new insight for their
worldview. Healing is a matter of transforming people's perceptions
of a critical or painful situation by making it somehow meaningful.
Healing in some way invokes Christ, especially his death and resurrection, and these as paradigmatic of his service to others.

Ritual, especially the Mass, plays a fundamental role in the pursuit of transformation, serving both a salvific function—situating
the crisis in the larger narrative of faith in Christ—and a redemptive
one—exhorting believers to activities that will benefit the social entity
as a whole and the hurting individuals therein. Healing is needed
when communal relations, whether vertical or horizontal or both, are
somehow broken off, eliciting the need for reconciliation and forgiveness not only among people but also with God. Healing, therefore, is
sought not individualistically but amid the community of faith. Healing comes through doing actions that, even if only as verbal protest,
seek to enact change in the situation. At the same time, symbolic action (word and sacrament) must function in tandem with medical,
psychological, social, and financial assistance.

Much of the wisdom, criteria, and goals for healing that I have just
gleaned from the words and actions of American Catholics in their
ecclesial crisis is actually also operative in the church's reformed sacramental rites for the sick, dying, dead, and alienated. The challenge for
those rites, however, is to discover and advance those powerful qualities, which clearly do matter to the faithful, such that the rites might
contribute to a genuine renewal in the liturgical life of the church. As
we saw in chapter 1, this reform is not for the liturgy's own sake but
rather for its pastoral service to the members of Christ's Body such

[14] See below, chaps. 5, 6, 7.

31

that the rituals can manifest the presence of God in their lives, their care for one another, and their mission in the world. The crisis experience of the church in recent years indicates that the discourse of healing and its associated activities clearly resonate with contemporary believers. Significant differences, nonetheless, also exist between the scenarios I have analyzed here and the types of situations the rites of anointing, Viaticum, and funerals serve.

What I am pursuing in this opening part of our investigation are the promising and problematic aspects of contemporary believers' own metaphors and practices of healing. The practical terrain covered here will provide theoretical insights into the pastoral theology of the rites we will investigate in chapters 5 through 7. I have just summarized the positive criteria for healing emergent from the current ecclesial crisis. I now must also consider the problems and challenges to a renewal in sacramental-liturgical healing those scenarios imply, as well as the limits to correlating those scenarios with the pastoral situations associated with the sacramental rites.

As much as the discourse and symbolic actions of healing bespeak wholeness (spiritual, social, interpersonal, communal) as their goal, their performances also indicate problematic divisions in the thought and relationships among the faithful. Perhaps the most prominent of divisions in the modern context of religious practice is between the public and private spheres of life.[15] Churches and other religious institutions may hold a measure of public visibility, and religious leaders are certainly expected to function to some extent publicly. The practices of individual believers, however, are largely considered private, as are their ethical and moral decisions. Likewise, when it comes to the experience of illness, Americans largely consider sickness shameful and, therefore, a condition preferably kept quiet and managed in private. Illness and mortal decline may carry senses of failure, with the financial, personal, and social burdens that so often accompany sickness only adding to the sense of shame.

[15] See Robert N. Bellah and others, *Habits of the Heart: Individualism and Commitment in American Life*, rev. ed. (Berkeley: University of California Press, 1996), 55–84, 142–65, 219–45. See also, Johann Baptist Metz, *Faith in History and Society: Toward a Practical Fundamental Theology*, trans. David Smith (New York: Seabury Press, 1980), 35–39; and *The Emergent Church: The Future of Christianity in a Post-Bourgeois World*, trans. Peter Mann (New York: Crossroad, 1987), 34–36, 41, 74.

The breaking open of the clergy sex abuse scandal in 2002 was symptomatic of these private-public tensions in the contemporary practice of religion. As scores of victims poured forth their years-old stories of abuse, they also lamented the force with which not only the church hierarchy but also their fellow parishioners (and sometimes even their parents) forbade them to disclose their stories. The recent diocesan programs for healing these people have included very clear lists of diseases and illnesses the victims now suffer, debilitating conditions that often bear shame and beg privacy. And yet one of the keys to the healing so many victims say they seek is their public vindication, their finally being heard and believed. The church's and even wider society's resistance to acknowledging the suffering of the clerically abused demonstrates how deceptive, in the end, are the conventionally drawn lines of public and private, both for religion and illness.

The same holds true for the late-modern momentum to privatize death. Not only do the diseases that terminally afflict fellow citizens confront all with the realities of human decline and mortality we culturally prefer left denied, but also the collision of limited economic resources with increasing medical capabilities to extend life press the question of death persistently into public and ecclesial awareness. As I will try to demonstrate in the third part of this book, only if the church's sacramental rites are freed from merely private functioning will its liturgical worship be able to offer original forms of genuine consolation that would otherwise remain unknown: squandered treasure.[16]

Another division in practical thought evident in the handling of the clergy sex abuse crisis is the tension between seeking rapid resolution of the symptoms of scandal (the "quick fix") and committing to more lengthy processes of recovery (healing "wounds" and "scars"). While different aspects of these complicated situations may well warrant such a dichotomy of tactics (legal strategies, for example), still the mentality of wanting to get past the suffering quickly would seem to coincide to some extent with the modern expectation of instant pain relief.[17] The promise of an instant cure is one rarely realized in

[16] See Bernard Häring, *In Pursuit of Wholeness: Healing in Today's Church* (Liguori, MO: Liguori Publications, 1985), 54–55.
[17] "The public taste for quick fixes through drugs and surgery, as deeply rooted as the taste for fast food and the fifteen-minute oil change, helps keep the biomedical model in business at a time when a number of doctors and

modern medicine, and yet people find themselves believing in—and expecting—its occurrence more than might readily be acknowledged. This, however, is to take a shortcut past what very often are humanly important processes of interpersonal solidarity and personal reflection practiced in light of time-tested traditions: the multivalent work of healing. It is not for nothing that people decry the lack of effective rituals today, whether for the sexually abused or the seriously ill or the dying.[18] Rituals, when practiced in a larger complex of communal worship and pastoral care, afford real possibilities of healing.

Still another division evident in the efforts at healing during the church crisis has been that between clergy and laity. The human disaster of clergy sexual abuse has shed stark light on the clericalism that so persistently afflicts Catholicism. Victims' typical explanation for why they concealed the abuse was the absolute, even god-like, power the laity afforded the priesthood ("We were taught the priest is Christ here on earth"). Distressing to read were not a few victims' testimonies to the beating they could expect not only from their fathers but even their mothers should they have dared describe what the priest had done to them. While the trauma visited upon these sufferers must be our primary concern, I note the disastrous dark side to the nearly divine status the hierarchy has expected from an, at least up until now, largely cooperative laity. Clericalism not only perpetuates a religious division of labor that cuts off the overwhelming majority of believers from claiming a more active responsibility for the praxis of the faith, including the liturgy, but it also reinforces attribution of magical or otherworldly power to the ordained ministers of the Gospel that, in the end, distances those in need from the genuine paradoxical power that is the Gospel's unique gift.[19]

People's images of God and Jesus have often functioned in mutual reinforcement with their understanding of the priest and the sacra-

---

caregivers are coming to recognize its limitations." David N. Morris, *Illness and Culture in the Postmodern Age* (Berkeley: University of California Press, 1998), 16–17.

[18] See Thomas F. Driver, "What Healthcare Professionals Need to Know about Ritual: A First Lesson," and Laurence J. O'Connell, "Ritual Practice and End-of-Life Care," *The Park Ridge Center Bulletin* 5 (August–September 1998): 3, 14, 17.

[19] That paradoxical power will be continuously explored in the ensuing chaps., below.

34

ments he dispenses. We must ask ourselves: What god inspires such dread in people as to insight them to beat their children?[20] What god expects church hierarchs to endanger their children and youth in order to defend the reputation of the institution and its clerical caste? What god are people worshiping when they silence and ostracize fellow believers who muster the courage to reveal their personal violation? These questions stand alongside the observation that so many clergy and laity were content to keep on celebrating the Mass and other sacraments, to worship liturgically the God of biblical tradition, even as they worshiped other gods in their practical behavior. This gap between the church's sacramental and ethical actions is, of course, nothing new, let alone unique to the current crisis.[21] The liturgical-ethical gap is a recurrent prophetic concern that has arisen over and again since the earliest generations of the church.

We have touched upon what has proven mortally dangerous for the human enterprise of the faith at this moment: a breakdown in Catholic religious-business-as-usual, demanding reform on the part of both clergy and laity, a renewal by returning to the primary sources of word and sacrament. History teaches us that facing the danger, the disaster, is the key to knowing once again our total dependence on the God of Jesus, our fundamental need for grace. This is not the god of clerically dominated and passively received rites, magical acts of sacred power divorced from the joys, struggles, and sorrows of the real world. The

---

[20] Here I follow the example of N. T. Wright, whose biblical scholarship will figure significantly in the next two chapters, especially chap. 4, below. Wright explains his methodological decision to refer to "god" with a lowercase g: "This is not an irreverence. It is to remind myself, as well as the reader, that in the first century, as increasingly in the twenty-first, the question is not whether we believe in 'God' (with it being assumed that we all know who or what that word refers to), but rather to wonder which god, out of the many available candidates, we might be talking about. . . . The alternative is to adopt the standard usage and thus fail, for most readers most of the time, to alert them to the most important question which underlies this entire series [Wright's current multivolume study of the New Testament]." N. T. Wright, *The Resurrection of the Son of God*, Christian Origins and the Question of God, vol. 3 (Minneapolis: Fortress Press, 2003), xviii; see also, 6.

[21] See Bernd Wannenwetsch, *Political Worship: Ethics for Christian Citizens*, trans. Margaret Kohl (New York: Oxford University Press, 2004), 34–36, 159–62; see also, Gordon W. Lathrop, *Holy Ground: A Liturgical Cosmology* (Minneapolis: Fortress Press), 182–88.

God revealed through Jesus in word and sacrament, rather, trusts believers' capacities to join with Christ in the patient growth and transformation essential to human healing. The sacraments are thereby freed from the mechanistic clerical realm and reoriented in ritual service to the pastoral work of all the people of God. Liturgy, then, serves life.

Can we trust such a God? Knowing the demands such a commitment to the God of Jesus entails, would we risk ourselves to such a way of life? These reflections bring us to a final division disclosed through the clerical abuse scandal: a practical dualism between the divine and the human that is utterly antithetical to the humanity of God revealed in the death and resurrection of Jesus.[22] An overcoming of the dualism that imagines God's omnipotence to entail distance, indifference, or even capriciousness toward suffering people would seem to be at the heart of the "spiritual wholeness" that Archbishop O'Malley and others described abuse victims as so greatly desiring.[23] In the end, even when satisfactory measures of human justice, goodwill, and compassion have been attained, there remains, in the powerful words of Johann Baptist Metz, a "suffering unto God."[24] When people have exhausted blaming the clergy for the abuse, or when in cases of chronic sickness, disease, diminishment, and terminal illness people have exhausted whatever medical expertise and other resources are available, they are finally thrown back on God, the mysterious otherness of the God of the Gospel. To bring the suffering borne in one's own person-body or shared in compassionate solidarity with another into the presence of God, to experience an encounter with Christ through the proclamation of word, the sharing of prayer, and the affective touch of symbolic gesture, is to trust that the Spirit of the crucified and risen Christ continues to immerse the divine presence into the depths of our human condition. Salvation comes not in magical

[22] See Louis-Marie Chauvet, *The Sacraments: The Word of God at the Mercy of the Body* (Collegeville, MN: Liturgical Press, 2001), 161–64. We will explore Chauvet's exposition on the "humanity of God" as one contemporary systematic-theological interpretation of the paschal mystery in chap. 4, below.

[23] See Dorothee Soelle, *Suffering*, trans. Everett R. Kalin (Philadelphia: Fortress Press, 1975), 41–45.

[24] See Johann Baptist Metz, *A Passion for God: The Mystical-Political Dimension of Christianity*, trans. J. Matthew Ashley (New York: Paulist Press, 1998), 42, 66–71.

escapes from reality but rather in a renegotiation of our place in this world—before God and people—according to the paschal mystery.[25]

POSTMODERN ANALYSIS OF ILLNESS

The willingness and ability to trust the healing wisdom of the Gospel is challenged not only by difficulties within church culture but also the mentality of modern society. The praxis of faith happens not in a sacred vacuum but a cultural context. Cultural theorist David Morris has devoted much of his work to the human phenomena of pain and illness.[26] His research and analysis demonstrate how unrealistic dualisms, mechanistic thinking, and fantastic expectations have been endemic to modern Americans' views of illness and medicine. The modern valorization of scientific reason as a total worldview has abetted rigid distinctions between body and mind, reason and emotion, as well as attributed near-magical power and authority to the doctor and medical technology.[27] Morris finds, nevertheless, significant changes of attitude sporadically emerging in this now postmodern era. His work affords numerous insights into the sort of change in mentality necessary for the church's rites of healing to make a practical difference and salvific contribution to the struggles of people's lives—and deaths.

Early in his *Illness and Culture in the Postmodern Age*, Morris honestly confronts postmodernism's resistance to definition. What can be said about a worldview characterized by fragmentation, indefiniteness, and uncertainty is that it "indicates a world that we recognize as inescapably 'constructed,'" a recognition that is bringing about significant "change in human perception."[28] Negatively, this altered outlook entails a rejection of modernity's definition of health, its myth of immortality, and the hegemony of the biomedical model of illness. Morris sees the range of unrealistic modern expectations for total (if not permanent) wellness standing on the foundation of the World Health Organization's 1946 definition of health as "a state of complete physical, mental, and social well-being, and not merely the absence of

[25] This divine-human paradox, the paschal mystery at the heart of all authentic liturgical practice, I will pursue in depth in chap. 4.

[26] His *The Culture of Pain* (Berkeley: University of California Press, 1991) won a 1992 PEN award.

[27] See Morris, *Illness and Culture in the Postmodern Age*, 15.

[28] Ibid., 25, 27.

disease or infirmity."[29] An abstract ideal, this notion of health has set modern people on a relentless quest for a personally embodied utopia expected to be complete and uninterrupted. This is a culture "in which illness appears increasingly as an anomaly or scandal that must be excluded from the consumer paradise of pleasure and health," a myth played out in (unattainable) desires for instant cures, rapid weight loss, and world-class sex.[30]

Such widespread contemporary fantasies and their practical pursuits operate in league with the regnant modern biomedical model of health care. Biomedicine is a mechanistic approach to the human organism that, while having achieved undeniable human benefits from vaccinations to vascular surgery, is proving far too limited in its perspective on the rapidly changing physical, psychological, and social conditions of illness. Crucial to our present investigation into the viability of the church's liturgical ministry to illness and death is Morris's repeated observation that Americans largely embrace the biomedical model dogmatically, perceiving illness strictly in terms of biological causes, relegating other contributing factors to the pejorative category of the mental and psychological, seeking (total) cures for chronic or terminal conditions, overusing prescription and nonprescription drugs, and pushing aside pain and suffering as meaningless.

The postmodern era is generating not only a negative critique but also a growing array of positive alternatives to the modern understanding of illness, which Morris perceives as an emerging "biocultural model."[31] The biocultural view recognizes the human phenomenon of illness always to be a specific construction combining not only the physical matter and operating mechanisms of our human biology but also an array of interrelated cultural factors—ecological and environmental (the natural world as both received and manipulated by culture), economic (today, including marketing and consumerism), religious (and, in modernity, antireligious), legal and political, artistic (narrative and image, and now mass media), as well as conventional roles for personal identity. Illness therefore is never a condition purely imposed biologically by nature on humans and thus simply the object of medical cure. The individual person is the somatic site of an objectively verifiable disease that nonetheless is itself the product of

[29] Ibid., 241.
[30] Ibid., 245, and see 17.
[31] See ibid., 9, 12, 19, 71, 75–77.

not only nature but also culture.[32] The person experiences the disease as illness, but that experience is not just a matter of his or her seemingly individual or autonomous integration of the bodily with the mental or emotional. People continuously construct *meaning* for their experiences,[33] a human activity so tacit to everyday personal, interpersonal, and social functioning that its disruption by sickness, with attendant degrees of disorder, chaos, and incoherence, causes people to react with avoidance or suppression. The latter, of course, only contributes to people's suffering—another category outside the bounds of the biomedical model, as is the more holistic category of healing. Such are the socially learned and culturally sustained patterns of thought, behavior, and power that Morris sees "postmodern illness" beginning to address and, ever so gradually, to transform.[34]

The transformation to a more helpful biocultural model of illness and health is indeed gradual. Morris observes no small amount of evidence for the strength with which laypeople (not just medical professionals) cling to the Cartesian dualism inherent in the modern

[32] For a detailed review of how medical anthropologists distinguish between such terms as illness and disease, cure and healing, see chap. 3, pp. 72–79.

[33] See Morris, *Illness and Culture in the Postmodern Age*, 21–22, 38, 49, 57, 66–67, 158, 258, 271.

[34] An example of this transformation comes in the growing movement for patients' rights, especially their being treated as persons and not biological objects by medical professionals. One recent *New York Times* report opens with a description of how a women recovering from breast cancer surgery was visited by a team of doctors and medical students without introduction, stripped to the waist, and treated as a specimen. "Entering the medical system, whether a hospital, a nursing home or a clinic, is often degrading. At the hospital where Ms. Duffy was a patient and at many others the small courtesies that help lubricate and dignify civil society are neglected precisely when they are needed most, when people are feeling acutely cut off from others and betrayed by their own bodies." The story cites survey data and includes other anecdotes of the "loss of identity" that patients experience, a problem exacerbated by tight hospital budgets and reduced nursing personnel. Despite hospitals' increasing development of patient representative offices and other such efforts, national survey data in the present decade have found steadily decreasing satisfaction among patients, who "often feel resentful, helpless and dehumanized in the process [of medical treatment]." Benedict Carey, "In the Hospital, a Degrading Shift From Person to Patient," *New York Times*, 16 August 2005.

theory and practice of medicine.[35] A crucial symptom of this body-mind dualism is people's distorted attitudes toward the fundamental human phenomenon of pain. Descartes' philosophy of the mind as a passive observer (receptor) of bodily sensations has heavily influenced modern medicine's relegation of pain to practical meaninglessness. Medicine dismissed the contradictory, complicated, and "prescientific" human efforts to find meaning in pain—especially the religious—from what really matters in practice, with a great number of the general populace following suit.[36] And yet, as Morris reports, chronic pain is a steadily increasing phenomenon in postmodern society, an observation confirmed by a more recent (2005) scientific survey that found more than half of Americans saying they have chronic or recurrent pain, with broad numbers reporting it "interferes with their mood, activities, sleep, ability to do work or enjoyment of life."[37]

Morris has long argued that chronic, as opposed to acute, pain especially lends itself to biocultural analysis and treatment. An incorporation of the gains achieved by biomedicine into a more comprehensive, holistic model would entail recognizing that meaning is often fundamentally at issue in people's experiences of pain, that chronic pain sufferers and those caring for them can enlist powerfully helpful resources in the historical, psychological, and cultural dimensions of a given person's life. The 2005 survey would seem to support Morris's argument, while also indicating that biocultural approaches have only realized limited practice to date. The study found that for all pain

[35] Describing how medical educators in the United States have been trying to address the breakdown of the doctor-patient relationship due to the latter's perception of the former as unfeeling technicians, philosopher and physician William E. Stempsey analyzes the challenges facing the medical school reform: "[S]tudents are already well conditioned to see science and technology as the heart of medical practice. What we are seeing is a creeping acceptance of scientism, the view that science gives us the best and most complete description of our world. Science is seen as something quite distinct and far removed from the humanities." "The quarantine of philosophy in medical education: Why teaching the humanities many not produce humane physicians." *Medicine, Health Care and Philosophy* 2 (1999): 3–9, here 7.

[36] See Morris, *Illness and Culture in the Postmodern Age*, 117–19.

[37] For Gary Langer's analysis of a telephone survey conducted 13–19 April 2005 by ABC News, USA Today, and the Stanford University Medical Center, see "Poll: Americans Searching for Pain Relief," at http://abcnews.go.com/Health/print?id=732395, accessed 16 August 2005.

sufferers—chronic, recurrent, and acute—the entire range of remedies from prescription and over-the-counter drugs to bed rest to prayer to homeopathy, massage, meditation, yoga, and acupuncture only offers limited relief. The most tried were over-the-counter drugs and home remedies (in the eightieth percentile), followed by prescription drugs, prayer, bed rest, and massage (all around 60%). The best-rated were prescription drugs and prayer, which each earned a 51 percent effectiveness rating of "very well." Chronic pain sufferers (compared with recurrent and acute) were most likely to have tried prescription drugs (80%) and prayer (69%), yet "they were much less likely than others to say these have worked very well."[38] Prescription drugs were very effective for only 30 percent of chronic, compared to 64 percent of acute, sufferers. As for prayer, the three groups reported very effective rates as follows: chronic = 37 percent, recurrent = 45 percent, and acute = 61 percent. These statistics, of course, are open to numerous lines of inquiry for analysis. For the moment I would simply both note the intransigence of chronic pain (its resistance to all treatments) and question (with Morris's arguments in mind) whether greater effectiveness from such practices as prayer might be possible if people became more engaged in liturgical and other traditions as comprehensive practices, not stop-gap measures. Crucial, as well, is the question of whether people envision the desired outcome to be the curing of a disease, that is, the elimination of an individual's biomedical symptoms, or the healing of the total person, that is, an arrival at personal meaning in the illness, even if the physical pathology persists. The distinction is important for grasping how people understand the relationship between prayer and healing.

Morris's analysis provides insight into why contemporary American Catholics might adopt the metaphor of healing so readily in response to social, institutional, and even interpersonal troubles, such as the

[38] Ibid. "Six in 10 Americans rate their last experience with pain as moderate or worse, and for two in 10—about 40 million individuals—it was severe. Nineteen percent suffer chronic pain, meaning ongoing pain that's lasted three months or more. An additional 34 percent report recurrent pain; the rest say their usual pain experience is acute, or short-term." The overall rate of pain is highest among people 65 years and older, although "50 looks to be one breaking point for pain." On the other hand, for those experiencing pain, the average age for acute sufferers is 39 years old; recurrent, 48; and chronic, 53.

crises of the clerical sex abuse scandal, yet be highly skeptical of claims that "real" healing takes place when the sacrament of the anointing of the sick is celebrated for a wide range of health misfortunes other than the deathbed. In light of Morris's research, the fact that many Catholic clergy and laity have so persistently held to the notion of "extreme unction" for this sacrament, despite both the Council of Trent's and Vatican II's teaching it as a sacrament for the sick as well as the dying,[39] is not terribly surprising. Those councils may arguably be described as occurring at the nascent and latter stages of the modern era. Popular clerical and lay restriction of the sacrament's meaning exclusively to a mechanistic release of the soul from the temporal punishments of sin after death would seem to align quite nicely with how the biomedical model mechanistically treats the human body. Likewise, the apparent widespread ignorance or resistance of the lay faithful, as well as a distressing number of the clergy, to the profoundly eschatological texts, symbols, and gestures of the Order of Christian Funerals would seem to complement their practice of the funeral Mass as the eulogizing and commendation of a soul that has "passed away."[40] Morris reports: "Biomedicine, with a few distinguished exceptions, has left the issue of suffering nearly untouched, delegating (or relegating) it to pastoral care."[41] The sad irony is that the church's rites are often an underutilized, if not in many places ignored, pastoral resource for helping not only the sick and dying to experience healing during all the stages of their struggles, but also the loved ones and professionals who accompany and care for them.[42]

---

[39] See Michael Drumm, "The Practice of Anointing and the Development of Doctrine," John M. Huels, "Ministers and Rites for the Sick and Dying: Canon Law and Pastoral Options," and Genevieve Glen, "Going Forth in the Spirit: The Road Before Us," in *Recovering the Riches of Anointing: A Study of the Sacrament of the Sick*, ed. Genevieve Glen, 53–55, 99, 119 (Collegeville, MN: Liturgical Press, 2002).

[40] I will explore this perhaps provocative statement in chap. 7, below.

[41] Morris, *Illness and Culture in the Postmodern Age*, 192.

[42] In her concluding presentation for a 2001 international symposium on the sacrament of anointing the sick, Sr. Genevieve Glen, a longtime specialist on the topic, offered the following assessment: "Apart from 'healing Masses' that have become regular practice in many parishes, personalized sacramental care of the sick and dying at the optimal moment for their participation and full benefit has not yet been fully implemented. That implementation requires a considerable investment in individualized rather than programmatic ministry,

In drawing connections between Morris's analysis of illness in postmodern culture and the current celebration of the church's rites I am, of course, writing in generalities and, moreover, emphasizing the difficulties and challenges entailed in the reform and renewal of their pastoral practice. I do so not to be negative or pessimistic but rather to raise critical awareness of both impediments to and opportunities for promoting the implementation of the post–Vatican II rites at this point in their history. While likewise working within the limits of anecdotal evidence from the pastoral field, Lizette Larson-Miller, in her recent study of the sacrament of the anointing of the sick, repeatedly argues from the perspective of the revised rite's widespread use in American parishes: "[T]he popular shift in understanding from an anointing of the dying to an anointing of the sick was not only fairly smooth but, in many places, enthusiastically embraced by active Roman Catholic parishioners, so much so that the opposite concern was also considered necessary to state in the general and specific introductions to the sacrament, namely that the anointing of the sick be sought only for serious illness, and not for every minor illness or injury."[43] The key to that overview of the situation would seem to lie in Larson-Miller's careful identification of the practitioners as "active Roman Catholic parishioners." Toward the end of her study Larson-Miller explains how many Catholics do not consider the purpose of sacramental anointing to be for either only the sick or only the dying but rather as appropriate to both. This flexible, more comprehensive view of the sacrament, not surprisingly, is found "in some parts of the United States" where parishes have "a vibrant and engaging ministry to the sick by many members," integrating communal anointing liturgies with the full complement of rituals in the Pastoral Care of the Sick.[44]

The advancement of such an integrated approach to this and other rites, holistic both in human and ecclesial terms, is the fundamental motivation of this present book and the primary objective of chapters 5 through 7. Even with her helpful emphasis, however, on how well the rites have flourished in certain regions among more liturgically engaged Catholics, Larson-Miller acknowledges, "In a world of

---

as well as in the catechesis necessary to restructure expectations." Glen, "Going Forth in the Spirit," 119.

[43] Lizette Larson-Miller, *The Sacrament of Anointing of the Sick*, Lex Orandi Series, ed. John D. Laurance (Collegeville, MN: Liturgical Press, 2005), 63.

[44] Ibid., 135.

impoverished literalism, of post-symbolic, post-metaphorical interests, sacramental reality is a hard sell."[45] The question of what is meant by healing, then, persists. My own concern is with the prevalence of mechanistic thinking, which in late modernity is found not only in the biomedical model of illness but, I will argue in chapter 4, certain popular views of sacraments and ordained ministry in the church. Such thought is inimical to the liturgical work of healing.

HEALING, PRAYER, AND THE MIRACULOUS

The growing interest of doctors and other medical professionals in a more biocultural approach to illness that Morris noted in the mid- to late-1990s has certainly found confirmation in one area of American culture: the practice of religious faith. A 2003 *Newsweek* article quoted a neurologist at the University of Pennsylvania studying the effects of prayer and meditation on the brain as saying, "There's been a tremendous shift in the medical profession's openness to this topic."[46] A *New York Times* article published a year and a half earlier reported, "More than 70 medical schools offer instruction in how to address patients' religious beliefs."[47] While related within a broad professional debate, those two statements are not exactly addressing the same questions or necessarily seeking the same outcomes. The latter statistic is indicative of doctors' recognition that attention to the entire person one is treating promises better medical care than only focusing on narrowly identified disease symptoms or pathologies. Mounting numbers of studies, moreover, indicate that people who regularly attend church live significantly longer than those who do not—a holistic health indicator many physicians now consider relevant to the treatment of their patients.[48]

[45] Ibid., 71.

[46] Claudia Kalb, "Faith & Healing," *Newsweek*, 17 November 2003, 48–56, here 50.

[47] Mary Duenwald, "Religion and Health: New Research Revives an Old Debate," *New York Times*, 7 May 2002, D5.

[48] See Kalb, "Faith & Healing," 54. The U.S. polling data behind the 2003 *Newsweek* article include the following findings: 84% believed "praying for others who are sick or injured can have a positive effect on their recovery," 89% believed "a patient's religious faith can have a positive effect on his or her recovery from an illness or injury," while 53% reported personally having "relied on religious faith to get through a major illness." "Prayer" and "Religion" (New York: Newsweek, Inc., 1 November 2003), accessed 17 October 2005

There has been much agreement on the potential benefits of religious or spiritual practices for overall mental health and well-being. The debates have arisen, however, around the attempt to quantify scientifically the impact of prayer on the healthy functioning of the body, especially the correlation between prayer and the cure of specific episodes of disease or acute sickness. The key move entailed in this latter line of investigation has been the growing conviction, pursued in nearly a dozen different studies, that the correlation between prayer and cure can be scientifically proven. Fueling speculation around the debate was a decade-long, $2.4 million study of 1,800 cardiac patients led by a physician who emphasizes the benefits of personal prayer and meditation. The eagerly anticipated results were made public in 2006.[49] In this study some people undergoing surgery were assigned members of religious communities to pray for them, while others were not. Furthermore, among those assigned intercessors, some were told of this fact while from others that information was withheld. In the end the scientists found no difference in the number of postoperative complications experienced by those who received prayers and those who had not, while those who had been told they were being prayed for actually suffered a significantly higher rate of complications (59%) than those who had not (51%). Dr. Richard Sloan, a professor of behavioral medicine at Columbia University and vocal critic of the entire medical foray into faith and healing, found the publication of these results an occasion for reiterating his doubt that prayer is an appropriate subject for scientific study: "The problem with studying religion scientifically is that you do violence to the phenomenon by reducing it to basic elements that can be quantified, and that makes for bad science and bad religion."[50] The reaction from the director of a "prayer ministry" in

---

at http://poll.orspub.com/poll/lpext.dll/ors/p/prayer/001759-2003i.htm; http://poll.orspub.com/poll/lpext.dll/ors/r/religion/001935-2003i.htm; and http://poll.orspub.com/poll/lpext.dll/ors/r/religion/001937-2003i.htm.

[49] See Benedict Carey, "Long-Awaited Medical Study Questions the Power of Prayer," *New York Times*, 31 March 2006, A1, A15. For the published study, see Herbert Benson and others, "Study of the Therapeutic Effects of Intercessory Prayer (STEP) in Cardiac Bypass Patients: a multicenter randomized trial of uncertainty and certainty in intercessory prayer," *American Heart Journal* 151, no. 4 (April 2006): 934–42.

[50] Ibid., A15. See also, Richard P. Sloan, *Blind Faith: The Unholy Alliance of Religion and Medicine* (New York: St. Martin's Press, 2006).

Missouri, on the other hand, was to aver that a person of faith might "say that this study is interesting, but we've been praying a long time and we've seen prayer work, we know it works, and the research on prayer and spirituality is just getting started."[51]

I agree with Sloan in his insistence that the practice of medicine is an activity of a different order (subject to scientific research) than the religious practice of faith (which is not). This distinction does not mean that a physician should ignore the importance of faith in the life of a patient, should the patient either explicitly mention it to the doctor as part of her or his way of maintaining health or demonstrate it in any number of ways, such as the presence of religious objects, use of a Bible, reference to a pastoral minister, and so forth. Doctors increasingly enlist or encourage whatever human resources a patient demonstrates that would contribute to her or his health. Indeed, the postmodern turn in medical practice is described precisely in terms of physicians working with other medical personnel and the wider circle of caregivers, family, and various community members to cooperate in helping people live healthy lives or recover from health misfortunes. Crucial, however, is the need for recognizing the differences and there-fore complementarities in the various types of practices that together comprise a biocultural approach to health and sickness. Otherwise, as Sloan warns, people end up practicing "bad science and bad religion."

William Stempsey, a physician (MD), philosopher (PhD), and priest (Jesuit), has identified another way in which too facile a conflation of medicine and religious (or other paranormal) beliefs can serve people poorly. In an article exploring the concept of miracles and the limits of medical knowledge, Stempsey warns about the extent to which the rhetoric of miracles has become commonplace in medical practice and hospital publications. Finding the apotheosis of this trend on the cover of a children's hospital magazine proclaiming "Expect a Miracle," Stempsey explains why this should be a cause for concern: "Since 'miracle' is not understood in any univocal way, and since the knowl-edge most patients have about the capabilities of modern medical technologies is not sophisticated, such advertising can create quite different expectations for patients and physicians. We might well ask whether such talk about miracles is leading people to have false expec-

[51] Carey, "Long-Awaited Medical Study Questions the Power of Prayer," A15.

tations about the capabilities of medical practice."[52] It would seem that those false expectations would include the late-modern assumption that a quick-fix solution to a complicated medical problem must exist and, therefore, should be available. The burden of Stempsey's own argument is that the concept of the miraculous cure functions on theological and philosophical grounds, namely, belief in divine power acting upon nature in ways beyond human comprehension. In contrast, all physicians can do in (rare) startling cases of unexpected recovery is to ascertain that a particular cure cannot be explained within the epistemological standards of biomedicine. They do not, however, have anything to say about whether a miracle has occurred, for that would be a theological proclamation based on metaphysical beliefs about the nature of God and the created order of the world.

One of the implications of Stempsey's essay, then, is that the meritorious desire for more holistic approaches to health care must not muddle people's thinking about what they can and should expect from medical professionals. [53] A biocultural approach is a matter of an array of people working together in communities of care and service. In such cooperative efforts we need doctors to offer the scientific expertise that is intrinsic to their profession, delivered in ways appropriate to particular patients and their families' affective and cognitive capacities. Other care and service providers, of course, need to be competent in their own fields, including those whose ministry is to provide sacramental pastoral care to the sick, dying, bereaved, and alienated. I will lay out the scriptural and traditional foundations (in Stempsey's language, the theological and philosophical grounds) for such competent pastoral-liturgical ministry in part 2, the next two chapters of this book.

Another implication of Stempsey's article is that late-modern people do indeed expect miracles. Otherwise, the strategy of the public

[52] William E. Stempsey, "Scientific Contribution: Miracles and the limits of medical knowledge," *Medicine, Health Care and Philosophy* 5 (2002): 1–9, here 1.

[53] "Physicians today live simultaneously in different worlds with worldviews that are not always completely consistent. Physicians often maintain that each case is unique, yet they practice with a scientific worldview that is based on regularities in nature. Even when physicians are wonderfully humanistic and even religious, and even when they see each patient as a unique individual, they still tend to see the science of medicine in the way that scientists see it—deterministically." Ibid., 7.

relations office of that children's hospital would not make much sense. The data from a 2000 *Newsweek* telephone poll conducted in the United States give compelling evidence for the extent to which Americans, regardless of religious affiliation, believe in miraculous cures. Over three-quarters (77%) of the respondents answered yes to the following: "Regardless of whether you have ever personally prayed for a miracle, please tell me whether you believe that God or the saints perform the following kinds of miracles today. . . . What about curing or healing the sick people given no chance of survival by medical science? Do you think God or the saints perform this kind of miracle today or not?"[54] Note that the question does not ask how such belief ties in with the respondents' larger religious worldviews, beliefs, and practices, if any. A political scientist studying the contemporary social-scientific literature seeking to explain the relationship between beliefs in Christian doctrine and in paranormal phenomena has argued that the prevailing theories, which tend to correlate the two, fall far short of data recently collected in the United States. His study "suggests that millions of Americans are doubters when it comes to traditional Christian paranormal dogma, but have no problem believing in classic paranormal phenomena [such as ESP and psychic healing]."[55] Having correlated the new data into tables, he concludes that explanations for which Americans hold paranormal beliefs and why need revision:

> One reason may be that the nature of spirituality has changed in recent decades. Beginning with the counterculture movement of the late 1960s, people have increasingly rejected traditional religions in favor of more personalized belief structures . . . In this new environment, people pick beliefs 'cafeteria style' rather than being constrained by traditional religious dogma or social structures. The result should be a more even distribution of beliefs across social background variables . . . [and] individual belief systems that include an amalgamation of religious and classic paranormal phenomena . . . If this thinking is correct, then people may be making choices about what paranormal

[54] "Miracles" (New York: Newsweek, Inc., 15 April 2000), accessed 17 October 2005 at: http://poll.orspub.com/poll/lpext.dll/ors/m/miracles/021252-2000.htm. The exact breakdown of responses to this scientifically conducted poll of 752 people was: yes = 77%; no = 16%; don't know = 7%.

[55] Tom W. Rice, "Believe It Or Not: Religious and Other Paranormal Beliefs in the United States," *Journal for the Scientific Study of Religion* 42, no. 1 (2003): 95–106, here 104.

phenomena to believe based more on psychological factors than on social factors.[56]

That particular study considered "social factors" to include educational and income levels, gender, regional location, and religious denomination. A further social-cultural factor contributing to people's ideas and feelings about miracles warrants consideration: the news and entertainment industry, which includes a continuous stream of television programs and movies about paranormal phenomena. While televangelism and other Christian religious broadcasting have been part of American and global entertainment for decades, I turn to one particular case that demonstrates how the commercial television industry's mediation of the miraculous can influence people's religious imaginations.

The story concerns the cult of a "victim soul" centered upon a silent body. [57] In 1987, just shy of her fourth birthday, Audrey Santo nearly drowned in her family's swimming pool in Worcester, Massachusetts. The accident left her in a state of akinetic mutism—paralyzed, mute, unconscious, and on a respirator. Whereas medical professionals expected the child to be institutionalized, her parents brought her home, and during the ensuing years family and other supporters provided the girl (by then a young woman) with full-time care. The family perceived Audrey's survival as a miracle demonstrating the superiority of God's power to that of modern institutions. From this belief, and in the context of a European and American popular cult of victim souls,[58] those devoted to Audrey developed the further conviction that she took on the sufferings of others, offering them to Christ. Audrey had become an agent of healing and hope to the medically incurable, as

[56] Ibid., 104–5.

[57] See Mathew N. Schmalz, "The Silent Body of Audrey Santo," *History of Religions* 42, no. 2 (2002): 116–42. See also, Susan Rodgers, "The Sacramental Body of Audrey Santo: A Holy Mystic Girl in Ritual and Media Spaces in Worcester, Massachusetts, and Beyond," and Mathew N. Schmalz, "Performing the Miraculous in Central Massachusetts," in *Practicing Catholic: Ritual, Body, and Contestation in Catholic Faith*, ed. Bruce T. Morrill and others (New York: Palgrave Macmillan, 2006), 203–6, 227–28. *Note:* Audrey Santo died April 14, 2007.

[58] See Paula M. Kane, "'She offered herself up': The Victim Soul and Victim Spirituality in Catholicism," *Church History* 71, no. 1 (2002): 80–119; and Schmalz, "The Silent Body of Audrey Santo," 120–23.

well as a living sign of God's loving care for those deemed worthless, especially children. Such are the convictions of the Apostolate of the Silent Soul, Audrey's parents, family, and supporters who for years arranged for those seeking physical cures or various sorts of spiritual or psychological deliverance to pray at her bedside, take with them an intercessory prayer addressed to the girl, and assist at large annual Masses held on the date of her accident. The latter reached their climax in 1998 when a crowd of eight thousand worshipers converged on a nearby college football stadium to participate in an elaborate liturgy that included some forty concelebrating priests and the bedridden Audrey, visible through the picture window of a specially outfitted travel trailer located near the altar.

The rapid growth of the cult of Little Audrey, Silent Victim Soul, during the 1990s was due in no small part to the mass media's picking up on the purported miraculous, paranormal occurrences in Audrey's bedroom. Newspaper and magazine coverage spread from the local arena of Worcester publications to regional, national, and then international readerships, including the *Boston Globe*, *New York Times*, *Washington Post*, *Tablet* of London, and *USA Today*. Hagiographic video documentaries gradually emerged, and when EWTN, a conservative-traditionalist Catholic cable television station with international reach, began airing one of these, interest in, as well as pious devotion to, Audrey increased dramatically. Indeed, it played no small part in growing the numbers of devotees who eventually comprised the great crowd at the 1998 anniversary Mass. CBS News and the BBC produced feature stories, the Learning Channel included the Audrey-phenomenon as part of a full-length program on paranormal occurrences, but a 1999 broadcast of the ABC newsmagazine *20/20*, entitled *Miracle of Audrey*, may well have been the apex of the secular news coverage. In a production that anthropologist Susan Rodgers critiques as having disingenuously "eschewed any serious social scientific, historical, or investigative journalism," the program's anchors and reporters presented the story as one of "magic, mystery," and "spiritual experiences," challenging viewers to judge whether miracles really do occur.[59] Implicit in Rodgers's essay is the acknowledgment of the powerful role television plays in how contemporary people shape their ideas, beliefs, and values. That viewer interest ran high is attested by the fact that 20/20 did a follow-up story in 2003,

[59] Quoted by Rodgers in "The Sacramental Body of Audrey Santo," 117–18.

a report on that year's annual commemoration of Audrey's deliverance from drowning, which the Spanish-language television channel Univision also covered.[60] While the ritual scale and numbers actually attending that later event had diminished, the multilingual televised reach of the paranormal, miraculous images and those who engage them only grew.

In her description and analysis Rodgers seems surprised by the way in which ABC's first 20/20 broadcast about Little Audrey focused uncritically on the miraculous angle of the events, persons, and objects, thereby achieving a presentation seemingly "designed to re-enchant small sectors of the American landscape."[61] Rodgers describes how the ABC program repeatedly asks its television audience, "Do you believe in miracles?" The segments of the hour-long broadcast give sound bites from bus-riding pilgrims as they approach the stadium, close-ups of Audrey and her parents' ministrations around her body, dramatic angled shots of statues and flashbacks about the dripping phenomena, only at the end of one segment to have these all overlaid into photos of an unrelated church façade with its niches of statues and a looming crucifix.[62] In other words, the television network blends these specific believers and their practices into generic images of the American church—its buildings and other objects. As for narrative, the interviews focus on the paranormal phenomena, quoting key players on the inexplicability of these miracles, but not on their convictions about what these marvels religiously and ethically *mean*. A further segment considers the proceedings of church bureaucracy in the whole affair,

[60] See Schmalz, "Performing the Miraculous in Central Massachusetts," 227–28.

[61] Ibid. A sociologist of religion confirms Rodgers's analysis, as well as an interpretation of Catholic sacramentalism that isolates images from doctrinal and ethical beliefs: "By downplaying the verbal in the favor of the visual feast of holy pictures, saints, and Audrey close-ups, ABC was more in tune with what sociologist Andrew Greeley has called the Catholic imagination. Though produced by a presumably secular crew at ABC News, the 20/20 documentary effectively conveyed a Catholic sense of the sacramentality of the material world (including Audrey's suffering body)." John Schmalzbauer, "Catholic Sacramentalism as Media Event: A View from the Sociology of Religion and Media Sociology," in *Practicing Catholic: Ritual, Body, and Contestation in Catholic Faith*, ed. Bruce T. Morrill and others, 224 (New York: Palgrave Macmillan, 2006).

[62] See Rodgers, "The Sacramental Body of Audrey Santo," 220.

explaining that nothing conclusive has been determined about the miraculous phenomena.

MEDIATING THE MIRACULOUS IN CONSUMER CULTURE

Television broadcasts, including major news magazine shows that earn high Nielson ratings (e.g., 60 Minutes, Dateline, 20/20), would seem to have a significant impact on how Americans individually shape their ideas and images about religion, Christianity, and Roman Catholicism. In *Consuming Religion* theologian Vincent Miller teaches us to understand the function of television and other media industries within the larger context of postmodern consumer culture. Miller's important methodological insight for theology (and a fortiori, liturgical theology) is that the key to assessing and promoting Christianity's actual role in the lives of contemporary believers lies not in arguing about and presenting doctrinal content (ideas) but rather in analyzing and transforming people's life practices. The "deep workings of culture" reside in *practices*, "social actions that have a profound power to form us as persons in ways in which we are not aware," rather than the overtly articulated principles and ideas of academics, prelates, and television or talk-radio commentators.[63] While the latter certainly do influence people's beliefs and opinions, they are only able to attract sympathetic ears among persons habituated in specific social structures of using and interpreting the symbols of their daily lives, that is, who participate in a particular culture.

Postmodern advanced capitalist society has evolved as a consumer culture, a situation in which people are habitually disposed to engaging everything, including traditional symbols, beliefs, and practices, as commodities. At the economic base of contemporary society, the dynamics of commodification entail the reifying and abstracting of products from their place of origin and agency so as then to advertise them as not only desirable but personally necessary for consumers. Employment structures and commercial marketing have largely succeeded in creating a culture of consumers, people who desire goods abstractly produced by anonymous others yet felt to be urgently attractive or necessary. Indeed, pleasure for consumers resides more in the desire experienced in shopping than in finally having the product

---

[63] Vincent J. Miller, *Consuming Religion: Christian Faith and Practice in a Consumer Culture* (New York: Continuum, 2004), 19, 22.

itself.[64] Economic profitability in consumer culture depends upon corporations always having more "stuff" to market to well-practiced consumers.

With durable and disposable goods now basically available to the vast majority of people in advanced capitalist societies, "corporate cultural production"[65] seeks further profits through the proliferation of technologies, especially those that make each consumer an agent of his or her own entertainment and personal communication. With the proliferation of both cable television networks and internet-based delivery systems, the entertainment industry constantly needs more content, which they obtain by commodifying elements out of cultures—from music to the arts to clothing to traditional stories to mythic and even historical personages. Corporations then fashion these into cultural commodities that, like all marketed products, "are abstracted from their conditions of production, presented as objects valuable in themselves, shorn of their interrelations with the other symbols, beliefs, and practices that determine their meaning and function in their traditional contexts."[66] Once severed from their integral contexts, cultural commodities can be manipulated for uses unrelated and even contradictory to original meanings by not only the industries that produce and market them but also by those who consume them. Culture and religion are increasingly matters of individual choice, as commercially mediated celebrities, spectacles, and products shape consumers' unreflective practices of mixing and matching, taking up and casting aside images and symbols.

While the benefits of modern freedom (from oppressive social structures and statuses, for example) are undeniably evident in the greater personal agency afforded individuals in consumer culture, there is also an impoverishment of the human condition: "When we relate to cultural religious traditions as commodities, they lose their power to inform the concrete practice of life."[67] Personal fit, rather than communal commitment, becomes the norm for decision, as does personal spirituality rather than institutionally based religion. But that marks a profoundly different practice of faith and thus a different faith itself. For example, rather than standing amid an assembly at liturgy hear-

[64] See ibid., 116–26.
[65] Ibid., 29.
[66] Ibid., 72.
[67] Ibid., 13.

ing the word of God and witnessing the sacramental anointing of the sick, an American Christian sits in front of a television set that asks, "Do *you* believe in miracles? Watch for this hour and judge for yourself." What possible good will such passing exposure to paranormal spectacles do for the individual viewer in his or her hour of need? Will the television provide a community's commitment, personal care, sacramental touch, listening ear? Can the individual religious consumer learn the wisdom, experience the joy, and value the struggle of giving and receiving faithful service to, from, and with others such that he or she has a repertoire of practices ready to hand in moments of need? Is "need" only a matter of one's own satisfaction, or is one habituated in empathy and expectant of encountering the divine in human care for and accompaniment with the neighbor?

One final scenario from the Little Audrey affair affords an excellent example of how the entertainment industry abstracts and reifies the content of religion, presenting the practices of specific believers in a commodified fashion that conforms to consumer reception. Historian of religions Mathew Schmalz has published a study of the two television networks that covered the sixteenth annual commemoration of Audrey's accident in 2003. The day's events, which took place at the Santo home, drew busloads of pilgrims attracted to the miraculous girl, statues, and stories of healing. Schmalz describes and analyzes the pronounced difference in the way ABC's 20/20 and the Spanish-language Univision cable station performed that day. Univision's cameraman chronicled a communal luncheon some one hundred fifty pilgrims from New Jersey had spread, as well as their preparations for celebrating a Spanish Mass later in the day. Univision's correspondent inserted herself among the pilgrims, who "talked about their conversions to Christ and prophecies made by Mary at Medjugorje" but especially of Audrey "and of the miraculous oil from the statues at the Santo Home, oil that they had distributed to relatives far beyond the confines of Worcester."[68]

In sharp contrast, Schmalz observed, the ABC cameraman and sound technician, far from interviewing let alone eating with the people, "essentially ignored the pilgrims except as rather objects to be gazed down upon" from the second floor of the neighboring house, where they repeatedly returned to get an overview of the Santo's

---

[68] Schmalz, "Performing the Miraculous in Central Massachusetts," 228.

driveway and yard.[69] What interested the 20/20 team was the display and sale of rosaries and other items that had been placed near Audrey. The crew switched between getting overhead panoramas of the buying and selling and close-up shots of various items on the vendors' tables. Upon gaining access to Audrey's bedroom, the ABC cameraman did not take in the human composition of place and persons but rather "penetrated the space surrounding Audrey so that the camera would bear down upon her from above."[70] Thus did Audrey become a cultural commodity for the eventual television audience who, in turn, became individual voyeurs of objects and spectacles disassociated from narratives of communal faith.

LITURGICAL MINISTRY OF WORD AND SACRAMENT: THE SALVIFIC WAY FORWARD

The opportunity for postmodern Catholics (and other Christians, of course) is to discover and share the Gospel as a living, saving word through sacramental rites that empower people struggling with the misfortunes of illness, aging, and death to narrate their suffering in concert with that of Christ. Morris reports that narrative, in a variety of forms including prayer, is proving a crucial postmodern strategy for finding meaning in suffering.[71] Narrative enables people to situate their experience of pain in a consoling, and at times empowering, company of voices, breaking the silence modernity has imposed on suffering. In her prophetic challenge to modern apathy Dorothee Soelle argues that the language of prayer and liturgy has the power "to move [the afflicted] from purely passive endurance to suffering that can humanize them in a productive way . . . go[ing] over to the speaking God of a reality experienced with feeling in pain and happiness. It was this God with whom Christ spoke in Gethsemane."[72] Celebrations of such rites as bringing Communion from the Sunday assembly to the housebound,

[69] Ibid., 237.

[70] Ibid. Schmalz's essay includes a number of photos taken by his sister, photojournalist Julia Schmalz, that capture the ABC cameraman positioning his sizeable, bulky apparatus within inches of miraculous statues or relics on vendors tables, followed by a most compelling shot of his tripod positioned against Audrey's bed, with the camera, and him hulking behind it, angling down over Audrey's head. See ibid., 233–36.

[71] See Morris, *Illness and Culture in the Postmodern Age*, 89, 194–98, 201.

[72] Soelle, *Suffering*, 75, 78.

laying hands on the sick, sharing Eucharist as food for the final journey (of death), keeping vigil with the bereaved, and confidently invoking eternal rest for the faithful departed are all powerful experiences revealing through proclaimed Word and tangible symbols the strong and loving presence of the Christ so often hidden and intangible in the ambiguities of life and death. The liturgical tradition of the church thus presents itself as an original way forward in the postmodern search for practices of healing.[73]

In part 3, chapters 5 through 7, we will explore how the liturgical economies of the Pastoral Care of the Sick and the Order of Christian Funerals are renewed forms of Christian tradition capable of placing believers in active, meaningful engagement with Christ in his Body, the church, through his power, the Spirit. Before attending to these rites in detail, however, we need first to consider the elements of Scripture and tradition crucial to their humanly beneficial celebration. Fundamental to the reform of the rites has been the church's rediscovery of Scripture as the irreducible source of liturgical tradition. Not only did Vatican II endorse a reform that made the proclamation of the word essential to the celebration of every sacrament, the council also declared the paschal mystery—the content of which is utterly biblical—to be at the heart of the entire sanctifying mission of the church's rites.[74] Narrative, in other words, is essential to the human healing that divine worship has to offer. But just as this narrative dimension of sacramental liturgy resonates with the description and analysis of contemporary crisis, illness, and healing we have surveyed in this chapter, so also the recurrent temptation to seek "quick fixes" I reported in those domains likewise constitutes an ongoing problem for the way believers approach sacramental grace. Fetishistic practices of sacred presence, excessive claims to and practices of clerical mediation, and a broader cultural consumerist mentality of immediate possession can all impede people's giving of themselves over to the mystery of salvation that unfolds in the process of biblically informed rites and liturgically healed lives.

For Christians the antidote to errant ritualism is the content of biblical faith and the life of action to which it calls us. That simple

---

[73] For another discussion of Christian healing and ritual today, see John Koenig, "Healing," in *Practicing the Faith*, ed. Dorothy Bass, 149–62 (San Francisco: Jossey-Bass, 1997).

[74] See *Sacrosanctum Concilium*, nos. 5, 6.

statement, nonetheless, belies the complex interpretive process whereby we humans place ourselves (our world) in front of a text, get behind the words of the text, and ultimately enter into the world of the text.[75] The next two chapters will follow that hermeneutical pattern by studying contemporary biblical scholarship on Jesus as healer (chapter 3) and expounding faith in the paschal mystery as the theological key to encountering the healing Christ through celebrations of word and sacrament in service to one another (chapter 4).

[75] For a clear overview of hermeneutic theory that makes the work of Gadamer and Ricoeur accessible, see Sandra Schneiders, *The Revelatory Text: Interpreting the New Testament as Sacred Scripture*, 2nd ed. (Collegeville, MN: Liturgical Press, 1999), 13–26.

Part 2

Scripture and Tradition

Chapter 3

Christ the Healer: The World of Biblical Witness

THE WORD OF GOD: PRIMARY SOURCE FOR
RENEWED SACRAMENTAL TRADITION

As has already been noted more than once in the previous chapters, Scripture is the irreducible, essential source for Christian tradition and thus a key to the reform and renewal of liturgy in the Latin Rite.[1] Constant recourse to biblical texts prevents the reduction of the faith to some ersatz "Catholic imagination."[2] The pastoral and theological impact envisioned, and slowly but steadily being realized, by the renewed engagement of the Bible in the practice of Catholic tradition cannot be overstated. The council's mandate that the proclamation of Scripture be integral to the liturgy (a primary form of the tradition) has changed the content, tenor, and length of sacramental celebrations. Whereas prior to the council liturgical reading from Scripture was cursorily done, if at all, often in an unintelligible language, the Mass and other sacraments now include substantial and sustained readings focused around the Gospels and other New Testament texts, but also drawing from the Old Testament, especially the psalms. For believers intellectually and emotionally capable of engagement in the Liturgy of the Word during the celebration of Mass or other rites, gospel stories of Jesus' words and actions contribute to their image of the Christ who is salvifically present in the sacramental ritual. When done with even a modicum of care (i.e., well-paced reading, some reflection or preaching, opportunity for voiced or silent response), proclamation of the Word prevents sacramental celebrations from devolving into mere

---

[1] See George H. Tavard, "Tradition," in *The New Dictionary of Theology*, ed. Joseph Komonchak and others (Wilmington, DE: Michael Glazier 1989), 1037–41; and Sandra Schneiders, *The Revelatory Text: Interpreting the New Testament as Sacred Scripture*, 2nd ed. (Collegeville, MN: Liturgical Press, 1999), 67–86.

[2] See above, p. 51, n. 61.

ritualism. While the faithful may well draw consolation from the doctrine that sacramental grace is assured in the validly performed rites of the church, the tradition has much more to offer than this conceptually held belief. The recovered and enhanced tradition of the proclaimed Word in all the church's rites offers an encounter with the person of Jesus the Christ, who comes to confront and console us with his revelation of who God is, what God has done, what God desires, and how we are invited into that God's reign. This altogether amounts to a deepened experience and understanding of grace.[3]

What distinguishes Scripture as proclaimed Word in liturgy from all other ways whereby believers might engage biblical texts is the church's belief that Christ is truly speaking in the present moment amid his assembled Body.[4] In liturgy the scriptural passages are not merely read or studied or personally reflected upon but, rather, the Word comes alive among a people, making present a living encounter with the Lord Jesus. Christ is present in liturgy because of the paschal mystery that every celebration of the rites enacts.[5] An article from the *General Introduction to the Order of Christian Funerals* exemplifies this treasure of the tradition:

> In every celebration for the dead, the Church attaches great importance to the reading of the word of God. The readings proclaim to the assembly the paschal mystery, teach remembrance of the dead, convey the hope of being gathered together again in God's kingdom, and encourage the witness of Christian life. Above all, the readings tell of God's designs for a world in which suffering and death will relinquish their hold on all whom God has called his own. A careful selection and use of readings from Scripture for the funeral rites will provide the family

---

[3] See Bernard Cooke, *Sacraments and Sacramentality*, rev. ed. (Mystic, CT: Twenty-Third Publications, 1994), 224–32.

[4] See Louis-Marie Chauvet, *The Sacraments: The Word of God at the Mercy of the Body* (Collegeville, MN: Liturgical Press, 2001), 43–49.

[5] "The mystery of the Lord's death and resurrection gives power to all of the Church's activity. 'For it was from the side of Christ as he slept the sleep of death upon the cross that there came forth the sublime sacrament of the whole Church.' The Church's liturgical and sacramental life and proclamation of the Gospel make this mystery present in the life of the faithful." International Commission on English in the Liturgy, *Order of Christian Funerals* (1989), no. 2; hereafter, OCF.

and the community with an opportunity to hear God speak to them in their needs, sorrows, fears, and hopes.[6]

While the priority given to the paschal mystery in the present example might seem due to the pastoral circumstances of the funeral rites, that priority is actually essential to all liturgical celebrations. It is only because God has raised the crucified Jesus from the dead and continuously sends his Spirit into the midst of those assembled in his name that the celebrating community enters into the very world of Jesus, sharing in the company of his kingdom, "God's designs for a world in which suffering and death will relinquish their hold . . ." While we shall consider more closely the fundamental liturgical concept of the paschal mystery in chapter 4, the point here is to appreciate how in the celebration of the Word the members of a given liturgical assembly are not left to speculate, "What would Jesus do?" Rather, they respond to the personal offer of grace the living Jesus gives in that moment. The assembled faithful do not hear about God but rather they "hear God speak to them." This God does not communicate by some sort of mental telepathy but through the activity of the liturgical assembly and its ministers, whose faithful pastoral practice of the rites meets the people in their thoughts, experiences, and emotions—in this case, "in their needs, sorrows, fears, and hopes." That this is not merely wishful thinking is assured by the biblical witness, especially the gospel narratives, wherein the humanity of the risen Jesus comes alive in the stories of his encounters with the women and men among whom he taught and healed, proclaiming the in-breaking of God's reign.

In addition to the proclamation of the Word in the liturgy (including the readings, psalmody, and homily), biblical words and imagery suffuse the entire content of the rites of the postconciliar church: "It is from the scriptures that the prayers, collects, and hymns draw their inspiration and their force, and that the actions and signs derive their meaning."[7] Indeed, the reformed rites of the church find their *pastoral* promise fundamentally in the biblical witness of the person and mission of Jesus. For example, the *General Introduction of the Pastoral Care of the Sick* opens with a blunt acknowledgment of the troubling

---

[6] OCF, no. 22.

[7] *Sacrosanctum Concilium* (Constitution on the Sacred Liturgy), no. 24. *Vatican Council II: The Conciliar and Post Conciliar Documents*, ed. Austin Flannery, OP, rev. ed. (Northport, NY: Costello Publications, 1992), 10.

questions suffering and illness pose to the human condition only to assert confidently that "Christ's words" reveal "meaning and value" in people's struggles with illness both "for their own salvation and for the salvation of the world." This stunning assertion about individual and universal salvation coincides with believers' personal knowledge of Christ's love for them in their illness, a conviction grounded in the fact that Jesus "during his lifetime often visited and healed the sick."[8] Even as Christians find the promise of the world's salvation in the resurrection of the crucified Christ, this faith does not abstract him into the realm of philosophical principle or mythical deity.[9] The gift of genuine faith in Jesus as the Christ, the Son of God, entails a yearning to know Jesus of Nazareth that is as ancient as the communities from which the canonical gospels emerged. A crucial distinction between the gospels the early church discerned to be God's Word and the various Gnostic texts that vied with them for the claim to revelation was the latter's general disregard for the stories of Jesus' life and work among his fellow Palestinian Jewish people. To give revelatory status to those stories is to embrace the mysterious ambiguity of our created bodily condition as the very medium of our divine redemption.[10] Thus Gnostic gospels largely include sayings by Jesus but little if any narrative of his actions—his miraculous work with the physically and spiritually afflicted, his table fellowship with "sinners," his emotional investment in the lives of the poor. It is the revelation of this Jesus as Christ that makes Scripture the inspiring, empowering source of meaning in the liturgy's symbolic words and actions.

---

[8] International Commission on English in the Liturgy, *Pastoral Care of the Sick: Rites of Anointing and Viaticum* (1983), no. 1; hereafter, PCS.

[9] "[W]henever the post-Easter and pre-Easter Jesus are allowed to drift apart, we run into the problem of high versus low Christology. The only Jesus Mark knows is Jesus risen, but the Jesus he loves and follows is unknowable without his cultural particularity and history." William Reiser, *Jesus in Solidarity with His People: A Theologian Looks at Mark* (Collegeville, MN: Liturgical Press, 2000), 191–92.

[10] "Narrativity, after all, inevitably involves materiality. To have the good news revealed in a human story represents an affirmation of the body and of time . . . But precisely that conviction is incompatible with the Gnostic perception of materiality as a ghastly error or malicious trick." Luke Timothy Johnson, *The Real Jesus: The Misguided Quest for the Historical Jesus and the Truth of the Traditional Gospels* (San Francisco: HarperCollins, 1996), 150.

A significant portion of the total biblical portrait of Jesus entails healings and other wondrous deeds. While modern Scripture scholars debate the definition of miracles and the exact parameters of the healing pericopes in the gospels, the sheer volume and cumulative impact of the stories lead Leander Keck to conclude, "Whoever will interpret the Gospels has no option but to come to terms with miracles."[11] Keck tallies some thirty-two different miracle stories (exorcisms, healings, raisings of the dead, so-called nature miracles) appearing a total of sixty-four times in the four gospels, not counting additional general summaries of Jesus' deeds. While people regularly address Jesus as teacher in Mark, for example, nearly a third of the total verses in that gospel (ending at 16:8) directly or indirectly relate miracle traditions. If one considers just the first ten chapters (that is, up to the passion narrative) the proportion of miracle material leaps to 47 percent.[12] Now consider what such statistics imply about the Jesus the assembled faithful encounter in the three-year Sunday cycle of gospel readings. As the church moves through the Synoptic Gospels in Ordinary Time, accounts of exorcisms and healings occur both serially and intermittently. In addition, Johannine accounts of miraculous signs constitute key passages for Lenten Year A, while all three Easter cycles include some accounts of the apostles' similarly marvelous deeds, as the first reading is taken exclusively from Acts throughout that season.

Clearly, Christ the healer constitutes no small part of the Word proclaimed in the church's regular worship, let alone in those rites serving sickness and death, and yet the question remains as to how that Word is broken open through the clergy's preaching and the people's imaginations. The danger lies in the disjointed, isolated hearing of the pericopes, especially when this constitutes many worshipers' only engagement with Scripture. Taken in isolation, accounts of Jesus' curing blindness or releasing a person from demonic possession and the like can lead contemporary hearers to reduce them to fantastic tales of the paranormal or of a God who (through Jesus and the disciples)

---

[11] Leander Keck, "Excursus: Interpreting the Miracle Stories in Matthew," in *The New Interpreter's Bible,* vol. 8, *Matthew, Mark,* 244 (Nashville: Abingdon Press, 1995).

[12] John P. Meier, *A Marginal Jew: Rethinking the Historical Jesus,* vol. 2, *Mentor, Message, and Miracles* (New York: Doubleday, 1994), 618–19. Treating Matthew's Gospel, Keck reports that it contains more miracle stories than any of the others. See ibid., 241.

episodically breaks the laws of nature and/or arbitrarily chooses to eliminate the physical pain of only certain sufferers.

How the substantial portion of the gospels depicting the healing deeds of Christ is preached and received in the liturgical assembly over time cannot but have a significant impact on how today's believers—clergy and laity—interpret God's presence and action in both the church's sacramental rites and the personal, social, and religious dimensions of their own lives. Facile homiletic explanations of Jesus' healings as magic feats whose time frame was limited to his "earthly mission" and whose purpose was to lead all subsequent generations only to "spiritual" healing may shore up some clerical sense of authority in the sacraments or allay those committed to modern rationalism.[13] Still, diminishing numbers of not only regular lay participants at Sunday Mass and other rites but also actual priests available to perform them would seem to indicate that such simplistic, even dismissive, interpretations of such a large part of the gospels' treasury is a practice the church can ill be allowed to continue. The rhetoric of saving souls does not seem to speak to younger and middle-aged (baby-boom) generations of American Catholics for whom, for better or worse, the threat of eternal damnation has become largely untenable. Searches for holistic spirituality have been underway now for decades, largely pursued as alternatives to institutional religion and, more specifically for Catholics, mechanistic sacramental rites. That the rites themselves actually bear resources for healing this situation, that the church's sacramental liturgies of healing offer the very integral ministry to body, mind, and spirit contemporary believers rightly desire, is the burden of the present and remaining chapters of this book.

THE CHALLENGE AND PROMISE OF
THE BIBLICAL WITNESS TO JESUS AS HEALER

To argue that the gospel texts comprise a key resource for the renewal of the church's liturgical ministry of healing is not to deny the obvious: the miracle stories in the New Testament pose formidable challenges to their modern readership. A number of reasons for

[13] For a discussion of how "Cartesian dualism" has come to afflict the church's pastoral ministry to "souls," as well as how a communal approach is needed in an era that denies suffering and hides sickness, see Bernard Häring, *In Pursuit of Wholeness: Healing in Today's Church* (Liguori, MO: Liguori Publications, 1985), 51–55.

hesitating to delve into the miraculous healing narratives present themselves. Taken in isolation, the action in a given gospel episode happens so fast, with the marvelous result so soon reached, that these types of narratives might seem merely to aid and abet the "quick fix" mentality that David Morris describes in his critique of modern people's reactions to health crises. We likewise noted a similar quick-fix mentality operative in some people's recourse to paranormal interventions in the hope of miraculous turnarounds in desperate cases. The miracle accounts in the gospels can correlate with reports and depictions of the paranormal in news programs and video (film and television) entertainment such that people might relegate the healing stories to the realm of the bizarre. The problem becomes one of credulity, as we saw in the media's handling and various responses to the Little Audrey phenomenon. The educated modern Christian may react, "these things just don't happen in the real world," while looking nervously over one's shoulder to be sure he or she is not being associated with the ignorant or superstitious. Embarrassed dismissal of the gospel miracles can become an apologetic exercise, if only in self-reflection, among secularized and agnostic friends and colleagues.

This sentiment, which biblical scholar John Meier calls "the academic sneer factor," has roots reaching back to the Enlightenment philosophies of Spinoza, Voltaire, Hume, and Lessing, whose arguments against the possibility of miracles (biblical or otherwise) not only were consistent with their closed-universe cosmologies but also sought to counter confessional claims to miracles as proofs of Jesus' divinity.[14] Bultmann asserted the inability of moderns both to avail themselves of electricity and medical science and to believe in New Testament miracles, setting a course for Scripture scholars' rationalistic, mythological, and other such interpretations of the miracle accounts. While N. T. Wright perceives "a quiet revolution" in the current Historical Jesus Quest's acceptance that Jesus did actions that his contemporaries considered beyond the regular cosmic order, Meier warns that the miracles in the gospels remain "perhaps the most intractable problem" in any historical-critical sifting of the Jesus traditions."[15] Given the complexity and discomfort caused by the modern historical quandary

[14] Meier, *A Marginal Jew*, 519–21. See also, N. T. Wright, *Jesus and the Victory of God*, Christian Origins and the Question of God, vol. 2 (Minneapolis: Fortress Press, 1996), 186–87; and Keck, "Excursus," 248–49.

[15] Wright, *Jesus and the Victory of God*, 186; Meier, *A Marginal Jew*, 454.

over miracles, the contemporary preacher, pastoral minister, or any member of the faithful may well want to avoid delving too deeply into the miracle traditions in the gospels, if at all. On the other hand, Meier criticizes his fellow academics, enclosed, it would seem, in the proverbial ivory tower, for ignoring polling data that show an overwhelming majority of Americans believe that God works miracles to this very day.[16] His criticism coincides with my work in the previous chapter and serves as a reminder that many of the assembled faithful do not necessarily react incredulously to gospel accounts of miracles proclaimed in the liturgy.

Against the Historical Jesus Quest's dissecting of texts to determine whether recounted incidents "really happened" or are "historically sound," some biblical scholars have mounted counterarguments for the narrative integrity of each gospel as a whole.[17] This presses the enterprise beyond the limiting criteria of modern historical scholarship to "the domain of philosophy and theology,"[18] just as we saw William Stempsey argue concerning miracles in the context of contemporary medical practice. But to speak of a philosophy or theology is basically to entertain the question of *meaning*, the effort to understand how the New Testament authors, as well as the characters they portrayed, constructed their world and interpreted events within it. For first-century (CE) Jewish people the cosmos was not a self-functioning, closed system called "nature" but rather a world continuously sustained by the will of God, who could at any time act in marvelous ways. Meanwhile, Hellenistic culture abounded with stories of divine and superhuman beings performing miracles. Asking today whether miraculous events could have happened back then poses a question to the biblical sources they neither considered nor even conceived.

[16] Meier cites a 1989 Gallup opinion survey that found 82 percent of Americans, polled across the American social spectrum, agreed that "even today, miracles are performed by the power of God," while only 6 percent completely disagreed. See *A Marginal Jew*, 520–21. A decade later a *Newsweek* poll found 77 percent of Americans believe God works miraculous cures of the sick today. See above, chap. 3, p. 48, n. 54.

[17] Johnson further criticizes many of his colleagues ("questers") for limiting the question of the historical Jesus only to the four gospels rather than engaging the entire New Testament. See *The Real Jesus*, 151.

[18] Meier, *A Marginal Jew*, 514–15.

What people in that world did contest, on the other hand, was the meaning of such marvels—their agency, authorization, purpose, implications—what New Testament and subsequent generations of believers in Jesus' lordship articulate as *faith*. One places one's faith in Christ Jesus and the coming reign of God he revealed, not in miracles. The gospels relay miracle stories not as journalistic accounts of incidents (as with modern historical biography), nor as *proofs* of Jesus' divine or superhuman status (as with the Greeks), but as *revelations* of the person, message, and mission of Jesus.[19] Keck thus offers this sound principle for interpreting miracle stories: "The question of faith/non-faith must be posed in terms of *what* message the miracle story wants to communicate. Do not permit the offense of the miracle story to replace the offense of the gospel."[20]

The offense of the Gospel, of course, is the scandal of the cross and the mystery of the resurrection. It is this paradox that must take charge of believers' imaginations and shape their own lives. Luke Timothy Johnson demonstrates how the "pattern of obedient suffering and loving service" is the consistent image of Jesus that pervades the entire corpus of the New Testament, a message so theologically and anthropologically scandalous, he suggests, as to motivate current "Historical Jesus questers" to deconstruct the gospels in search of a more sociopolitically tenable Christ: "In our present age, in which the 'wisdom of the world' is expressed in individualism, narcissism, preoccupation with private rights, and competition, the 'wisdom of the cross' is the most profoundly countercultural message of all."[21] To that list of contemporary conventional wisdom we could add the exclusively biomedical view of sickness and healing, the suppression of pain, and the marginalization of aging and death. In a trenchant analysis of contemporary society and widespread Christian apathy toward suffering, Dorothee Soelle recognizes from the earliest generations of the church forward a tendency to suppress the (scandalous) paradox essential to the faith. Soelle argues that various developments in trinitarian theology and Christology, through repeated efforts at guarding the image of divine supremacy from the paradox of the cross, historically silenced the very prophetic, liberating word that is the church's heri-

[19] See Keck, "Excursus," 246–47, 249. See also, N. T. Wright, *Jesus and the Victory of God*, 187–88, 194.

[20] Keck, "Excursus," 251.

[21] Johnson, *The Real Jesus*, 166.

tage and mission.[22] The sad irony is that Christians thereby abandon the unique salvific (healing) gift the Gospel offers, a paradoxical lived knowledge of a compassion that "cannot be derived directly from nature or grounded in it . . . the unending affirmation of life that arises in the dark night of the cross."[23]

The paschal mystery is, indeed, the key to Christian faith and thus to the sacraments. While ecclesial documents and theologians regularly articulate the death and resurrection of Christ as grounding the sacramental efficacy of the church's rites, my concern here is with how those climactic events cohere with Jesus' entire public mission. This connection, N. T. Wright argues, was vital at the church's origins: "The earliest Christians regarded Jesus' achievement on the cross as the decisive victory over evil. But they saw it, even more, as the climax of a career in which active, outgoing, healing love had become the trademark and hallmark. It is so easy to turn this point in a sentimental or pietistic direction that a historian may well be shy of raising the matter. But when we put the historical package together . . . this is the theme that emerges."[24] Only when Jesus' end is grasped in conjunction with how he got there can the entire breadth of the gospel narratives have the force to inspire the pastoral effectiveness of the various healing rites of the church's liturgy. Otherwise, we are left in our liturgical celebrations with hearing disjointed stories about Jesus doing good that variably warm the heart or confound the head, only to fall back on the image of Jesus' crucifixion as an exhortation to trust that our suffering is somehow part of God's will. Such words too often fall flat on the ears of the sick or the bereaved or those accompanying them, leaving people to seek support from other resources they may well already have exhausted. At worst, Soelle passionately argues, a simplistic call for submission to God's will as revealed in Jesus' death too often has proven a practical Christian masochism.[25] The Gospel, as we shall see in the remainder of this chapter, reveals a God compassionately present *in* human struggles with alienation, sickness, and death *through* the specific words and actions Jesus performed among his people. Solidarity in human suffering is the revelation of divine love.

[22] See Dorothee Soelle, *Suffering*, trans. Everett R. Kalin (Philadelphia: Fortress Press, 1975), 43–44.

[23] Ibid., 157–58.

[24] Wright, *Jesus and the Victory of God*, 607.

[25] See Soelle, *Suffering*, 17–28.

Once we recognize the priority of the paradoxical paschal mystery in approaching the content of the miracle stories in the gospels, we are enabled to discover the depths of what they reveal about both the human condition and God's gracious salvation in Christ Jesus.

> The miracle stories were first told not as constituent elements of a 'life of Jesus,' but each as a complete story, summing up some aspect of the meaning of the Christ-event for Christian faith. Each one shows some aspect of human need, symbolizing human separation from God, authentic life, and the need for salvation (from hunger, sickness, meaninglessness, subjection to demonic powers and the accidents of nature, sin, death). Each one pictures the act of God in Christ to deliver human beings from this threat to authentic life. Each one looks back on the life, death, and resurrection of Jesus and sums up the meaning of the whole Christ-event in one brief narrative.[26]

While the primary danger for Christian faith is the rejection of the offensive—but thereby life-giving—wisdom of the cross, we risk further deprivation of the gospels' personally and socially transformative power if we presume we already understand all there is to know about that list of human misfortunes Keck has gleaned from the gospel stories. Here the otherness of the biblical world—the particularity of its anthropology, cosmology, psychology, social structures, and institutions—comes as a likewise promising offense to the common attitudes, assumptions, or even entire worldviews Christians may unreflectively hold in modern society. Faith in Jesus heals, but Jesus the healer works the marvel of salvation precisely in and through the concrete circumstances of peoples' living and dying. While baptism into Christ's death has immersed us in the pattern of his life, the various healing stories in the gospels contain a treasury of details about the human condition that promise to disabuse us (at least to some degree) of our modern biomedical blindness. Salvation in sacramental rites can thereby be delivered from the realm of abstract theological concepts to the concrete experiences of life.

THE BIBLICAL PARAMETERS OF HEALING:
COMPARISON AND CONTRAST TO LATE MODERNITY

Exploring the world of Jesus the healer requires a clear delineation of terminology, a challenging task given both the profound

---

[26] Keck, "Excursus," 245.

sociocultural differences between the New Testament and late-modern worlds and the fact that our analysis (in English) must work in translation of the texts' original language (Greek).

We could begin by asking whether Jesus was a physician. While in Christian history the term has shared with many others (e.g., lamb, shepherd, redeemer, mother, king, etc.) the function of symbolizing who Jesus is in the life of believers or communities, the historical question posed to the biblical texts can only yield an unqualified no. In the two situations in the New Testament where Jesus is called a physician, Jesus is using the word analogously about himself in defending his prophetic mission: "Surely you will quote this proverb to me: 'Physician heal yourself!'" (Luke 4:23, NIV), and "It is not the healthy who need a doctor, but the sick" (Mark 2:17//Matt 9:12//Luke 5:31, NIV). Physician, then, is a metaphor figuratively communicating something about the person and work of Jesus.[27] The biblical world, Palestinian and Mediterranean, did have literal doctors, practitioners learned in medical arts (such as they were) whom people paid for their services, as depicted in Mark's account of the hemorrhaging woman: "She had suffered a great deal under the care of many doctors and had spent all she had, yet instead of getting better she grew worse" (Mark 5:26, NIV). Sick people also, in fact more often, availed themselves of other resources, especially home remedies and what anthropologists generally call folk healers, including healers associated with divine powers and/or sacred sites. The latter category seems the most adequate for analyzing the gospels' descriptions of Jesus' care of the sick and afflicted.

Still, the methods of ancient physicians and healers had much in common. While Greco-Roman physicians worked from learned treatises, most notably the large collection associated with Hippocrates, their practices were necessarily a matter of trial, error, and accumulated wisdom and skills—some of which overlapped with home and folk healer remedies. Furthermore, some of the Hippocratic treatises attributed conditions or cures to the sacred or divine. Descriptions of medical symptoms and physicians' procedures by the first-century Jewish writer Josephus likewise indicate that the line separating

---

[27] See Harold Remus, *Jesus as Healer*, Understanding Jesus Today, ed. Howard Clark Kee (Cambridge: Cambridge University Press, 1997), 15; and John J. Pilch, *Healing in the New Testament: Insights from Medical and Mediterranean Anthropology* (Minneapolis: Fortress Press), 63–64, 77.

professional doctors from folk healers was not nearly so distinct as today. Physicians' dismal success rates for cures, on the other hand, were in sharp contrast to other healers' regularly achieving successful results.[28] Such a claim, so counterintuitive to conventional modern thinking, should pique our interest. A further conclusion, the consensus among New Testament scholars, that available textual evidence is insufficient for determining whether Jesus the *healer* actually *cured* anybody,[29] surely presses us to look more closely at how scholars are using these and related terms.

Over the past two decades John Pilch has taken the lead in demonstrating how the cross-cultural work of medical anthropology offers a wealth of knowledge about human sickness and health that New Testament scholars can utilize in their analysis of the healing narratives in the gospels. Comparative ethnomedicine, an anthropological subdiscipline that studies how illness is socially constructed through a given culture's practices and beliefs about disease, has afforded Pilch a framework for attaining numerous insights into gospel texts that have heretofore evaded biblical scholars biased by their own medicocentric environment.[30] The basic goal for people confronting sickness in any sociocultural context, Pilch reports, is efficacy, "the perceived capacity of a given practice to affect sickness in some desirable way."[31] Efficacy is a matter of perception, which, in turn, is a function of how people go about constructing meaning for their lives and world. For those committed to a biomedical worldview, treatment is efficacious when medical professionals have diagnosed and altered the physical symptoms presented by a patient according to the scientific categories of pathology, epidemiology, genetics, and so forth. The subject of treatment

---

[28] See Remus, *Jesus as Healer*, 3, 6, 11; Pilch, *Healing in the New Testament*, 77, 13–44, 34, 60.

[29] See Pilch, *Healing in the New Testament*, 72, 142; Remus, *Jesus as Healer*, 112; and Meier, *A Marginal Jew*, 517, 661, 706.

[30] Anthropologists have coined the term "medicocentrism" in reference "to the belief that scientific Western medicine is the only truth relative to health and sickness questions," a bias contemporary historians too often unwittingly impose on ancient texts. Pilch, *Healing in the New Testament*, 91, and see 103. The concept is comparable to Morris's biomedical model, reviewed above in chap. 2, pp. 37–38. See David B. Morris, *Illness and Culture in the Postmodern Age* (Berkeley: University of California Press, 1998), 5, 14.

[31] Ibid., 34, quoting Allan Young, "The Anthropology of Illness and Sickness," *Annual Review of Anthropology* 11 (1982): 277.

is the individual functioning as a biological unit, a view of the autonomous person consistent with what anthropologists identify as the egocentrism or individualism of Western culture. Eighty percent of the global population today, however, as well as all who lived prior to modernity, do not share this perspective. For people in sociocentric or collectivistic non-Western cultures, healing has been affected when "the individual experience of illness has been made meaningful, personal suffering shared, and the individual leaves the marginal situation of sickness and is reincorporated—in health or even death—back into the social body."[32] Health, then, is a matter of restoration not only for the sick person but also for the shared social order, its values and coherence. The difference between this conception of well-being and the Western therapeutic model of the individual regaining self-sufficiency, Pilch argues, leads to disparate reactions to the World Health Organization's definition of health. As we saw with David Morris, Pilch notes how Western professionals are uneasy with the definition, while non-Westerners are very comfortable with the WHO's description of health as a comprehensive state of well-being, "physical, mental, and social . . . and not merely the absence of disease and infirmity."[33]

With the phenomenon of health being such a complex social construction, it is not surprising to learn that its opposite is likewise a complex human affair. With characteristic erudition John Dominic Crossan has summarized the fruits of Pilch's research: "Society (and its systemic structures) can not only exacerbate the *illness* that follows from a *disease*, it can create the *sickness* that leads to *disease*."[34] Sickness, disease, and illness are etic ("outsider") terms, that is, categories created by anthropologists to conceptualize phenomena they observe in given cultures (as opposed to emic ["insider"] terms, which are the way the people of a given culture themselves conceptualize and articulate their experience of phenomena).[35] Sickness refers to persons' actually having a disease and/or illness, a reality they undergo.

---

[32] Pilch, *Healing in the New Testament*, 34. See also, 93.

[33] Ibid., 24. See also, above, chap. 2, p. 38.

[34] John Dominic Crossan, *The Birth of Christianity: Discovering What Happened in the Years Immediately After the Execution of Jesus* (San Francisco: HarperCollins, 1998), 295.

[35] For the remainder of the paragraph, see Pilch, *Healing in the New Testament*, 24–25, 60, 63, 92–94. For parallel treatment of this subject matter, see also Morris, *Illness and Culture in the Postmodern Age*, 21–23, 36–37.

Disease, in contrast, is not a personal reality but a biomedical concept for describing dysfunction or abnormalities in bodily organs or systems. Biomedicine works at strategies for explaining, controlling, and predicting physical symptoms using such terminology as diagnosis, prognosis, and therapy. Illness is likewise a conceptualization, but its concern is with how a given society constructs the experience of disease, sickness, or some other malfunction according to its cultural norms, values, perceptions, and conventions. Illness, then, is the subject field of ethnomedicine. "Cure" refers to the effective control or removal of the disease in a person's body. "Healing," on the other hand, is an intervention affecting an illness. To heal somebody is to bring personal or social meaning to the misfortune experienced in illness such that the person attains a new or renewed sense of value and purpose in his or her world.

Before we turn to the gospel depictions of Jesus' healing work, some crucial differences in the understanding of sickness and health are notable between modern society (with its scientific, individualist, and consumerist orientations) and preindustrial or peasant societies (marked by pre-Enlightenment and collectivist, or group-oriented, thought). First, the general expectation of Western people is that disease-inflicted sicknesses will be cured, with the correlative assumption being that health and illness are dualistically opposed. The modern neologism of wellness bespeaks an expectation of the highest level of physical health as the standard for quality of life. As Morris reports, despite doctors' growing realization of and efforts to modify the hegemony of the biomedical model of illness, late-modern people largely continue to cling to the notion that any illness can and should be diagnosed as an organic disease and successfully cured. Health, then, is imagined as a biological state free of any illness, injury, or disability.[36] The people of the New Testament world would not have shared these assumptions nor, for that matter, do the vast majority of the lower economic classes and poor in so-called developing countries today.

That people facing acute, life-threatening sickness always have some moment or measure of hope for a complete turnaround is a cross-cultural generalization we may safely venture. What is different about the modern version of this hope is its singular focus on a biomedical cure, as well as the simple equation of such a cure with the restoration

---

[36] See Morris, *Illness and Culture in the Postmodern Age*, 74–77, 118–20, 130–34, 241–43.

of physical health. The fact is, however, that cures remain relatively rare in the total picture of human illness. Studies published in leading medical journals have found, for example, that "firm" diagnoses of illness occur only 50 percent of the time, while the complete cure of specific diseases is actually rare in individual cases (much of the laudable advances in biomedicine are achieved by long-term accumulations of data, which is a different phenomenon from individuals' actual struggles with their own sicknesses).[37] Medical anthropologists observe, on the other hand, that when the intervention takes the form of healing an illness, the perceived rate of success can be very high. In the case of written or folkloric accounts of healers, only positive achievements are recounted so as to build up the healer's or deity's reputation.[38] More broadly, in the popular sector, both ancient and modern, "the healing of illness takes place always, infallibly, since everyone ultimately finds some meaning to given life situations: accidents, fate, will of God, providence, etc."[39]

The reasons for Western belief in the complete and permanent cure are undoubtedly complex but certainly include the influence of the mass media's ubiquitous images and narratives of physically vital, beautiful people obtaining all they desire. Meanwhile, news reports and commercial advertising continuously announce advances in medical science and the sure benefits of products resulting from them. With these medical and other cultural images comes the fantasy of living indefinitely in good health. The physical diminishment of old age is denigrated, and death becomes a scandalous interruption of the script.[40] Failed recovery from physical setbacks are probable causes for litigation, while chronic illness (which Morris cites as the fastest growing type of health misfortune in late modernity) can make people desperate for a biomedical diagnosis lest their illness be regarded as "purely" mental or "merely" psychological—and their personal character thereby denigrated.[41] Contributing social, political, and economic factors affecting both chronic and acute illness tend to recede from popular analysis. Witness, for example, the struggle of hunger advo-

[37] See Remus, *Jesus as Healer*, 2, 108; and Pilch, *Healing in the New Testament*, 33, 93.

[38] See Remus, *Jesus as Healer*, 11.

[39] Pilch, *Healing in the New Testament*, 60.

[40] See Morris, *Illness and Culture in the Postmodern Age*, 2, 15, 159, 245, 278.

[41] See ibid., 71.

cacy groups to raise awareness that fully 20 percent of American children live below the poverty line and are malnourished, making them more susceptible to sickness.

At the base of modern conventional images and expectations of health is the unprecedented, still changing, and rapidly intensifying notion of the autonomous individual. The combined forces of electronic communications, marketing, and private consumerism has brought about a new type of body, a self-creating utopian site for which physical health functions not as a means to the good life but the highest good itself: "Health no longer refers, via metaphor, to the ideal social state that generates it but instead signifies the perfection of a single private self. Further, good health is not exactly the issue. What matters is that the individual body *appear* healthy."[42] Here another contrast with the ancient world becomes pronounced. As members of collectivist cultures who constructed their identities in dyadic relationships with others, the people of the New Testament perceived health as a function of their inextricable role in a large social web. While what we call disease was certainly often the fearsome cause of illness, first-century Palestinian and Mediterranean people were well aware that numerous social, economic, and environmental factors, as well as familial or other interpersonal relations, were all capable of dragging one's own well-being (health) down with them. In seeking a more adequate understanding of Jesus as healer we can expect comparative dialogue between the collectivist anthropology of the New Testament world and the Western notion of autonomy to challenge us postmodernists with insights into the human condition that tend to evade us. Such insights arise from attention to both cross-cultural patterns of human misfortune and healing and the specific historical circumstances that exacerbated human need and thereby shaped the particularities—divine and human—of salvation recounted in the gospels.

Jesus lived in a conflicted, indeed dangerous, historical moment for his people, the Jewish nation. The health crises he confronted were not exacerbated by material excess and exaggerated human autonomy but, rather, by widespread poverty and multiple overlapping power struggles in a strongly group-oriented culture. To enter that world we must bracket modern conventional thinking that separates public and private, physical and spiritual, politics and religion, market practices and family values. The presence of the Roman military and

[42] Ibid., 139.

occupational government impacted all aspects of life: politics, economics, religion, and kinship. The populace in Galilee was comprised largely of peasants constantly on the verge of economic destitution and religious marginalization, struggles that strained the bonds of family life. The family was one's primary social safety net, although forms of fictive kinship (family-like groups bonding members in loyalty and solidarity) might be a given person's source of support. Oppressive agrarian and tax policies kept peasants constantly one step from losing their small farms due to illness, some other misfortune, forces of nature, or human interference. For those already dispossessed from the land, the added rental burdens of tenant farming made them all the more susceptible to natural or social misfortunes casting them into penury.[43] Such chronic struggles could impede people's capacities to practice acceptably the highly communal religion of Judaism, setting them up for possible official condemnation and/or social ostracism and, thus, further destitution.

The ongoing saga of foreign occupations, diasporas, and the incursion of Hellenistic culture and pagan religions created the classic conditions for a people such as the Jews to preserve their group identity through customs and practices designed to reinforce strong boundaries between themselves and a threatening world.[44] Typical of ancient Mediterranean peoples, they considered the individual human body a microcosm of the social universe, personal purity the marker of communal identity, social activity the arena for winning honor and guarding shame—prized values in a collectivist (group-centered) culture.[45] The ongoing Roman occupation posed profound, mutually impacting practical and theological questions for the Jews, making the social body susceptible to fractures along ideological and class lines

[43] Even biblical colleagues who disagree with Crossan's theoretical reconstructions of Jesus' mission and death and the origins of the Jesus movement acknowledge their debt to his analysis of the social, economic, political context comprising the first half of *The Historical Jesus: The Life of a Mediterranean Jewish Peasant* (San Francisco: HarperCollins, 1991). See also, Johnson, *The Real Jesus*, 45–46.

[44] See Wright, *Jesus and the Victory of God*, 398–99.

[45] Mary Douglas produced the classic theoretical work in this field. See her *Purity and Danger: An Analysis of Concepts of Pollution and Taboo* (New York: Praeger, 1966); and *Natural Symbols: Explorations in Cosmology* (London: Barrie and Jenkins, 1973). See also, Bruce J. Malina, *The New Testament World: Insights from Cultural Anthropology*, rev. ed. (Louisville: Westminster John Knox, 1993).

(Sadducees, Pharisees, Herodians, Zealots and other revolutionaries, tax collectors and other Roman collaborators, rich men and women, displaced peasants, destitute urban beggars, to mention but a few). If an individual was suffering from some sort of physical, mental, or spiritual affliction, the person could be perceived as a malignant symptom of the larger distress of the social body as a whole—and thereby alienated. To imagine this we need only reflect on how in our own times ethnically, socially, economically, or religiously marginalized people consistently become scapegoats for larger societal problems, whether at the local or national level. When groups—be they churches, families, nations—find themselves losing cohesion, strength, livelihood, or purpose, time and again certain subgroups emerge as being "sick." Individuals thereby end up bearing the brunt of the anxieties festering in the members of the larger social body. In the far more group-oriented world of the New Testament, the state of what we would call a person's health or, better yet, overall well-being, was integrally and overtly a function of one's status within the concentric circles of family, town or village, and nation.

In the collectivistic culture of the New Testament reputation was a crucial social value; a person's sense of worth was linked to multiple others and thus conditioned by their states of well-being. Likewise, illness was "a socially disvalued condition or state that involv[ed] and affect[ed] many others besides the stricken individual."[46] Families, friendships, and patron-client relationships were fundamental building blocks for one's thriving or even survival. Gospel stories of healing include numerous instances of afflicted people being brought to Jesus by or through a kin-type group, while others are poignant in their portrayals of unfortunate individuals left to struggle alone. Here I shall survey a representative sampling of cases with a view to both the human dynamics of illness and healing and the way they point toward the evangelical message of a Jewish prophet announcing something more largely transformative for the people of Israel, a revelation about their God that proved subversive to some, liberating or redemptive to others. As prophet, Jesus fit the tradition of such figures being called by God to speak an effective word to a people in crisis due to injustice, poverty, inauthentic ritual worship, overpowering foreign forces, and contested religious leadership. In this total matrix, people's health and

---

[46] Pilch, *Healing in the New Testament*, 76.

illness took place. For Jesus, it was the very medium for encountering God, the in-breaking of God's reign.

JESUS' HEALING WORK IN THE GOSPELS

Prophet-Healer: The Symbolic Power of Healing

In all four gospels, Jesus clearly functions as what historians and anthropologists identify as a healer. The sorts of crises and conditions with which unfortunate people present him, the way in which they and he perceive these illnesses within their cosmic and social universe, and the outcomes of his actions all align with descriptions of healers (whether folk or professional) found in the extant writings of antiquity. Surveying Mark, for example, Harold Remus finds the methods of Jesus and those who come to him—including the use of touch, gestures with saliva and other materials, power-laden words, terms from other languages, confrontation with demons, the invocation of names or titles—comparable with the descriptions of divine or miraculous power working through human agency in biblical as well as contemporary Jewish, Hellenistic, and other pagan sources.[47] What distinguishes Jesus from others as a healer is the fact and content of his teaching. While Remus generalizes that most first-century healers (professional or folk) would not also have been teachers, Pilch explains the teaching and exorcising functions of a Jewish prophet (especially as developed in Luke) as the way Jesus developed his identity as a folk healer. In any event, a broad consensus exists among scholars that specific attention to the Jewish identity of Jesus and his people, to the characteristics of leadership prophets in second-Temple Judaism, is crucial for grasping how healing and teaching are tandem activities in Jesus' mission, to the point of death.[48] The key to comprehending this

[47] See Remus, *Jesus as Healer*, 16–27. For a more radical thesis proposing Jesus (as well as his disciples and their followers) as primarily a medium, that is, a spirit-entranced healer comprehensible in both cross-cultural and Jewish terms, see Stevan Davies, *Jesus the Healer: Possession, Trance, and the Origins of Christianity* (New York: Continuum, 1995), 147–69. Wright, on the other hand, leans toward scholarship that downplays parallels between Jesus' techniques and those of other healers and exorcists, pressing for the distinctiveness of his practice from both Jewish and pagan contemporaries. See *Jesus and the Victory of God*, 190–91.

[48] See Remus, *Jesus as Healer*, 11; Pilch, *Healing in the New Testament*, 94–95; and Wright, *Jesus and the Victory of God*, 196–97.

80

crucial dimension of Jesus' prophetic mission lies in recognizing that the gospels portray Jesus as healing, not curing, that he is interpreting situations of illness and changing the meaning of people's experiences therein. This assertion need not discount the miraculous or magical character of much of Jesus' activity, as experienced by those with Jesus.[49] Indeed, the reported range of positive and negative reactions to his healings demonstrate how these marvels required people to make a decision about Jesus' claims concerning God's will in the contemporary state of human affairs, as well as about his own role therein.[50]

As a (folk) healer confronted by a sick person, Jesus would have perceived the person's affliction as an intensely social and communal event wherein multiple values, concepts, and collective narrative-memories (traditions) about illnesses and their outcomes all come into play. Medical anthropologists understand religious healing (which would include the work of prophets), shamanism, and Western psychotherapy as cross-culturally similar activities: the therapist or healer mediates culture through a process of symbolic healing that affects not just the individual but all functioning within the social system.[51] With the goal being both the reduction of symptoms and restored meaning for life, a demonstrable cure (total symptom alleviation) is possible, but more often the result is some physical sign indicating present relief plus the hope for further recovery. The primary remedies are symbolic therapies that manage a person's condition and renegotiate his or her status in the community. The healer works with the sick person and those concerned to put a name on the chaotic, life-threatening experience and to apply mutually recognized symbols (words, mythic narratives, gestures, objects) with the expectation of a positive outcome. The resolution does not require the total absence of illness or difficulty,

---

[49] "A miracle is a marvel that someone interprets as a transcendental action or manifestation." Crossan, *The Birth of Christianity*, 303.

[50] "I hold, in sum, that Jesus, as magician and miracle worker, was a very problematic and controversial phenomenon not only for his enemies but even for his friends." Crossan, *The Historical Jesus*, 311. Noting Crossan's prominent work in establishing the miracle accounts among the earliest strata of gospel materials, Remus reports how Morton Smith's earlier work reaches "a similar conclusion: Jesus' popularity, and the opposition he aroused, are credible only if he was perceived by the populace as performing miracles (*Jesus as Magician*, 1978)." *Jesus as Healer*, 107. See also, Wright, *Jesus and the Victory of God*, 189–90.

[51] See Pilch, *Healing in the New Testament*, 28–35.

nor is it presumed to be a once-and-for-all solution. Not surprisingly, then, bringing about meaningful death figures prominently in what anthropologists call traditional health care. Healing takes place when the healer, the sick person, and others involved agree that it has. It is a matter of meaning and transformation, the human power of symbol, narrative, and metaphor to renegotiate and resolve life crises.

Whereas contemporary moderns continue a long Western history of denigrating symbols as mere semblances of reality, such is not the practical epistemology of most peoples in the world. In point of fact, despite their tendency to oppose symbol and reality in thought, in practice Westerners engage in robust symbolic activity when working out their own interpretations of what is life-giving and life-threatening, what is worth sacrificing and even dying for, what should be cause for dread or hope. Scientific terminology and images are not only not immune to such symbolic functions in modern constructions of meaning, the hegemony of biomedicine in people's coping with health misfortunes is exemplary of how the realm of the scientific often furnishes the primary symbols laypeople employ to deal with reality. In his own caution against our dismissing biblical peoples' interpretations of illness, Crossan warns: "They talked about evil spirits and demonic forces responsible for sickness and death. We speak of sanitation and nutrition, of bacteria and germs, of microbes and viruses. How are they not wrong if we are right, and vice versa?"[52] Morris comments on the extent to which Americans prove ready to attribute almost any bodily ailment to contaminated air, water, or food, to the point that pollution has nearly replaced germs "as the all-purpose, postmodern explanation for bad health."[53] These too constitute exercises in narrative and symbolism in the effort to bring meaning to life problems too complex for the controlled environment of the biomedical laboratory. The challenge in postmodern culture, Morris concludes, is to find narratives and representations of health as "the manner in which we live well despite our inescapable illnesses, disabilities, and trauma."[54]

The people populating the gospels practiced a fulsome symbolic repertoire for interpreting health misfortunes and healing. Anthropological (etic) analyses parse that multilayered symbolism of the social and physical body according to several taxonomies, including

[52] Crossan, *The Birth of Christianity*, 293.
[53] Morris, *Illness and Culture in the Postmodern Age*, 86.
[54] Ibid., 244.

boundary preservation and transgressions, mythic world constructions, and the identification of bodily parts or zones (e.g., eyes, mouth,
feet) with specific aspects of personal agency. Guided by Pilch, I will
survey Jesus' healing work along these heuristic lines, beginning with
boundary issues.

Restoration to Wholeness: Leprosy and Hemorrhaging

The clearest, most telling case of biblical illness as boundary trans-
gression—or uncleanness—is the misfortune called leprosy. Decades
of preaching based on modern exegesis have made contemporary
Christians widely aware of the fact that the skin conditions afflicting unfortunate individuals in the Bible were not the contemporary
Hansen's disease, a germ-borne pathogen caused by one of the first
bacilli discovered in the latter nineteenth century (*mycobacterium le-
prae*). The highly charged symbolism of the word "leper," however,
has contributed to continual misconceptions about even this modern
biomedical condition, which is just mildly contagious, neither sexually
transmitted nor lethal, and only causes physical deformations if left
untreated for more than fifteen years.[55] The leprosy recounted in biblical texts, on the other hand, refers to a range of rashes (such as eczema,
psoriasis, fungal infections) characterized by discoloring, breaking the
surface of, and excreting liquids through the skin. What made those
afflicted with such skin ailments so abhorrent within the socioreligious
system of ancient Judaism was the fact that the individual person's
bodily surface was cracked, broken open, vulnerable. The danger to
the wider social body was not contagion but pollution. The purity of
the group and each member's body were expected to replicate each
other. The uncleanness on an individual's body, in this case, the flak-
ing or oozing of skin surfaces, manifested a lack of wholeness in the
social body, a breach in the bulwarks of the communal identity. Thus
biblical leprosy is a prime subject for ethnomedical analysis.

Postexilic Judaism, as noted in the previous section, was particularly
preoccupied with the integrity of its ideological boundaries, given its
subjection to continual waves of foreign invaders and their deities,
beliefs, customs, and mores—the symbolic makings of group identity.[56] The Torah's call to holiness (Lev 17–26) was a matter of integral

---

[55] Pilch, *Healing in the New Testament*, 45.

[56] Pilch notes how in 2 Kings every time Israel undergoes attacks from foreign hostile forces the king suffers from various skin afflictions. See ibid., 82.

wholeness on the part of the people before the God of their ancestors. The repulsiveness of lepers' bodily surfaces symbolized the religious-national group's anxiety over their rightness with God ("You shall be holy, for I the LORD your God, am holy"—Lev 19:2), who alone created and could sustain them. The consequence for lepers was their stigmatization, their being labeled unclean or outside the boundaries of the holy. In such a highly group-oriented society, wherein reputation, kinship ties, and patronage networks were the sources of personal sustenance, such shunning was deadly. The severity of the misfortune lay not with the physical symptoms of the skin but with the whole range of personal consequences resulting from being categorically excluded.[57]

What the leper in the parallel story of Matthew 8:1-4, Mark 1:40-45, and Luke 5:12-15, therefore, asks of Jesus is highly specific: to be made *clean*. He is asking for deliverance from the physical-social-traditional bodily condition that isolates him from life in the community and thereby, in a very practical sense, life itself. Jesus heals the man by declaring him clean. His touching the leper seems to symbolize welcome into the body of the community. The word and gesture of purification make the leper whole and, thus, capable of presenting himself to the priest and offering sacrifice to God, returning him to participation in the holy community.

As usual, the Synoptic authors take the original story about the leper and incorporate it into their theologies of how Jesus is the Messiah, the Christ. Mark includes the story early in his gospel in a string of marvels illustrating the power and authority of Jesus' teaching. In Matthew the account leads off two chapters of stories on the nature of faith and discipleship, with the leper's calling Jesus "Lord" and Jesus' healing command together implying that Jesus continues as healer in the church now.[58] Luke's version likewise highlights discipleship, its source and inclusiveness. Later, in chapter 17 (vv. 11-19), the account of Jesus' healing ten lepers completes a series on the nature of faith. Once again, Jesus sends the leprous to the priests, but this time it is en route that they find themselves cleansed (v. 14). Luke's account again teaches about discipleship. The ten called out as one for mercy from Jesus, a cry implying their recognition of his power and demand that he exercise it in justice toward them. The proper response is gratitude,

[57] See ibid., 41, 48, 50.
[58] See Remus, *Jesus as Healer*, 45–46.

which only the Samaritan, the "foreigner" (v. 18), expresses. Brendan Byrne concludes, "The episode well illustrates Luke's sense of the 'knowledge of salvation' (1:77): beyond physical healing or rescue, salvation means praising and thanking God who has set you free."[59]

The controversial point, then as now, concerns what it means to be set free, what such a state of human life both offers and, once received, demands. The accounts of Jesus healing lepers, along with the larger ensemble of his actions and words, amount to a redefinition of holiness within the socioreligious system. Jesus is not rejecting but working with and radically revising the Jewish understanding of what it means to be sound of mind and body before God and people.[60] But this requires a rethinking of perfection, divine and human. Matthew's account of the leper's healing follows directly upon the conclusion of the Sermon on the Mount (chapters 5–7), wherein Jesus explains his purpose as fulfilling the Law and the Prophets (5:17), exhorting his followers to be perfect as their heavenly Father is perfect (5:48). That perfection is not a matter of posturing over against the outsiders, the pagans (who love their neighbors and hate their enemies—5:43-47) or keeping only the letter of the Law concerning murder, adultery, divorce, oaths, and charity toward the needy (5:21-42). Jesus proclaims, on the contrary, through both his declaration of the lepers' cleanness and his words in the Sermon, that godly perfection or holiness lies in mercy and compassion. The purity of the community likewise is not fundamentally about the externals (bodily conditions or dietary regulations), but compassionate mercy and faithfulness arising from within: "genuine purity is a matter of the heart."[61]

The authenticity of Jesus' teaching coincides with the authority exuded in his healings. By means of both he announces a realignment of the boundaries of human interaction in the presence of God. The chronically hemorrhaging woman, categorically cut off from the touch of fellow humans and the communal worship of God, not only has faith in Jesus' power to heal her physical malady; by touching his garment (Mark 5:28) she risks publicly defiling Jesus (see Lev 15:19-30), as well as broaching the ban on individual women initiating contact

---

[59] Brendan Byrne, *The Hospitality of God: A Reading of Luke's Gospel* (Collegeville, MN: Liturgical Press, 2000), 140.

[60] See Pilch, *Healing in the New Testament*, 51; and Wright, *Jesus and the Victory of God*, 371.

[61] Wright, *Jesus and the Victory of God*, 396; see also, 282–87.

with men in public (hence her fear of coming forward in the crowd).[62] Yet Jesus' concern to know who touched him is not to condemn the woman as either a source of his own potential defilement or a threat to his manly honor. His desire, rather, is to free a person from her suffering (social, religious, financial)[63] and send her in peace into the life of the community (see 5:34). The sickness and the defilement are gone not just for this individual but for all who accept Jesus' interpretation of what it is to be God's people, a light to the nations, participants in God's reign. In her newfound freedom the woman becomes a living symbol of the freedom God is now offering in the person and mission of Jesus.

Dislodging Demons: Healing and Forgiveness

While the taxonomy of purity and impurity may well be the most prevalent in New Testament accounts of healing, this by no means exhausts the complex system of health and illness those people maintained. Another means of analysis is what anthropologists broadly call the mythic worldview of a people, the ensemble of beliefs, practices, symbols, and narratives whereby they interpret the world they experience. A prominent aspect of the mythic world of the gospels is the pervasiveness and power of spirits and, concerning misfortune and illness, demons. Noting the extent to which Luke attributes people's bodily aliments to demons, Pilch concludes that spirits must have comprised a key dimension of that community's world. Satan and other evil spirits cause illness as well as incite people to evil actions, while Jesus (and subsequently, the apostles in Acts) heals people by the Spirit of God.[64] Demons and spirits, of course, appear in other

---

[62] See Remus, *Jesus as Healer*, 34; and Pilch, *Healing in the New Testament*, 67.

[63] "The woman 'had been suffering from hemorrhages for twelve years,' Mark explains, a condition that likely rendered her ritually unclean in her society's eyes, and so strictly limited her physical contact with others and objects, including bedding and, crucially, clothing. Mark's report that she had spent all her savings on 'many physicians' signals not only her loss of hope but also her loss of social status, since only the wealthy elite could afford a physician at all, to say nothing of 'many' of them (Mk 5:25-26). That is, this woman was once rich but now poor, once healthy but now suffering, once clean but now unclean, once elite but now ostracized and isolated." Matthew Myer Boulton, "'Your Faith Has Made You Well': Healing Liturgies in Reformed Theological Perspective," *Liturgy* 22, no. 3 (July 2007): 25.

[64] See Pilch, *Healing in the New Testament*, 104–6.

gospels as well, and taken altogether, their prevalence indicates yet again that the healings described in the biblical stories occur in the folk or popular (as opposed to professional) sector of society.

While modern biomedicine has certainly given us far greater sophistication in identifying and diagnosing diseases, we must resist imagining that ancient Mediterranean physicians lacked precise medical terminology and therapeutic protocols of their own. Whereas the evangelists describe the people and the prophet/healer Jesus evaluating a sick person as demon-possessed, physicians learned in the Hippocratic treatises would have shunned such assessments and prescribed medications or diets appropriate to a diagnosed disease. Such professional medical diagnosis, however, is not the concern for those finding their entire world refashioned in relation to Jesus. The bodily afflictions the gospels recount Jesus healing cover "a wide range of vague pathologies."[65] The evangelists vary in their interpretations of symptoms in a given common story, use broad concepts such as leprosy or lameness in individual cases, and employ general (Greek) terms like "sick," "weak," and "illnesses" in summary statements about the many who came to Jesus for help. Typical of the popular sector, their concern for precision lies with not *what* but *who* has caused the health misfortune a given individual is suffering: Peter's mother-in-law is possessed by a demon named Fever (Luke 4:38), a woman has been bound by Satan for eighteen years and is stooped over by a "spirit of infirmity" (Luke 13:10-16), and so forth.[66] The personified cause of sickness may be human or more-than-human (spirit, demon, god or goddess), individual or corporate, sociopolitical, or cosmic. In any given situation, in fact, the agency is usually a combination of these. Therein lies the powerful force of demon possession: it manifests a malignancy not only in the individual's illness but also in the community, revealing both an individual and a social body endangered amid the larger historical and cosmic scene.[67]

---

[65] Meier, *A Marginal Jew*, 678. See also Remus, *Jesus as Healer*, 14–55.

[66] See Pilch, *Healing in the New Testament*, 69, 106.

[67] For a treatment of Mark's pericope of the crazed Gerasene man possessed by a "Legion" of demons (5:9) as an exemplary case of the cross-cultural phenomenon of demonic possession as individual embodiment of "the almost schizoid position" of people living under foreign occupation and colonial oppression, see Crossan, *The Historical Jesus*, 313–18.

As noted earlier, family was the fundamental social unit in the New Testament world and, thus, played no small part in the popular healthcare system. The family's honor rode on the health (again, in the broadest sense of complete well-being) of its members, with fathers and mothers having key responsibilities for winning and guarding (respectively) the good reputation of the family. Illness in one family member, then as now, could wreak physical, spiritual, emotional, and/or fiscal havoc on not just the individual sufferer but also all one's kin. William Reiser offers a pastorally sensitive and theologically insightful interpretation of Mark's story of the demon-possessed boy and his father (Mark 9:14-29//Matt 17:14-21//Luke 9:37-43).[68]

Noting how Mark treats the positive final outcome for the boy, namely, the exorcism of the demon (9:25), as a foregone conclusion, Reiser finds the greater witness to healing in the dialogue between Jesus and the distraught father. Years of caring for and trying to prevent harm to the boy (v. 22) have worn down the father's own emotional and religious life to the point of peril, which he expresses in the cry, "I believe; help my unbelief!" (v. 24).

> The poor father needed healing too; and from one point of view, he may have needed forgiveness for his greatly weakened confidence in God's providential love. In contrast to the disciples, whose faith had not yet been fully tested, Jesus understood the situation of the father's soul; he knew what it was like to wrestle with powerful, relentless doubts. Whenever Jesus exclaimed, 'If you are able!—All things can be done for the one who believes,' he was speaking from conviction, from experience, from having learned for himself that one can emerge

[68] Matthew alone uses the word *seleniazesthai*, literally "moonstruck," to describe the boy's condition (17:15) and, likewise uniquely among the evangelists, includes the term in a summary statement of Jesus' healing activity (4:24). Noting that contemporary exegetes nearly all translate the term as epilepsy, Pilch warns against the danger of anachronism here. He argues rather that the literal "moonstruck" better represents ancient Mediterranean peoples' widespread beliefs in the sun, moon, stars, planets, and constellations' powers to cause people's health misfortunes. Such historical-anthropological awareness once again indicates how the gospel narratives of healing function within the folk (or popular) sector of society. It also invites us contemporary believers to assess our own biomedical and ethnomedical assumptions so as to consider how the Gospel might come as salvation in present contexts. See *Healing in the New Testament*, 80, 85.

from being tested by demons with seasoned faith. For that reason Jesus replied to his disciples that this kind of spirit can only be driven out through prayer (Mark 9:29)—not the spirit that had infested the boy (his physical condition was not objectively worse than that of the paralytic or the crazed man who lived among the tombs) but the spirit that had begun to take up residence in the father's soul. What we may have in this scene, therefore, is a deeply moving story about forgiveness, understood in this instance as the rebuilding of shattered hope.[69]

In the New Testament world evil spirits cause illness in the comprehensive sense. The misfortunes, acute and chronic, personal and corporate, afflict not only certain persons' physical body parts and systems. They also are capable of causing the whole range of what we today would parse as psychological, interpersonal, social (familial, economic, legal, political), spiritual, and religious conflicts that non-modern people are much better at acknowledging include guilt and sin. Thus, in this as in all gospel narratives, something much bigger than a narrow biomedical cure is coming about. The something bigger entails all who are engaged with the sick person. Not only the sick individual but also the family members (and others, as the case may be) need healing, are seeking meaning, confidence, hope, faith, and with these, forgiveness. A powerful event of healing causes all to renegotiate their understandings of and relationships among each other and God. The promise of healing, nonetheless, comes through the process of change (*metanoia*), repentance of and release from habits, decisions, and (in the case of the social and political body) customs and policies that can bind persons chronically in illness.

The popular religious tendency to make sense of sickness and other misfortunes by attributing them to personal agents, such as demons, inevitably carried the possibility of ascribing causality to the sins of human agents as well. The book of Job is the complex, multilayered Wisdom text exploring the range of problems and solutions associated with sin, suffering, humanity, nature, and God. The prophetic literature, likewise, holds no small amount of teaching about the biblical God's word on the sins of social injustice, the ability of those in political and religious power to deceive themselves and others, as well as God's concern for the poor who suffer as a result. The gospels portray Jesus as speaking and acting in that prophetic line, contesting the

[69] Reiser, *Jesus in Solidarity with His People*, 78.

ruling religious and political leaderships' condemnation of the peasantry for the sinfulness associated with their personal misfortunes.

Crossan provides a succinct evaluation of the unjust religious and economic bind the Jewish peasantry suffered in conjunction with sickness in first-century Palestine: "Excessive taxation could leave poor people physically malnourished or hysterically disabled. But since the religiopolitical ascendancy could not blame excessive taxation, it blamed sick people themselves by claiming that their sins had led to their illnesses. And the cure for sinful sickness was, ultimately, in the Temple. And that meant more fees, in a perfect circle of victimization."[70] Reporting that the "poorer classes evidently regarded the Temple as symbolizing the oppression they suffered at the hands of the rich elite,"[71] Wright incorporates this religious-economic-political dimension into his construction of the historical Jesus' mission: Through his acts of healing and forgiveness Jesus was prophetically revealing God's long-awaited defeat of evil. Satan was behind not only the oppressive Roman occupational government but also the misguided nationalism among the Jewish people, of which Jesus proclaimed their need to repent. Jesus' eventual symbolic destruction of the Temple, Wright argues, was consistent with his claim that in his own person and, ultimately, the death he would surely suffer, God was delivering the people out of exile into life as a light to the nations.

While not sharing Wright's larger view of how Jesus understood his mission, Crossan likewise sees Jesus' healings as "religiopolitically subversive." By removing people's sickness Jesus was also nullifying their sinfulness and thus their need for forgiveness, thereby contesting "not the medical monopoly of the doctors but the religious monopoly of the priests."[72] Crossan thereby makes compelling sense of the argument Jesus has with the teachers of the Law as he cures the paralyzed man brought on the mat by his friends (Mark 2:1-12//Matt 9:1-8//Luke 5:17-26): If Jesus is curing the paralysis, he likewise is forgiving the sin and thus revealing how God really is at work. In light of his demonstrated power to heal, Jesus makes the question of which is

---

[70] Crossan, *The Historical Jesus*, 324.

[71] Wright, *Jesus and the Victory of God*, 412.

[72] Crossan, *The Historical Jesus*, 324. Wright offers support for this evaluation by noting that one of the earliest acts of the revolutionaries in the war of 66 CE was to take over the temple and burn the record of debts. See *Jesus and the Victory of God*, 412.

easier, curing or forgiving, moot. The only question that remains is one of faith: does one accept and embrace—trust—what God is revealing in Jesus?

Bodily Agency: Blindness and Faith

A third taxonomy of illness useful for interpreting gospel narratives of healing analyzes the ways in which ancient Mediterranean peoples associated certain bodily parts or zones with specific aspects of human agency. In contrast to the modern introspective personality, biblical persons understood the soundness of their thoughts and actions in terms of how others in society observed and judged the state or activity of their bodies. The conditions of certain bodily parts or zones were the (real) symbolic indicators of a person's motivation and character, of one's health and wholeness or, on the contrary, sickness and sinfulness. One's health and honor, then, were very much a socially constructed condition, such that much of the hardship in sickness was due to a person's being ill-regarded and even displaced from society. Pilch, drawing on the work of Bruce Malina, describes three zones of bodily organs symbolizing different functions of human agency: *heart-eyes* was associated with emotion-fused thought, *mouth-ears* with self-expressive speech, and *hands-feet* with purposeful action.[73] Affliction or misfortune in any of those zones was indicative of a lack of rightness in one's relationship with God and people.

Particularly prominent in Luke-Acts, Pilch notes, is blindness, a misfortune of the eyes indicative of an illness of the heart, that is, of misguided if not evil understanding and emotions. Such, however, is the very matter for conversion to faith, which in Luke's gospel is a wholehearted (insightful, comprehending) embrace of Jesus as the Christ, the inaugurator of God's reign. When Luke, therefore, summarizes Jesus' healing work in terms of curing diseases, expelling demons, and giving sight to the blind (7:21), the latter should not be understood in a narrow biomedical fashion. The people in Luke's world did not sharply distinguish the physical and metaphorical conditions of blindness. Thus, the deliverance from blindness in Luke-Acts includes the sociocultural (and religious) transformation of how people understand God's will and action in their midst, as well as their participation

---

[73] See Pilch, *Healing in the New Testament*, 106–7.

therein.[74] Jesus gives priority to being-in-becoming over doing-and-achieving as the personal and socially recognizable dimension (zone) of human existence that manifests faith. Thus, the interspersing of healings of physical blindness in Luke and Acts with numerous proverbs, parables, and speeches engaging sight (lamps, blindness, witnessing events, recognizing natural signs, etc.) altogether indicate that healing for Luke is fundamentally about a change of heart, a conversion in faith, a transformed state of being in relation to Christ.

Likewise in the Gospel of John the state of blindness symbolically manifests human sinfulness. In the healing of the man born blind (John 9:1-41), Jesus shifts the locus and content of sinfulness away from physical to a metaphorical blindness. As they observe the blind man in passing, the disciples interpret his health misfortune as the result of human culpability, either his own or his parents' (v. 2). Later, as the Pharisees find their interrogation of the healed blind man turning into an indictment of their own lack of knowledge (v. 30), they resort to an *ad hominem* attack on the man's state of being, "You were steeped in sin at birth; how dare you lecture us!" (v. 34, NIV). This charge rests upon the ancient mythic worldview whereby light symbolized human life itself: "This living light derived from the heart and emerged from the eyes in the seeing process. The eyes were made of fire, the stuff that causes light. When this emanated from the eyes, the human person was able to see. Jesus observed: 'The eye is the lamp of the body' (Matt. 6:22). Aristotle said: 'Vision is fire' (*Problems* 31, 959b); 'Sight (is made) from fire and hearing from air' (*Problems* 960a)."[75] Blindness, especially as a condition from birth, was not merely the absence of physical sight, not only a lack of heart-fueled light, but the malevolent presence of darkness. Physical blindness indicated darkness rather than light in the heart, dark stuff rather than life-giving fire emanating from the eyes. Indeed, blind people were constantly suspected of casting the *evil eye* upon others, a widespread Mediterranean belief (still held by many today) in the malevolent person's supernatural ability to affect harm. Among the folk remedies for the evil eye was spitting and the rubbing of saliva, the very type of symbolic action Jesus uses in healing the man born blind (v. 6). Jesus' healing of the man born

---

[74] See ibid., 113–16. Remus notes how in the Synoptic Gospels the healing of blindness includes the restoration to full participation in society. See *Jesus as Healer*, 84.

[75] Pilch, *Healing in the New Testament*, 133.

blind sets up the conflict exposing the real (metaphorical) blindness of the Pharisees, who reject Jesus' claim to authority and eject the healed man from the community. The irony is that the one who from the start was considered as good as dead ends up coming to know the true light (life) that has come from God, joining the fellowship of Jesus and his followers (the man's new fictive kin group). Jesus heals by transforming the blind man's "psychophysiological process (whatever it might have been in this instance) into meaningful experience."[76]

ENCOUNTERING CHRIST THE HEALER: LIFE-REDEEMING FELLOWSHIP

A primary objective of this chapter has been to situate Jesus' miracles in the perspective of ethnomedical healing, as opposed to biomedical curing. The investigation into what healing, as opposed to curing, entailed *then* can enable a better understanding of how the church's pastoral-liturgical service to the sick, dying, deceased, and bereaved are encounters with the living Jesus of Scripture and tradition *now*. Tradition affirms the continued active presence of Jesus in the sacramental healing ministry of the church, but Scripture is what both grounds and gives shape to Christ's ongoing work therein. Our survey of current biblical scholarship has demonstrated how the healing Jesus performed as part of his prophetic mission responded to a broad range of illnesses and misfortunes that, far from being narrowly defined biomedical diseases, were complex personal somatic, spiritual, and social (religious, economic, political, and so forth) constructions. For the church, therefore, to carry on the same salvific mission in the power of Christ's Spirit requires an awareness of and availability to a similar breadth and depth of human illness in our own day.[77] It is

[76] Ibid., 137.

[77] Pilch wisely avers that using the analytic tools of cultural anthropology can prevent us from anachronistically reducing the gospels' descriptions to what we think we know about the human phenomena of sickness, disease, and illness. We thereby become better disposed to making respectful conclusions about those stories and gaining insights relevant to contemporary pastoral circumstances. See *Healing in the New Testament*, 71–72, 142–43. This coincides with Morris's description of the postmodern "biocultural" approach to illness, an effort to reform "American illusions about health" due to an exclusively biomedical culture that "has almost burned away the memory of its prescientific ancestors." This entails learning to recognize the external and internal, physical and social threats to personal and collective health today

true that the symbolic activity whereby Jesus the Christ healed then, namely, by mighty deeds experienced as miraculous or magical, is of a different type than the primary symbolic rituals through which he heals now, that is, through liturgical rites of the church.[78] Still, the purpose in both cases remains the same: healing as a transformation of people's experiences of illness, misfortune, and death such that they find renewed meaning (faith, trust) for life and death in the presence of God and within their world.

Still, if we desire to hear the Gospel as the living Word of God in the assembly, then the most important difference pervading the texts lies between neither miraculous feats (then) and liturgical rites (now) nor the culturally specific ways ancient and modern peoples interpret illness, but rather in the seismic shift in human meaning revealed in Jesus' resurrection. Scripture itself proclaims God's having raised the executed Jesus from the dead to be *the* divine act of salvation, a revelation recasting the meaning of all life experiences for those who believe. Such a rethinking of life, divine and human, was the very call and task for the evangelists (and their communities) themselves. Whatever Jesus exactly thought God was bringing about, historically and cosmically (socially and religiously), through his prophetic mission up to his death remains as enigmatic to us as it did to both the disciples who were actually with him and the first generations of believers who produced the gospels. Once the resurrection occurred, however, they could not but remember the stories of Jesus' prophetic mission through the perspective of his death and glorification. The only Jesus believers have is the resurrected Jesus.[79]

This chapter has demonstrated how the gospels have much to teach us in our postmodern need for a broader human understanding of illness and healing. We can now return to Keck's caution that the miracles are not cumulative episodes in a "life of Jesus" but complete stories revealing how Christ Jesus restores "authentic life" (faith, hope,

---

across the cultural spectrum: economic, scientific-experimental (cloning, environmental hazards, etc.), epidemics (alcoholism, obesity), etc. Morris, *Illness and Culture in the Postmodern Age*, 13, 76. Such principles will guide my arguments for who are the proper subjects and what, therefore, are the most promising liturgical-pastoral approaches to the rites for the sick, dying, deceased, and bereaved in part 3 of the book below.

[78] See Crossan, *The Historical Jesus*, 138.

[79] See Johnson, *The Real Jesus*, 143–46.

and love) across the spectrum of human need and alienation.[80] "The early Christians did not invent miracle stories about Jesus from whole cloth, but as the appropriate form for conveying their faith that the eschatological age had been inaugurated by the way Jesus had actually lived and by God's vindication of him by the resurrection."[81] Since healing in any concrete instance of life is fundamentally a matter of renegotiated meaning, all Christian healing comes through a restoration of afflicted persons' sense of self and world in relation to Christ Jesus and the reign of God he has inaugurated: divine solidarity with human brokenness, God's glory in human wholeness.

Daniel Harrington, for example, in commenting on the healings in Matthew's ninth chapter notes that the primary message is about power over death, chronic illness, blindness, and speechlessness, while "every detail not relevant to the theme of faith in Jesus' power is omitted. The words that are translated as 'get well' and 'restored to health' [9:21-22] are part of the New Testament vocabulary of salvation."[82] Furthermore, in the story of the ruler's dead daughter, "the way in which the girl's restoration to life is described in verse 25 ('got up') connects this miracle to Jesus' own resurrection."[83] In his analysis of the demon-possessed boy and broken father Reiser likewise notes how in the process of exorcism the boy becomes so corpse-like that the onlookers proclaim him dead, whereupon Jesus takes him by the hand and *lifts him up*. The symbolism of death and/or rising features in a number of the healing stories (Mark 1:21-28; 5:1-20, 35-43), supporting Reiser's argument that Easter pervades Mark's gospel: "The restoration to life, to wholeness, and to community, which is so evident in the healings and exorcisms, prepares us for Easter. Those earlier stories dispose us to hear with understanding the great revelation underlying the whole life of Jesus."[84] Similarly, resurrection-from-death imagery pervades Luke's healing accounts. A notable example is Jesus' raising the widow's only son from the dead. In so doing, Pilch argues, Jesus redeemed a doubly tragic situation, since the widow would have been

---

[80] See above, p. 69.

[81] Keck, "Excursus," 249.

[82] Daniel Harrington, *The Gospel According to Matthew*, The Collegeville Bible Commentary, New Testament, ed. Robert Karris, vol. 1 (Collegeville, MN: Liturgical Press, 1983), 43.

[83] Ibid., 42.

[84] Reiser, *Jesus in Solidarity with His People*, 79.

reliant on her male next-of-kin for her livelihood: "Jesus effectively saved *her* life by restoring her son to *his* life."[85] These stories effectively bring to life for *us* the bodily and spiritual, interpersonal and social dimensions of healing borne of faith in the resurrected Jesus, the experiential knowledge that God can be trusted.[86]

In the Gospel of John the conflict between Jesus and the Judean authorities reaches its climax with the sign (*semeion*) of Jesus raising Lazarus from the dead (John 12:9-11), whereby the ultimate healing is revealed to be one's belief in (knowing, trusting) Jesus, "the resurrection and the life" (11:25).[87] The life-and-death tension, nonetheless, is at work throughout the course of the signs Jesus performs. Recall in John 9, for example, how in the ancient Mediterranean world the condition of blindness indicated a person's lifelessness, the absence of the animating fire within that *is* life. For the reader of the gospel, Jesus' healing of the man born blind is a sign pointing toward his ultimate act: "Above all, Jesus dies to give life."[88] Such interplay between Jesus' mighty deeds and his death and resurrection indicates that we who now hear the Gospel witness the wonders he did for and through people through the perspective of the definitive event of salvation. "John, like all the gospels, is a post-resurrection document, written after Jesus . . . is crucified and rises from the dead. Thus while we observe the earthly Jesus speaking to the people of his day, as readers we are expected to hear the risen Jesus speaking to us through the earthly Jesus, imparting insider information of a kind that invites and challenges us to make our own decisions about Jesus' identity and thus our own identity—whether we will want to be healed, to open ourselves to having life 'abundantly' (10:10)."[89] What the Christian discovers repeatedly through life's challenges and consolations is that the way one renegotiates one's sense of well-being and purpose is always a matter of faith, a search for the living Jesus who is always seeking us out. In their variety and detail the healing narratives in the gospels are a treasury of images and invitations for us to discover, by any number of angles, specific human needs—our own and others'—and the definite character of the salvation Christ is offering.

---

[85] Pilch, *Healing in the New Testament*, 97.

[86] See Reiser, *Jesus in Solidarity with His People*, 11, 23.

[87] See Remus, *Jesus as Healer*, 90.

[88] Pilch, *Healing in the New Testament*, 133.

[89] Remus, *Jesus as Healer*, 80.

A crucial insight Remus draws from John's gospel, evident in the extended quote above, is how fundamental to the healing process is the question of whether the person of misfortune does indeed want to be healed.[90] Insofar as illness entails the loss of meaning in one's life, healing inevitably requires a renegotiation (if not total rethinking, at times) of one's priorities, God-images, relationships, memories, practice of tradition, view of authority, and so forth. Jesus' asking the paralytic by the pool of Bethesda whether he wants to get well (John 5:6) is no mere throwaway line, especially in light of Jesus' concluding exhortation to the man to stop sinning (5:14). Here Pilch's anthropological research proves especially helpful. Whereas readers often find that warning contradictory to Jesus' later insistence that the man born blind's condition is due neither to his own nor his parents' sins (9:2-3), Pilch demonstrates how the danger for the paralytic is categorically different than for the blind man.[91] The key detail is the fact that the paralytic has neither family nor friends to help him into the pool. In such a highly group-oriented society, making friends is essential to a man's honor and, if suffering misfortune, survival. The poor man is somebody with no social standing; sin is a breach in social relations. To sin in this context is to cut off one's relationship with one's family, fictive kin group, or community. Thus the paralytic's lack of anybody to help him would seem to indicate that he has so alienated others as to be left in isolation. Jesus' concluding words to him, then, would be an encouragement not to behave so as to end up ill—not necessarily sick—again, that is, not to bring upon himself the misfortune of being without any loyalty or solidarity, of being unloved, a sinner.

As for the man born blind, his healing likewise brings about a radical change in his identity and relationships, but in his case the alienation from parents and rejection from the (Pharisaic) Jewish community is due to his newfound friendship with and loyalty to Jesus. This aspect of the story is a stellar example of how two time frames overlap in the gospel, that of the evangelist's community and that of Jesus' mission among his fellow Jewish people. Whereas in the Synoptic Gospels those whom Jesus heals are regularly reintegrated into the community, John's account of the blind man reflects the alienation that had developed between the Pharisees and local synagogue(s) and his own community due to their belief in Jesus as the Christ. Those who

---

[90] See ibid., 76–77.
[91] See Pilch, *Healing in the New Testament*, 128–31.

publicly profess faith in Jesus must join a new fictive kin group, the evangelist's community: "There they will find the life and light that make whole as Jesus seeks and finds them, just as he once sought out and found the man in our story."[92]

The reconstituting of group membership, the forging of new communal bonds, points to the other crucial feature of Jesus' prophetic mission that the first generation of believers in him as risen Lord understood to be essential to following him: his open table fellowship. Those whom Jesus healed he called to communion in the reign of God, and thereby to share in his healing life; feasting was a sign of healing and forgiveness. There is near unanimous scholarly agreement that Jesus' open commensality, his egalitarian dining with sinners, was one of the most prominent, highly symbolic, and ultimately dangerous features of his prophetic mission.[93] True to classical Jewish prophetic tradition, Jesus' open fellowship with the poor, the sinners, the nobodies, was a highly symbolic enactment of his claim that God was taking a new initiative to deliver his exiled people, inaugurating a new interpretation of Torah for the life of the people. "For a first-century Jew, most if not all of the works of healing, which form the bulk of Jesus' mighty works, could be seen as the restoration to membership in Israel of those who, through sickness or whatever, had been excluded as ritually unclean. The healings thus function in exact parallel with the welcome of sinners, and this, we may be quite sure, was what Jesus himself intended. He never performed mighty works simply to impress."[94] Both the healings and the table fellowship were shocking acts challenging social conventions and the regnant organs of power, religious and political, countering their claims to divine authority with an enacted proclamation of mercy and forgiveness as the hallmark of God's sovereign rule. As essential elements of the entire gospel

[92] Remus, *Jesus as Healer*, 85.

[93] See Wright, *Jesus and the Victory of God*, 431, 532; Meier, *A Marginal Jew*, 149; Remus, *Jesus as Healer*, 66; Crossan, *The Historical Jesus*, 261–64, 341–44; and Reiser, *Jesus in Solidarity with His People*, 108–11.

[94] Wright, *Jesus and the Victory of God*, 191. Wright's point bears repeating: Jesus never performed miracles "simply to impress." This scholarly finding gives the lie to any preaching or catechesis that presents Jesus' healing works as dazzling proofs of his divinity or demonstrations of some sort of irrepressible autonomous power—notions that are theologically and pastorally bankrupt.

message, "miracle and table . . . magic and meal, healing and eating, compassion and commensality, spiritual and material egalitarianism"[95] comprise a bravely enacted vision proving to be a matter of life or death for Jesus. For believers from the first generations to the present, they are an invitation to life in "the Spirit of the one who raised Jesus from the dead" (Rom 8:11, NAB).

Several of the resurrection appearance accounts at the ends of the gospels include Jesus' eating in the midst of the astonished disciples—a strong indication of how important the practice of table fellowship was for establishing and maintaining the continuity between Jesus' historical mission and that of the nascent Christian communities. Among these, the "legend of the Emmaus road" emerges as the symbolic-ritual "pattern for the development of that remarkable sense of fellowship between the early Christians and the risen Lord which is such a feature of primitive Christianity—and which has had such an effect on the Jesus tradition."[96] The risen Jesus' "breaking of the bread" (Luke 24:35) is the climactic action that affectively unlocks the explanation of his death as the fulfillment of the Law and Prophets, opening into the mystery of his presence-in-absence and, with that, their empowerment to take to the road again. This is what the church has come to call the paschal mystery at the heart of the sacramental-liturgical encounter of Jesus with the faithful and their ongoing mission of meeting him in lives of service patterned on his historical mission. In the next chapters we will explore how celebrations of the paschal mystery comprise privileged means whereby believers enter into the world of the Gospel, rituals whereby we appropriate the Lord's vision as our own and thus take up his healing work of commensality and compassion in our world today.

[95] Crossan, *The Historical Jesus*, 344–45.

[96] Norman Perrin, *Rediscovering the Teaching of Jesus* (New York: Harper & Row, 1976), 107–8; quoted in Maxwell E. Johnson, *The Rites of Initiation: Their Evolution and Interpretation* (Collegeville, MN: Liturgical Press, 1999), 4–5.

Chapter 4

Embracing the Paschal Mystery:
Liturgically Practiced Faith Grounded
in Biblical Hope

INTRODUCTION

The purpose of this chapter is to arrive at a certain theological understanding of the paschal mystery. As the source of all liturgical celebration the paschal mystery is the de-centering center from which we can in faith meet the Jesus portrayed in the past world of the gospels as a present reality for our lives.[1] For over four decades now the Second Vatican Council's call for "full, conscious, and active participation" by all the faithful in the liturgy[2] has been a touchstone for liturgical theologians' theoretical and practical efforts at liturgical renewal, even as the complexity of the very concept has made agreement on its explanation evasive. While many have approached the notion of active participation through consideration of the elements of rite, musicality, space, functions, and so forth, some theologians have been especially helpful in arguing for how the disposition or mentality with which people approach the act of worship is of fundamental importance.[3] A certain theological understanding is, in the end, essential for the

[1] See *Lectionary for Mass; Introduction*, no. 3.
[2] See *Sacrosanctum Concilium* (Constitution of the Sacred Liturgy), no. 14.
[3] See David N. Power, *Sacrament: The Language of God's Giving* (New York: Crossroad Herder, 1999), 123–31; and Don E. Saliers, *Worship as Theology: Foretaste of Glory Divine* (Nashville: Abingdon Press, 1994), 25–31. In the 1960s and 1970s Alexander Schmemann argued passionately from patristic tradition and in opposition to scholastic theologies that a proper disposition to the biblical and symbolic nature of Christian liturgy is essential to its pastorally beneficial celebration. See, for example, *Liturgy and Tradition: Theological Reflections of Alexander Schmemann*, ed. Thomas Fisch (Crestwood, NY: St. Vladimir's Press, 1990), 37–48. For a comprehensive review of Schmemann's thesis, see Bruce

paschal mystery's being able actually to govern the practice of liturgy. Given the challenge of analyzing the complex phenomenon of human ritualizing, coupled with the profundity of the theology indicated by the very word "mystery," attempting such an adequate theoretical (theological) explanation is no small challenge.

To lead us, then, into this exploration of the paschal mystery I shall recount a liturgy that was so shockingly at odds with the church's theology of it that the narrative can (sadly) serve as a clear example of how the saving, kenotic truth of the mystery can be absent in the ritual execution. Put another way, I will start with an example of what I am arguing against. After explaining what is at stake for believers in the practice of liturgy as enacted paschal mystery, I will then turn to two systematic theologians who have produced compelling works on the mystery of faith, one through a close reading of Scripture, the other through a fresh interpretation of sacramental tradition. The chapter's concluding section will, with help of one more biblical scholar, explore the question—at once a challenge and an invitation—of what motivates and sustains our desires to encounter the crucified and risen Christ as healer in the liturgical proclamation of the Word and celebration of the sacraments.

A DISASTROUS LITURGY OF COMPLETE ANSWERS AND HALF-TRUTHS

A few years ago, I found myself riveted to the pew of a beautiful Catholic cathedral in an American city where I was attending a conference, unexpectedly stunned and hanging on every word of the bishop as he preached his homily for the vigil Mass of the feast of Pentecost. We had just heard the proclamation of John 20:19-23, wherein the resurrected Jesus, appearing on Easter Sunday evening to disciples fearfully huddled behind locked doors, shows them the wounds of his execution, wishes them peace, breathes the gift of the Holy Spirit into them, and charges them with the authority to forgive people's sins. As the bishop began to rehearse the story we had just heard he noted the disciples' fear, quoting with loud intensity the phrase, "for fear of the Jews." He paused to let the nearly shouted phrase resonate in the bright air of the dazzling stained-glassed vault above us.

T. Morrill, *Anamnesis as Dangerous Memory: Political and Liturgical Theology in Dialogue* (Collegeville, MN: Liturgical Press, 2000), 77–92.

Okay, I thought, that *is* a dark and threatening notion for us who hear John's gospel "after Auschwitz,"[4] in the wake of a century that brought anti-Semitism to such evil depths that the church finally had to address its own role in that history, an effort augmented by a Polish pope intensely devoted to reconciliation with the chosen people of the First Covenant. In that slight moment of silence I hoped, almost desperately, that this colleague of Pope John Paul II would take on directly the problematic notion he had thrown out to us in the nave, but against my worst fear, he made no comment at all. He seemed to want to let the accusation stand on some sort of plain sense of the text. I was reeling in my seat, wondering what the preacher intended by his performance, what he expected the sizable assembly of entirely middle-aged and older Catholics to take from this condemnatory phrase. Would not the menacing tone and unvarnished words together lend themselves to the worst of interpretations, the very ones to which church documents themselves admit Catholics have long been prone? Nothing; silence on the ominously delivered point; "for fear of the Jews" seemed an answer to an unarticulated question that left a pit in my stomach.

The bishop turned instead to another aspect of the disciples' fear. *How*, he asked, could these people be afraid? They had seen Jesus heal the lame, cure lepers, and even raise the dead, he exclaimed with what seemed like genuine indignation. Those three were the exact miracles he noted (having been shocked by the introduction, I was now engaging my listening and remembering skills to their utmost). "How could anybody who had seen Christ do those miracles have any fear?" he shrugged. Again, he provided no commentary or explanation to what was now clearly becoming a set of rhetorical questions that, as best this listener could interpret, amounted to an accusation against the disciples, as if to say: What a bunch! If you or I had seen such things would we not have demonstrated superior character and never again feared anything (not even "the Jews," perhaps)? The preacher, however, again gave no commentary to his observation-cum-accusation. The question appeared to strike him as obvious and simple. He did not attempt any review of what the four gospels actually say about the reactions of the disciples or the wider crowd in those various miracle

---

[4] See Johann Baptist Metz, *A Passion for God: The Mystical-Political Dimension of Christianity*, trans. J. Matthew Ashley (New York: Paulist Press, 1998), 39–42, 54–56, 122–29.

stories, a couple of which texts at least could have been allowed also to speak for themselves. Nor did he show any empathy for those disciples struggling with their fears that Easter night.

And so where did that leave us, we who were, then and there, the liturgically assembled Body of Christ? In the reformed rites of the Catholic Church, the homily is itself an original proclamation of the very word of God, addressed to the assembly, transforming texts that might seem like history lessons or stories about *other* people *back then* into a living and active Word working to save *us now*.[5] What were they or we supposed to make of the miracles of Jesus to which he had alluded? And on further reflection, after the homily, I found myself asking: what miracles, if any, did the bishop think *we* had seen?

If such empathetic exploration was beyond this preacher's purview, at least in the case of that one particular homily, a ready and definitive answer to the problem was not. How could the disciples have seen Jesus heal the sick and even raise the dead and still be afraid? His answer: they had not yet received the gift of the Holy Spirit. They needed the Holy Spirit in order to go forward to "preach and teach Jesus Christ" without any fear, not even, he repeated once more with renewed passion and pause, "for fear of the Jews." The answer was plain and simple, with no descriptive explanation of how the gift of the Spirit abates fear, of how the Acts of the Apostles or St. Paul's letters (or the gospels, for that matter) describe (and thus reveal) the sorts of chaotic shadows, cosmic and human, over which the Spirit of Christ hovers so as to create new qualities out of them, so as to "renew the face of the earth" (Ps 104:30, NAB). The preacher simply stated that the apostles (for thus he referred to the disciples in John's text) needed the Holy Spirit to lose their fear and to go out boldly preaching Jesus Christ.

For me the experience of listening had become painfully disconcerting. The preacher made no connection between the Spirit and Jesus' own mission of healing, forgiving, and raising the dead. Nor, at that close of the Easter season (Pentecost Sunday), did he make any reference to Jesus' death and resurrection, the paschal mystery. This, after all, would seem to constitute the greatest of miracles. Or would it? Perhaps not, if one imagines that the disciples already knew what it meant to call Jesus the Messiah while they accompanied him on

---

[5] See *General Instruction of the Roman Missal* (2002), no. 29; *Dei Verbum*, no. 24; and *Lectionary for Mass: Introduction* (1997), no. 24.

his mission in Galilee, if one imagined perhaps that his identity as the incarnate Son of God was evident from the start and tangible in his miracles. The resurrection would then indeed seem to amount to an afterthought: of course the eternal Son could not be kept down for long! The preacher had not treated Jesus or those disciples as the first-century Palestinian Jews that they were. It was as if Jesus had fallen out of the sky (the Son, the Second Person of the divine Trinity), walked around doing astounding miraculous feats (whose implications should have been obvious), and then left once again (perhaps the phrase, "for fear of the Jews," alluded to Jesus' arrest, trial, and execution). The Holy Spirit then comes, and the remaining couple minutes of the homily (for it was brief, six or seven minutes) focused on the apostles' and "our" call "to preach and teach Jesus Christ," a phrase he repeated several times as the final, main point of the homily. It was, of course, a very important point, true to the very heart of the Gospel, but it came with no elaboration, no examples or content of what this mission of preaching and teaching might entail today nor, and this came to worry me as well, just exactly who "we" are, we who now preach and teach Jesus Christ. Was the phrase, as well as the "we," primarily a reference to the office of the bishop? If so, that is true to the tradition[6] and therefore good for us all. But were we in the nave of the church, the assembly, the *ekklesia*, invited to do this as well? If so, how? What miracles had we seen, and how was the Holy Spirit working in the church?

An answer, different in ritual form but no less forceful in proclaimed assurance, came during the Liturgy of the Eucharist. While the preparation of the table and early part of the eucharistic prayer were characterized by the dignified and meticulous execution one might expect during a bishop's Mass in his cathedral, the bishop performed the consecration with such intense and elaborate attention to the rubrics of the Roman Missal that I found myself once again spellbound with amazement. As he read out the account of the Last Supper he took the oversized host in his two hands and leaned his upper body over it at about a thirty-degree angle. Having finished a slow, deliberate recitation of Jesus' words, he raised the host high, gazing up at it for what I am sure was at least fifteen seconds (that is a very long period of silence, should one want to verify it). He then lowered it very gradually, placed it delicately on the paten, and genuflected deeply, holding

---

[6] See *Lumen Gentium* (Dogmatic Constitution on the Church [1964]), no. 24.

the position for several seconds when his knee reached the floor. He then took the chalice with both hands, drawing it toward his stomach and centering it there, just above the edge of the altar. He leaned way down so that his mouth was directly over and within inches of the rim of the cup. As he spoke Jesus' words from the narrative he clearly was breathing into the bowl of the chalice. This moment struck me most, due not only to the great dramatic gesture but also the sheer length of its duration, for the bishop once again was articulating each . . . word . . . ver-y . . . slow-ly. The meticulous precision and physical intensity of the ritual words and gestures exuded a quality something between that of an alchemist and a magician. The breathtaking ritual action as a whole communicated ever so clearly that the food and drink on that altar were no longer what they had been prior to the words and gestures executed by the one authorized to do so among and for the people. As the lengthy elevation and extended genuflection ensued, I found myself thinking: here is the miracle of Jesus that this bishop wishes to impress on us as having seen today.

This still begs the question of who "we" were and are, and we as a church in relation to Jesus. To take the latter first: How do we connect sacramental liturgy to biblical stories? How do we connect the quite elaborate ritual we do in the church today, as well as our own lives in the late-modern world, with the words and actions of Jesus who, while present in the Spirit as the risen Lord among the church today, is nonetheless revealed to us in what we believers hold as the uniquely authoritative scriptural stories of his life and work in his native Jewish Palestine of the first century CE? The stories of Pentecost and Jesus' miracles had been presented so utterly out of context, not only their own biblical-historical contexts but also our own. The preacher, to my ears, had reduced both the events of Pentecost and of Jesus' healing activity to incredible magic events that could not but persuade any-body who saw them—or, by implication in that homily, who now hear about them from the authoritative source of the church—that Jesus is the simple solution to all questions, to all fears. To my observation, the choreography of the consecration, by the change in the rhythm of the words and the extensive performance of gestures, reinforced this sense of absolute yet isolated certitude, cut off from the rest of the eucha-ristic prayer's narrated history of human suffering and salvation and the *hope* for its final, *future* realization for all, living and dead.

To say that Jesus Christ is *the* answer is, of course, fundamentally true for Christians. The dangerous problem, however, is that the assertion of such an absolute truth in the powerful context of the church's liturgy—an action at once of divine *and* human power—can all too easily stumble into being a half-truth. Left alone on a magical-ritual terrain, lost without an integral connection to either the content of the Gospel or the stories of human brokenness and need today, the proclamation in liturgical words and gestures of Jesus as Lord and Savior too often rings hollow inside a sacred no-man's land, a clerical place of holy acts and incantations devoid of the humanity of both God's Son and ourselves.[7] This is tragic, for we find ourselves part of a world so greatly desiring the Divine Word's deep resonance with the joys and hopes, the fears and struggles of all humanity, especially the poor and suffering.[8] Half-truths may be ironic, but they are never inef-fectual. And when the truth in question is nothing less than the con-tent of our Christian faith, there is no such thing as benign neglect.

The half-truth I worry about in this case is an excessive clericalism and ritualism that can focus too much on the divine to the neglect of the human. Is it possible to overemphasize the divine? Yes, when it takes on the sense of "the transcendent" or miraculous but not the sense of the *biblical God* of Jesus. The latter is about the humanity of God.[9] It *is* hard to believe in that and easier to believe that God does not really get mixed up in human affairs as they move between what such religiosity delineates as the sacred and profane spheres of real-ity. We can go to Mass, witness a miracle, and then plug away alone, vacillating between guilt and smugness, self-condemnation and self-congratulation, striving to live so as to get ourselves to the ultimate sacred place, heaven. This makes a dead end of earth. Many people, it seems, are not seeking out such ritual, nor do they feel obliged to

---

[7] See Louis-Marie Chauvet, *The Sacraments: The Word of God at the Mercy of the Body* (Collegeville, MN: Liturgical Press, 2001), 64–65. Gordon Lathrop identifies excessive hierarchism as the major distortion of Roman Catholic lit-urgy, while sectarianism similarly plagues Protestant worship. See his *Holy Ground: A Liturgical Cosmology* (Minneapolis: Fortress Press, 2003), 182–92. Just as for Chauvet and Lathrop, to Bernd Wannenwetsch the ontological sacral-izing of objects and personages is what defeats the ethical import of Roman Catholic liturgy. See his *Political Worship: Ethics for Christian Citizens*, trans. Margaret Kohl (New York: Oxford University Press, 2004), 161–62.

[8] See *Gaudium et Spes* (Pastoral Constitution on the Church in the Modern World [1965]), no. 1.

[9] See Chauvet, *The Sacraments*, 155, 169.

do it on a weekly basis.[10] With liturgy lacking an integral, narrative connection between the stories of their lives and the story of God's salvific work in history, they end up fending for themselves in moments of crisis. Yet such are the very times we *need* religion. The churches are not emptying for nothing.[11]

The decline in active, regular participation in the churches, however, is due to other half-truths as well, other total systems and complete solutions that exert no small influence on the lives of individuals in our societies. For all the benefits they have offered in forms of material freedom for human beings, modern science and capitalist economies have also brought an unfortunate evolutionary logic, a myth of inevitable progress, that in its own totalizing agenda has proven a devastating half-truth of its own.[12] No reasonable person would question the good that has come of modern medicine, technology, and free markets. The scope, however, of the type of reason that rules the market and the laboratory has nonetheless reached well beyond its proper domain, replacing the values of friendship, tradition, respect, hospitality, and compassion with an increasingly exclusive view to profit, efficiency, domination, consumption, and convenience.[13] The worship of God in a Sunday assembly, let alone the content of so much of the Gospel that might be heard there, does not accord well with such reason and its practices. And so the churches are not emptying for nothing. And so also there was at least something right about the content of the preaching and the style of presiding I witnessed at that vigil Mass for

[10] For a summary of trends in American Catholics' attendance at Mass and other indicators of liturgical practice drawn from a half dozen recent studies and surveys, see Thomas P. Rausch, *Being Catholic in a Culture of Choice* (Collegeville, MN: Liturgical Press, 2006), 1–6.

[11] See Peter Steinfels, *A People Adrift: The Crisis of the Roman Catholic Church in America* (New York: Simon & Schuster, 2003), 165–202. A mainstay of Father Andrew Greeley's relentless critique of the contemporary state of American Catholic liturgy has been his attention to the poor quality of the homilies priests deliver. For a recent example, see his *Priests: A Calling in Crisis* (Chicago: University of Chicago Press, 2004), 9, 92–93, 96.

[12] See Dorothee Soelle, *Suffering*, trans. Everett R. Kalin (Philadelphia: Fortress Press, 1975), 103–8. See also Morrill, *Anamnesis as Dangerous Memory*, 26–34.

[13] See Johann Baptist Metz, *The Emergent Church: The Future of Christianity in a Post-Bourgeois World,* trans. Peter Mann (New York: Crossroad, 1987), 4–8. See also, Morrill, *Anamnesis as Dangerous Memory*, 190–91.

Pentecost. Unapologetic, enthusiastic proclamation of the centrality of Jesus for the life of Christians, acknowledgment of the wonder that his mission in ancient Palestine caused then and still elicits today, identifying the Holy Spirit as the sustaining source for following Jesus in that mission, and reverent sharing in the sacramental ritual are all thoughts and actions that bring a desperately needed counterpoint to the habits of a late-modern society driven by the reason of the market and technology. Still, this praxis of truth cannot achieve its purpose if pursued as an equally totalizing, question-free, complete, and closed system.

As Johann Baptist Metz has long insisted, Christianity took a bad turn when it became a religion with far too many answers and few if any questions.[14] At the very origins of Christian faith is a definitive event that nonetheless has, from the start, always stood as a question, namely, the resurrection of Jesus.[15] Faith in the resurrection refuses to let us fill our blank images of God with whatever we think the divine should be like. The proclamation of God's having raised Jesus from the dead always bears the terrible reality of what his death was like, as well as the story of how this man faithfully lived the divine mission that brought him to that end. The story of that specific life and death and the future its resurrection opened but has yet fully to realize is the foundation of all other Christian doctrine.

THE PASCHAL MYSTERY AS KEY TO LITURGICAL, AND THUS CHRISTIAN, LIFE

From its earliest years the church has referred to the actions and sufferings, death, resurrection, and glorification of Jesus—with the latter including the sending of the Holy Spirit and birth of the church—as mystery.[16] The Second Vatican Council and the entire reform and renewal of the liturgy place the paschal mystery at the heart of what we celebrate in our sacramental rites and keeping of the church year. The

---

[14] See Metz, *A Passion for God*, 56, 61–62, 125–26.

[15] For a survey of contemporary thought on the mystery of the resurrection, see Bernard P. Prusak, "Bodily Resurrection in Catholic Perspectives," *Theological Studies* 61 (2000): 64–105. See also, N. T. Wright, *The Resurrection of the Son of God*, Christian Origins and the Question of God, vol. 3 (Minneapolis: Fortress Press, 2003), 1–31; and Carolyn Walker Bynum, *The Resurrection of the Body in Western Christianity, 200–1336* (New York: Columbia University Press, 1995), 1–17.

[16] See above, chap. 1, pp. 9–10.

general introductions to the various rites articulate this principle as fundamental to the theology operative in each liturgy's practice, as is evident, for example, in the *General Introduction to the Order of Christian Funerals*: "The proclamation of Jesus Christ 'who was put to death for our sins and raised to life to justify us' (Rom 4:15) is at the center of the Church's life. The mystery of the Lord's death and resurrection gives power to all of the Church's activity. 'For it was from the side of Christ as he slept the sleep of death upon the cross that there came forth the sublime sacrament of the whole Church.' The Church's liturgical and sacramental life and proclamation of the Gospel make this mystery present in the life of the faithful."[17] To say that the paschal mystery empowers all the church's activity means that the liturgy functions to make possible a way of life, with the members of the worshiping assembly being formed in the gracious vision of the world offered in Christ. Worldview, as Vincent Miller taught us in chapter 2, functions most often as practical knowledge in our daily lives, as opposed to an explicitly argued articulation of the beliefs, images, and convictions that guide and motivate our thoughts and actions.[18] Symbols and rituals, therefore, play a constant, integral role in the daily enactment of persons' lives. This is no less true for the practice of the Christian worldview than any other. Indeed, this is the anthropological reason for why the liturgy is so central to, the "source and summit" of, the practice of faith.[19] Moreover, when we consider the liturgy itself, its actual ritual practice is normally the way in which the message of the faith is imparted to the people, both laity and clergy. Only in certain circumstances—such as when the peculiar challenges in a particular pastoral situation prompt questions for the minister or in the ongoing ideological "liturgy wars" over the meaning and execution of the rites—do people study the (theological) theory in the general introductions. At times, however, we do need to stop and question, as Lizette Larson-Miller notes, whether practices of the rites reflect the theology

[17] International Commission on English in the Liturgy, *Order of Christian Funerals* (1989), no. 2. The article cites *Sacrosanctum Concilium*, no. 5.

[18] See above, chap. 2, p. 52. For another exploration of the primacy of practice over argued principles in people's values, judgments, and commitments, see Kwame Anthony Appiah, *Cosmopolitanism: Ethics in a World of Strangers*, Issues of Our Times, ed. Henry Louis Gates Jr. (New York: W. W. Norton, 2006), 69–85.

[19] See above, chap. 1, pp. 5–7.

of their official introductions, for "the theological introduction and the ritual should say the same thing—one with prose, the other through people, gesture, words, things and actions."[20]

My concern here is with *the* big theological principle suffusing all the rites, the paschal mystery. Only if its content and implications are sufficiently grasped can the distinctive sort of healing that liturgy offers be realized. Louis-Marie Chauvet has argued vigorously for the fundamental importance of grounding the theology and practice of liturgy in the paschal mystery: "*To start from the Pasch . . .* is first to locate the sacraments within *the dynamic of a history,* that of a Church born, in its historic visibility, from the gift of the Spirit at Pentecost and always in the process of becoming the body of Christ all through history. To start from the Pasch is consequently to be obliged to build sacramental theology not only on the *Christological* but also the *pneumatological principle.*"[21] Chauvet's insistence on history is crucial to the implications of his argument. Embracing the scandalous particularity of history opens us to the liberating content of Jesus' life, to the words, actions, and decisions in his native time and place through which he revealed the character of God as boundless mercy, forgiveness, and strength. To insist on history as the medium of God's redemptive work is to accept the sometimes consoling, other times unsettling revelation that, like Jesus, we meet God in the concrete circumstances of our own lives, both as participants in various social bodies and in the waxing and waning of our personal bodies. For such was Jesus' life story unto death, empowered by the Spirit of the God who raised him from the dead and thereby revealed the divine presence in a life spent in self-sacrificing love for fellow humans. The risen Christ's gift of the Spirit sets the lives of believers in the same pattern of encountering the unseen God in the concrete circumstances of their own time and place.[22]

[20] Lizette Larson-Miller, *The Sacrament of the Anointing of the Sick,* Lex Orandi Series, ed. John Laurance (Collegeville, MN: Liturgical Press, 2005), xiv.

[21] Louis-Marie Chauvet, *Symbol and Sacrament: A Sacramental Reinterpretation of Christian Existence,* trans. Patrick Madigan and Madeleine Beaumont (Collegeville, MN: Liturgical Press, 1995), 487.

[22] In his overview of Paul's argument in 1 Cor 15, N. T. Wright explains: "Jesus' resurrection is the beginning of 'the resurrection of the dead', the final eschatological event, which has now split into two; the risen Jesus is the 'first-fruits', both the initial, prototypical *example,* and also the *means* of the subsequent resurrection of his people, because it is through his status and

The "eschatological memorial of the Pasch, that is, the very specificity of the Christian liturgy"[23] places the lives of each believer in the present-tense drama of the mystery of salvation.

This language of mystery should tell us that our faith is at once a profound trust in God's saving, redemptive, vindicating will for humanity but also an ongoing call to accept the incomprehensibility of that God of love, our inability to control how the human story of God will finally come to completion.[24] As St. Paul teaches, the same Spirit of the one who raised Jesus from the dead now lives as the first fruits of his resurrection in the lives of those baptized into his death, working all for the ultimate good in us, just as for Jesus.[25] What characterizes such a life of faith is hope: "Now hope that is seen is not hope. For who hopes for what he sees? But if we hope for what we do not see, we wait for it with patience" (Rom 8:25).

BELIEVING GOD CAN BE TRUSTED: THE MYSTERY OF TESTED FAITH

While the church's doctrinal instruction identifies the paschal mystery as the source of liturgy's empowerment of the Christian life, theologian William Reiser likewise argues from Scripture that "the resurrection is the only logical starting point for thinking about Christian faith."[26] Reiser explains how Mark's gospel is entirely an Easter story framed by the opening verse's (1:1) identification of Jesus as Christ and Son of God (titles presupposing his glorification) and closing with the young man at the empty tomb instructing the women to send the disciples back to Galilee to meet Jesus (16:8). Galilee, of course, is where the gospel opens, and so the implication is clear. If you want to see the risen Lord, go back to the beginning of the story and be with

---

office as the truly human being, the Messiah, that death and all other enemies of the creator's project are to be defeated (verses 20-28) . . . the risen Jesus is the model for what resurrected humanity will consist of, and also, through the Spirit, the agent of its accomplishment." Wright, *The Resurrection of the Son of God*, 317.

[23] Chauvet, *Symbol and Sacrament*, 485.

[24] See Edward Schillebeeckx, *Church: The Human Story of God*, trans. John Bowden (New York: Crossroad, 1991), 168–86.

[25] See Rom 6:3-4; 8:23, 28.

[26] William Reiser, *Jesus in Solidarity with His People: A Theologian Looks at Mark* (Collegeville, MN: Liturgical Press, 2000), 2.

the Jesus whose words and actions reveal God's loving, compassionate, forgiving presence with his people. "[T]he theological significance
of the resurrection is that in raising Jesus from the dead the God of
Israel has identified himself with the life and death of Jesus. . . . God's
identification with the life and death of Jesus is properly a mystery
of faith. This mystery is not something that can be reversed, it challenges the mind as well as the heart, and it powerfully colors the way
we understand human life and human history."[27] The resurrection's
revelation of God's identification with Jesus—the Jesus who claimed
God's reign to be active in his solidarity with the poor, sick, and sinful—requires setting aside our presuppositions about how God acts,
what God wants, and thus who God is. While people might think of
the resurrection in terms of God's rewarding Jesus for exemplary service or confirming how wrong Jesus' enemies were, neither argument
holds much weight given the number of venerable (non-resurrected)
prophets before Jesus, on the one hand, and the Roman and Judean
authorities' harsh treatment of the early church on the other. No, Reiser
concludes, the God revealed in Jesus' resurrection is engaged in something profoundly different from such human inclinations toward merit
or vindication: "a lasting oneness with the crucified men and women
of every time and place . . . the resurrection points the Christian soul
in the direction of living the same solidarity. For divine solidarity with
human beings is the beginning of their salvation."[28]

While the doctrine of the resurrection certainly includes belief in
personal immortality, Reiser avers, that general conviction is not
the primary good news imparted through the resurrection *of Jesus*.[29]
Around the globe and across the ages people have believed in some
sort of continuation of the human being or spirit beyond the boundary
of an individual's death.[30] The Gospel's proclamation of Jesus' resurrection, precisely in relation to the specific content of his historical
life, is about the gift and nurturance of *faith* in the way of life God
calls believers to embrace in this world. Faith is a praxis, a reflective
participation in the "new creation" that Jesus found dawning in his
earthly mission and that Christians continue to glimpse through the

---

[27] Ibid., 3. See also, 152–55.

[28] Ibid., 4. See also, 118–19.

[29] See ibid., 155n4.

[30] We shall consider this distinction and its pastoral implications more
closely in chap. 7, below.

enacted parables of the kingdom, their mutual service to one another and work for a just world. What Mark's text reveals about Jesus, from his baptism in the Jordan through his death on Golgotha, is that he was profoundly a man of faith. Jesus accepted the call from the God of his people and surrendered to the mystery of that God who continually drew him precisely through his encounters with the alienated and suffering to the climax of his mission in Jerusalem. Among those people he shared the quiet joy of divine mercy and forgiveness made practical in human compassion, nurtured through shared meals and biblically centered prayer, and affirmed in foretastes of the fullness of God's reign experienced in profound moments of healing. "The people who appear within [Mark's] story were not simply characters invented so Jesus could display his power or his compassion; they were the ones who evoked from Jesus the substance and style of his prophetic mission."[31] Mark portrays Jesus in this way *for us*, to reveal precisely that in our own mutual solidarity in suffering and joy as followers of this Jesus we experience the life of the same Spirit that is the very mystery of God.

Lest the notion of faith slip into religious abstraction or escapist imagination Reiser presses upon us "the most penetrating question into everyday faith" that emerges from Mark's gospel: can God be trusted?[32] To ask this question does not betray a lack of faith but, quite the contrary, a genuine practice of it. Indeed, the need to question, over and again, one's trust in God is a sign that one is engaged in a life imbued with the Spirit of Jesus. Whether it be the heartbreaking worry over a seriously ill loved one or exhaustion from advocating for human rights or the dejection of accepting a setback in one's personal well-being, the evidence abounds that nothing is sure or predictable about this life of faith.[33] Thus, Reiser reasons, it is not so surprising that fear pervades the Gospel of Mark. From the disciples' repeated resistance to Jesus' passion predictions to the women's fearful, speechless flight from the empty tomb: "Once having chosen to stand with

---

[31] Reiser, *Jesus in Solidarity with His People*, 21.

[32] Ibid., 173.

[33] Harold Remus concludes at the end of his study of healing in the New Testament: "[Jesus'] healings are presented in the gospels not as panacea— the end of all pain and suffering—but as signs—glimpses of the reign of God that Jesus proclaims." *Jesus as Healer*, Understanding Jesus Today, ed. Howard Clark Kee (Cambridge: Cambridge University Press, 1997), 117.

Jesus, the disciples could never escape the wrestling with God that inevitably follows. Easter, Mark knew, does not spare us anything."[34] The Gospel reveals that being the Son of God, the fully authentic human being, "above all means being a person of tested faith."[35]

Here we can recall from chapter 3 how this meditation upon the necessity of tested faith enables Reiser's profound insight into the reason for the disciples' inability to heal the demon-possessed boy and his desperate father.[36] Jesus' explanation to the disciples that this type of demon can only be driven out by prayer indicates the deep empathy that Jesus has with this father, whose anxiety, fatigue, and despair over his son's severe condition have tested his faith to its limit. In the scheme of Mark's composition, only once the disciples have gone through the trial of the cross with Jesus will they have the power to pray and heal with the same empathetic, liberating Spirit of the risen Lord. Harold Remus draws the same conclusion from Luke: Only once Jesus has undergone his baptism by the Holy Spirit and fire (see Luke 3:15) is it possible for his followers to undergo the same, and this still incompletely before the eschaton. Until the end of history, the members of the church heal and teach in the pattern of the crucified Jesus and the power of the Spirit who has raised him into the fullness of life that awaits them.[37] From a broader reading of the New Testament, systematic theologian Bernard Cooke likewise responds to the question, "In precisely what way(s) did Jesus of Nazareth act as savior?" in terms of freedom from fear through trust empowered by the Spirit.[38]

The strength of Reiser's theological interpretation of Mark lies not only in the years of scholarship he has brought to reading the gospel but also, and more profoundly, the prayerful reflection on pastoral experience informing that reading—in the language of hermeneutics, the

[34] Reiser, *Jesus in Solidarity with His People*, 17.

[35] Ibid., 26.

[36] See above, chap. 3, pp. 88–89.

[37] See Remus, *Jesus as Healer*, 67–69.

[38] "This [Jesus] did (1) by himself confronting the prospect of ultimate physical evil, death, and not allowing fear of that evil to deter him from total acceptance of his mission to overcome the more ultimate evil, sin; (2) by sharing with his disciples that Spirit which lead him and them to overcome fear by trust in the power and love of his Abba; and (3) by encouraging through his teaching a trust in God that would free people from a variety of fears." Bernard Cooke, *Power and the Spirit of God: Toward an Experience-Based Pneumatology* (New York: Oxford University Press, 2004), 40.

world in front of the text. Within the necessary limits of his successful study, nonetheless, Reiser does not provide a theological explanation of how members of the church share the formative biblical vision of life in Christ, how the ethics of everyday life meets Scripture as ongoing pastoral tradition, and how sacramental practice forges the link between the two. To this fundamental theological investigation Louis-Marie Chauvet has made a significant contribution.

SURRENDERING TO THE DIVINE MYSTERY:
LIFE AND DEATH IN THE REAL WORLD OF SYMBOLS

At the heart of Chauvet's fundamental liturgical theology is his recognition and insistence that the sacraments of the church are practices of *faith*. Chauvet describes faith as "the assent to a loss,"[39] a continuous letting go of our projections of what we imagine God should be like so that the totally other yet lovingly near God revealed in the crucified and resurrected Christ might really be present to us in our lived experience. Chauvet identifies our imaginary projections of God as part of the larger human challenge of struggling with reality in all the difficulties and surprises with which historical existence presents us. This imagining of total presence, of complete possession or perhaps fulfillment, most often does not result from a moral failure of the will but rather arises in individuals' unconscious as they face harrowing challenges or chronic disappointments or limited personal qualities. Yet upon reflection we realize that it is precisely the resistance of the other to our expectations that tells us that we are dealing with the real and not an emotionally driven projection of our own desires onto what is around us. Heavily influenced by Heidegger's phenomenology, Chauvet describes how genuine presence always entails absence. "The concept of '*coming-into-presence*' precisely marks the absence with which every presence is constitutively crossed out: nothing is nearer to us than the other in its very otherness . . . nothing is more present to us than what, in principle, escapes us (starting with ourselves)."[40]

Given the abstract density of Chauvet's philosophical theology, a couple of examples may help elucidate what I understand by this pervasive human phenomenon, as well as its implications for the life of faith. Perhaps most fundamental is the experience of loving another person. In the case of romantic love, the beloved comes as wondrously

---

[39] Chauvet, *The Sacraments*, 39.
[40] Chauvet, *Symbol and Sacrament*, 404.

other, a person whose qualities so enchant and exhilarate the lover that he or she feels intoxicated with the elusiveness of the beloved: "I just can't get enough of you!" If a real relationship is to grow and last, however, then the couple will discover ways in which the other poses challenges and even difficulties such that each must accept and work with their differences, disappointments, and so forth, as well as the setbacks life presents to them together. Crucial to the relationship's endurance is the couple's developing their own special ways of communicating, forging interpersonal bonds through bodily symbols, of which the most common are words and the most powerful, at times, are (sexual) gestures. Important as well are special symbols and memories they have forged over time, words and gestures and objects that bespeak what exceeds whatever each person could conceive on his or her own. This constitutes a further "otherness" in the relationship, a giftedness greater than the mere sum of the two of them that participates in the larger reality of their world, both drawing from and contributing to life around them.[41]

To consider another example, we might return once more to Reiser's treatment of parental love as portrayed in the ninth chapter of Mark. That the presence of his son in his life is a most important reality for the father is evident in the anguished exhaustion of his faith, but that exhaustion is the very evidence of the father's real presence to the son and vice versa. The son's illness presses upon the father a fearsome absence, the loss of the healthy son he once knew. The resistance of the boy's body and psyche to the image of the good life the father desires for him does not deflect the father from the son before him but rather only heightens his pained commitment to the boy as he is. Love does not get more real than that.

Still another example, germane to any type of relationship, is the experience of being hurt by someone or being the one who inflicts pain on another, which may well entail the sort of alienation within oneself to which Paul so honestly attests: "For I do not do the good I want, but the evil I do not want is what I do" (Rom 7:19). But precisely

---

[41] As Bernard Cooke has long taught, such love-relationships are paradigmatic of friendship as the basic human sacrament. See his *Sacraments and Sacramentality*, rev. ed. (Mystic, CT: Twenty-Third Publications, 1994), 6–55, 78–93. For a more rigorous treatment of the role of loving relationships in human knowledge and self-transcendence, see Bernard Lonergan, *Method in Theology*, 2nd ed. (Toronto: University of Toronto Press, 1990), 104–7.

in such wrestling are we at our most real, spared any illusions of immediate presence to ourselves or another, called to grapple with what
matters through the very bodily matter of our lives and, in so doing,
to construct our own subjectivity in the world that is given us. To
reflect upon the human engagement of reality in this way is to reject
the Western dualistic valuing of soul over body, mind over matter, invisible over visible, unchanging essence over becoming-in-existence.
Instead, one comes to recognize that "the sensible mediations of
language, body, history, desire" comprise "the very milieu within
which human beings attain their truth and thus correspond to the
Truth which calls them."[42] This lack of immediate access to reality is
what constitutes the human need for language, by which is meant
the entire range of symbols whereby humans submit to the otherness
intrinsic to life, to the rule-bound cultural layers through which they
perceive the raw data of the physical universe affecting their senses.
Constantly working with the signs, words, gestures, and narratives—
the "language"—of their societies, people participate in a world at
once given—through symbolism and language usually so conventional to the native user as to seem "natural"—yet continuously under
construction.

Such recognition of the bodily, historical dimension constitutive of
human identity likewise requires the (postmodern) correction of exaggerated notions of individual autonomy that have followed politically,
economically, religiously, and personally from the Enlightenment.
Late-modern people, especially the younger generations for whom
consumerism has been their cultural womb, tend to think and act according to immediate gratification and interpersonal contact, while the
commitment of time and energy to traditional social bodies (religious,
political, civic, and so forth) decreasingly figure in their construction
of personal agency. Thus, upon reflection, I realize that the three examples I just chose in the effort to make Chauvet's fundamental theology accessible to a contemporary audience all focus on the personal
and interpersonal experiences of individuals. Those examples are in
danger of implying to the late-modern reader that such experiences
occur over and above the always-already present cultural frameworks
by which we exercise our subjectivity—a personalism or privatism
that imagines individual experiences as most real in life outside the
shared knowledge, images, and behavior of the social body. Rather

---

[42] Chauvet, *The Sacraments*, 6.

than a committed, albeit critical, giving of oneself over to the practical wisdom of a tradition, the late-modern person consumes (takes up and puts aside) elements from traditions that serve immediate circumstances and desires. The problem for the practice of Christian faith, moreover, is exacerbated by the longer history of the Western instrumentalist view of symbolism.

What has too long plagued the Western Christian understanding, and therefore practice, of the sacraments, Chauvet argues, is the metaphysical notion that the (ideal) human subject exists prior to and outside the world of language (symbolism), that some level of immediate access to reality is available to humans. From this arises thought and practices that value the "internal" over the "external," the invisible over the visible, thereby mistaking language (the symbolic) for a mere instrument to be overcome so as to enter into the total presence or pure essence of reality. Nothing could be further from the truth! The very "language" of the symbols that people of a religious tradition share, specifically in the manner they choose to engage them, are what comprise their particular experience of the divine and their view of the world, their commitment to its order, their ethics, their willingness to spend their lives in its realization.

> To say 'there is speaking,' constantly in human beings is to say that every perception of reality is mediated by their culture and the history of their desire. In the absence of these, this reality would be left to its raw factualness and would be only a chaos or meaningless jumble. In order for the subject to reach and retain its status of subject, it must build reality into a 'world,' that is to say, a signifying whole in which every element, whether material (tree, wind, house) or social (relatives, clothing, cooking, work, leisure) is integrated into a system of *knowledge* (of the world and of society), *gratitude* (code of good manners, mythical and ritual code ruling relationships with deities and ancestors), and *ethical behavior* (values serving as norms of conduct). The infant as well as the adult have to deal with this world, *always-already* constructed, and not with things in their crude physical state. By these means, the universe and events form a coherent whole which is called 'the symbolic order.' Subjects can orient themselves by it because each thing can find in it its own signifying place.[43]

---

[43] Ibid., 13.

Thus, language is not the instrument but the womb of our subjectivity, society the "space" constructed of knowledge, gratitude, and ethical behavior wherein people dynamically engage the symbols already present as cultural tradition in ever-original acts of meaning, such that the subject and language/culture are contemporaneous.

Chauvet's theological move is to interpret the practice of Christianity, the ongoing formation of Christian identity, as a particular engagement in this essential anthropological structure of knowledge, gratitude, and ethics. Christian identity is not self-administered but rather lies in the "assent to faith in Jesus as 'Christ,' 'Lord,' 'Son of God,'" an assent to "the confession of faith from which the church was born."[44] The church is the milieu within which believers come to and exercise an empowering competence in the symbolic order given by the Spirit of the risen Christ. The ecclesial pattern of this ongoing performance of faith Chauvet finds in Luke's stories of the Ethiopian's baptism (Acts 8:26-40), Saul's conversion (Acts 9:1-20), and the two disciples' encounter with the risen Christ on the road to Emmaus (Luke 24:13-35). All three stories situate believers in the milieu of the church, living a faith that comes from God's initiative through the mediation of the church in a consistent pattern: the knowledge of faith's content through the proclamation of Scripture, the inscribing of that word on the bodies of believers through symbolic gestures, and the sacramental experience of Christ's absence as an indwelling presence compelling believers to missionary action.

The story of Emmaus is paradigmatic of the ecclesial pattern. By the time Luke completed his gospel, Chauvet argues, believers were well habituated to assembling as church, as those called to worship on the first day of the week. By making this the very setting of the narrative, namely, disciples in companionship on the day of the resurrection, Luke signals to his audience that the risen Christ present in the story is also the Christ present in the ecclesial assembly. Christ comes to the two disciples who have quit Jerusalem, leaving behind their expectations of immediate divine deliverance through Jesus, abandoning those hopes with the corpse of the would-be Messiah. Jesus fills the empty space of their long walk home with his exposition of the Scriptures as revelatory of the meaning of his life and death. The beginning of faith, then, is the renunciation of the immediate sort of divine deliverance they expected and their consenting to the meaning mediated

---

[44] Ibid., 19.

through the crucified and risen Jesus' interpretation of the Scriptures. While Christ's proclamation may have burned in their hearts, they only came to recognize him when they were drawn into the reality of that word for them through the ritual of his taking, blessing, breaking, and sharing the bread at table. The pattern of the symbolic gesture is identical to the evangelist's description of Jesus' action at the Last Supper, a tradition we know the earliest ecclesial communities practiced as having come from the Lord (see 1 Cor 11:23). Thus, "it is in the church celebrating the Eucharist as his prayer and his action, as it is in the church welcoming the Scriptures as his word, that it is possible to recognize that Christ is alive."[45] That climax to the Emmaus story, nonetheless, results in Jesus' immediate vanishing from their sight, an absence that, far from leaving them with a hopeless feeling of abandonment (as in the story's opening), inspires them with the power to go back to Jerusalem to share the Good News. This, Chauvet argues, signals the ethical dimension of ecclesial faith: the sharing in word and sacrament is verified—realizes its truth (verity)—in the *koinonia* of practical care, concern, and service among believers. Ethical praxis in daily life is as much a performance of the word written on the body as is sacramental rite, the work of one and the same Spirit.

Chauvet thus arrives at an explanation for the ecclesial practice of faith as a taking up and converting of the basic three-dimensional structure of human subjectivity. Chauvet's sacramental theology is a philosophical interpretation of how God's having taken up and saved the human condition in the life, death, and resurrection of Jesus becomes real in the lives of those baptized into that same paschal mystery. The church's symbolic order of Scripture, sacrament, and ethics makes of the human pattern of knowledge, gratitude, and ethics a sacrament—an embodied revelation—of the reign of God, the salvation of human beings. By *scripture* Chauvet means not only the canonical books of the Bible but all that "pertains to the knowledge of God's mystery revealed in Jesus Christ,"[46] including theological texts past and present, catechesis, homilies, sermons, and so forth. He uses *sacrament* analogously to refer not only to official rites assuring the Spirit's grace under the leadership of those ordained to preside in the name of Christ (*in persona Christi*) but also to all forms of prayer, petition, contemplation, and thanksgiving. Ethical conduct includes

[45] Ibid., 26.
[46] Ibid., 28.

"all that pertains to *action* in the name of the gospel (therefore also, and even primarily, in the name of humanity)."[47] What keeps this way of life explicitly Christian is ongoing balance between these three constitutive poles of the practice of faith. Only by submitting to the resistance of reality revealed in each dimension's juxtaposition to the others do believers continue to give themselves over to the otherness, the presence-in-absence of the God of Jesus. Such ongoing praxis of scripture-sacrament-ethics keeps the faith real in its sometimes consoling, other times painful openness to the revelation of the God of Jesus.[48] By submitting together as church to the performance of scripture, sacrament, and ethics—face-to-face in liturgical gathering, far and wide in daily living—Christians discover over and again that otherness, finally, is not a threat but an invitation, that the God of Jesus can be trusted.

The concrete corporality of the practice of the sacraments, precisely as language-laden, communal acts of symbolic mediation, is what makes their celebration so essential to knowing and living the Christ proclaimed in Scripture. Participation in sacramental liturgy, as an ecclesial body given over to both the Word in Scripture and symbolic gestures that inscribe that divine word on our persons, delivers us from the human tendency to imagine that there should be no distance, no gap, no otherness between ourselves and the fullness of God. The members of a liturgical assembly bring precisely their bodies to the celebration, their daily action (ethics) as persons engaged in the social and cosmic corporality of the human story being written in history. By participating in the traditional body of the church's sacramental worship we submit to the mystery of God revealed in the crucified and resurrected Jesus, a God who comes to us in and through the shared bodily medium of our human knowing, suffering, and loving. Thus does the God of Jesus become really present to our lives, even as that

[47] Ibid., 31.

[48] Here I find the burden of Chauvet's argument resonant with Gordon Lathrop's liturgical theory of juxtapositions, as well as his mentor Edward Schillebeeckx's mystical-political theology of the contrast experience. See Gordon W. Lathrop, *Holy Things: A Liturgical Theology* (Minneapolis: Fortress Press, 1993), 15–83, 204–25; and *Holy Ground: A Liturgical Cosmology* (Minneapolis: Fortress Press, 2003), 53–79, 197–225; and Edward Schillebeeckx, *Christ: The Experience of Jesus as Lord*, trans. John Bowden (New York: Crossroad, 1981), 817–19; *Church*, 5–14; and *The Schillebeeckx Reader*, ed. Robert Schreiter (New York: Crossroad, 1987), 272–74, 257–59.

sacramental ecclesial presence always recedes in its coming, sending us in the Spirit to discover the Word as living and active in us and our world.

The resistance to that divine receding, to the absence necessarily inherent to divine presence *if God is really to be God for us*, can be terribly strong. The challenges, difficulties, disappointments, fear, and tragedies in life, as well as such temptations as greed, lust, vanity, and dominance, all contribute to people's succumbing, either episodically or habitually, to the imaginary realm of immediacy lodged in the depths of our unconscious. Religion, as Feuerbach recognized, can prove to be the projection of people's own desires for power, control, total assurance, immediate fullness. History teaches that Christian religion is no less prone to being overtaken by human ideologies than any other. Chauvet suggests models of how such idolatrous distortions of the faith arise when there is an "overvaluation" of one of the three poles structuring Christian identity: biblical fundamentalism, righteous moralism, and magical sacramentalism.[49] By isolating the literal word of the text, the fundamentalist turns Scripture into an imagined conduit of immediate access to God's knowledge and will, leaving no space for the more realistic sacramental meeting of the Word with the complexities of the bodily life—physical, social, cosmic—we bear in liturgy. The inevitable result is a manipulation of biblical (or theological or doctrinal) texts into the image of what the fundamentalist wants reality (including God) to be, often to the harm or neglect of individuals and the common good. On the other hand, those who identify Christian faith excessively with the performance of ethical activity—morality, service, social activism—are prone to self-righteous indignation over others' lack of commitment or, alternatively, "burn out" amid intractable social situations or individuals' failures or inabilities to change. Without continuous encounter with the divine images, narratives, and wisdom imparted through Scripture coupled with expressions of gratitude, petition, and solidarity—human and divine—in sacrament, the Christian life becomes grim in its alienation from both God and humanity.[50]

---

[49] Chauvet, *The Sacraments*, 40.

[50] "Politics without prayer or mysticism quickly becomes grim and barbaric; prayer or mysticism without political love quickly becomes sentimental and irrelevant interiority." Schillebeeckx, *The Schillebeeckx Reader*, 274.

The third type of idolatrous denial of the distance, the absence, the otherness between God and us humans Chauvet characterizes as an overvaluation of sacrament, a mistaken equation of the risen Christ's presence in the church's rites with immediate, complete union with the divine, an imagined consummation of reality. The sacraments become practices of magic, the performance of words and gestures that guarantee supernatural results. Magical practice of the sacraments is nothing short of a disaster for Christian faith because it inevitably corners "God" into having to produce immediate results according to human imagining of what and who "God" is, how "God" must act to remove all otherness, all fear, all uncertainty.[51] The sad irony in such a distorted appropriation of the church's doctrine of the sacraments' functioning *ex opere operato* is that it wipes out the very practice of faith. By narrowly and exclusively focusing on the objects of sacramental action at the powerful hands of the priest, magical sacramentalism alienates God from the struggles and joys of human life, thereby negating the very essence of the Gospel. To be a "practicing Catholic" means assisting at rites, performing prayers and devotions, and witnessing the miracle of sacred (set-apart) objects and personages. It may also entail following moral precepts, but this not as an experience of embracing the word of God as written on one's body, as coming to realization in one's life, but rather, as clerical directives to be obeyed under pain of denied access to the sacraments.

On the contrary, the saving truth of *ex opere operato* lies in the apostolic *faith* that efficacy in the rites depends not on the worldly strength of those who preside over them but on the power of the Holy Spirit revealed in Scripture and imparted to the church through Christ's glorification. The doctrine recognizes that *biblical* faith is given, received, and practiced in the always imperfect conditions of human living. The celebration of the sacraments is for revealing the transformative presence of the (scriptural) God *of Jesus* in all the ambiguity of our (ethical) living,[52] not for repairing to some sacred precinct where we

[51] If one follows N. T. Wright's method for symbolizing the idolatrous, as opposed to biblical, projections of the divine, the word I put in quotes here, "God" would be written without the quotation marks and in lower case, thus: god. See above, chap. 2, p. 35, n. 20.

[52] "In other words, *every sacrament shows us how to see and live what transforms our human existence into a properly Christian existence.*" Chauvet, *The Sacraments,* 148.

get to witness god being completely god. Here trinitarian faith is not a puzzling theological abstraction but the heart of embodied faith. Here faith in the crucified God scandalizes theism (with its monolithic god). The Christ who comes to us in the sacraments is the one who lived a human solidarity unto death, revealing the *difference* in God that is the source of our salvation, crossing out the god of human imagination and establishing a similitude between God and humans.[53] In the paschal mystery the love between Father and Son becomes the love between God and humanity. The Spirit is the difference, the holiness, the otherness of love shared between Father and Son. The Spirit wrote that difference on the person-body of Jesus of Nazareth, raised him from death to glory, and now writes that difference on the bodies of believers in the rites of the church. In celebrations of the paschal mystery "God is revealed as the one who, through the Spirit, 'crosses God out' in humanity, giving to the latter the possibility of becoming the 'sacramental locus' where God continues to be embodied."[54]

If this explanation of the sacramental structure of Christian faith seems paradoxical to the reader, then all I can say is: welcome to the world of the Gospel! I offer the greeting not in irony or sarcasm but impassioned with the tragic beauty of the paschal mystery, God's revelation of salvation as the meeting of divine and human desire (the Spirit) in the human (bodily and historical, assured yet struggling, defeated but triumphant) person of Jesus. Any imaginary shortcut to the immediate presence of divine fulfillment is a sliding away from the faith, a misplacing of the hope, a malnourishment of the love that comes to us in the Spirit of the crucified and risen Christ. The assent to the particular symbolic order of human living that is the tradition of the church—the constant, mutually informing movement between word, sacrament, and ethics—is what nurtures the life of Christian faith. When the divorce of symbol from reality (body from spirit) slips into Christian practice, we lose the singular grace, the divine favor, the Gospel has to offer us. Rather than gracing us with original gifts that only God (in God's saving difference) can give, liturgy becomes a mere expression of what we already know, the sacraments mere instruments for one dimension or other of human experience. If the Eucharist is understood and practiced as a sacred object whose reality ("real presence") is only assured by its transcending (ascending from, leaving be-

[53] See ibid., 161–64.
[54] Ibid., 167.

hind completely) the physical and social body of the bread and people assembled, then the evangelically transformative power of this and all other sacraments cannot but be lost. Various power agendas (clericalism, consumerism, individualism, and so forth) move in to fill the void between the sacred and profane, projecting some other image of what practically matters, what really "can be done" in an undeniably tragic world. Because of the traditional centrality of the Eucharist for the church, the divorce between liturgy and life in the Eucharist influences a similar disaffection in all the other sacramental rites. Anointing remains mired in the misconception of "last rites" because we know people aren't physically going to survive. Funerals become exercises in eulogizing because that's all we know we've got: the memory of the deceased's life. As we shall see in the ensuing chapters, the reformed rites of the church have far, far more to offer if only we seek the grace of assenting to the paschal mystery.

CONCLUSION: HEALING AS REVEALING THE BODY OF CHRIST IN ITS MEMBERS

In the end, the liturgy does not exist except in actual communities' enactments of the rites, in the corporate and corporeal actions (the work, *leitourgia*) of a particular local church.[55] This is another way of saying what I asserted in chapter 1, namely, that the people, as assembled members of the Body of Christ, are the sacraments of the church. The reform and renewal of the church's liturgy, therefore, is not merely a matter of historically and theologically informed revision of the ritual texts. To the extent that the church, in its array of members and range of structures, is in need of healing, so is the liturgy. The liturgy itself needs to be healed, even as it serves as an instrument of healing. But that is only another way of saying that for the church's acts of divine worship to be authentic to the Gospel, they must always be revealing the God of Christ Jesus, the powerful healer who ended up

---

[55] See Gary Macy, "The Future of the Past: What Can the History Say about Symbol and Ritual?" *Practicing Catholic: Ritual, Body, and Contestation in Catholic Faith*, ed. Bruce T. Morrill and others (New York: Palgrave Macmillan, 2006), 29, 37; and Bruce T. Morrill, "Contemporary Ritual Practices of Healing: Introduction," *Practicing Catholic*, 81. See also, Kenan B. Osborne, *Christian Sacraments in a Postmodern World: A Theology for the Third Millennium* (New York: Paulist Press, 1999), 16–17, 57–59, 188–89.

"powerless, hanging on a cross."[56] This Jesus, in turn, only comes alive among bodies of the faithful who have come to know their profound need for him.

And so I return once more to the story with which I opened this chapter. The reader who has persevered through the highly theoretical portion of this chapter will hopefully have heard echoes of the alarms I sounded in my description and analysis of that one liturgy. While the challenges confronting further renewal of the liturgical life of the American Catholic Church arise from numerous dimensions of the ecclesial and wider social (economic, political, cultural) context, the ongoing practical consequences of clericalism and magical sacramentalism should not be underestimated. The diminishing percentage of American Catholics who regularly participate in liturgy leads one to ask whether people are finding a *real* connection between word, sacrament, and ethics such that they could not imagine trying to live their lives without joining in the church's rites. For me the problem was symbolized at that cathedral Mass by not only the near absence of people under the age of fifty but also the composition of the liturgical ministers. My memory of the appearance, deportment, location, and interaction of those ministers can serve as a contemporary parable for this conclusion to the chapter.

In the minutes before the liturgy's start, I observed a tall, strapping, well-groomed, thirty-something cleric impeccably dressed in the highest quality cassock and surplus ordering around a much older, bald, hunchbacked acolyte unable to zip neatly to his neck the alb that hung unevenly down his body. The latter man, who may only have been in his late fifties despite looking much older, struck me as probably having suffered polio in his youth. The only other lay minister was a late-middle-aged woman who eventually served as lector, but her ministry was not evident from the start because she was allowed neither a seat in the sanctuary nor a place in the entrance procession of the Mass. That was for men only. Last in the procession, of course, was the middle-aged bishop, wearing an unusually puffy chasuble with a shiny peach-orange background covered by impressionistic yellow swirls (not quite the color red mandated by the Roman *ordo*). In front of the bishop were two priest-concelebrants, less flamboyantly vested, one middle-aged and the other elderly, neither of whom had any

[56] Harold Remus, *Jesus as Healer*, Understanding Jesus Today, ed. Howard Clark Kee (New York: Cambridge University Press, 1997), 11.

explicit role in the liturgy other than to sit at one side of the sanctuary and eventually flank the bishop during the eucharistic prayer. Ahead of them, in the role of master of ceremonies, strode the younger priest in smart cassock and surplus. In poignant contrast to the straight posture and virility of that cleric, the stooped acolyte led the way, lurching forward with each step as he carried a tall processional crucifix that tilted significantly to the left as it rose from the awkward clutch of his disabled upper body. The image is a poignant cause for reflecting on where among the people of God we encounter Christ and what sorts of ecclesial statuses and liturgical practices might foster or hinder our encountering him. Clerics, young and old, may symbolize forms of worldly power variably attractive to us all (office, wealth, physical beauty), but for Christians all such capacities are salvific only in service to humans in need, bearers of the cross.

As we have seen in the previous and present chapter, Scripture is crucial to the renewal of the liturgy and thus the church's compassionate service in the sacraments. Approached intelligently and prayerfully, Scripture counters clericalism and ritualistic idolatry by animating liturgical celebrations in depth with the person of the biblical Jesus, the Risen One proclaimed in the gospels and present in the Spirit. Jesus, the joy of faith's desire, meets us not in some sacred muted isolation but in the narratives of a biblical world at once common and strange to us, populated by a cacophony of characters historically ancient yet humanly familiar: worried parents, confused companions, social rejects, dispossessed peasants, rich people, beggars, women and men, elderly and children, Jewish reformers and priestly authorities, Roman officials, supporters and opponents of the military occupational government, thrill-seeking crowds, demoniacs, cripples, blind people, visionaries and fanatics, the sick and homeless, a wealthy young man "who's got it all," numerous scorned women, and the list goes on. Those people essentially shaped the self-giving mission of Jesus because, Jewish prophet that he was,[57] Jesus experienced God's call and promise of faithful presence precisely among

---

[57] In the middle of the second of his massive volumes on the historical Jesus, John Meier asserts that "nothing seems clearer" than that "Jesus acted and was thought of as a Jewish prophet during his lifetime" and that he and others thought of himself as a distinct if not definitive eschatological prophet. John P. Meier, *A Marginal Jew: Rethinking the Historical Jesus*, vol. 2, *Mentor, Message, and Miracles* (New York: Doubleday, 1994), 699.

them.[58] For those baptized into Christ's Body the situation and invitation is similar. We verify—make true in our lives—our faith in the God revealed in word and sacrament only through ethically embracing the attractive and the revolting, the beautiful and the broken, the calming and the upsetting, the clear and the confusing in our own unsettled world and ever-changing lives.

To conclude these two chapters' attempt to pull together Scripture and tradition, the hermeneutics of biblically practiced faith, I draw on one more biblical scholar whose work on Luke-Acts has shed profound light on the experience of need as the fundamental condition for the human embrace of the divine Gospel. In *To Heal and To Reveal* Paul Minear acknowledges how difficult it is for modern readers to grasp Luke's message about Jesus, as well as about the church as the historical successor of his mission. Indeed, it is impossible without undertaking the hard work of trying to apprehend the consciousness or worldview that Jesus and his disciples lived (the reign of God), which is at odds with virtually every tenet of modernity. This is the consciousness of God calling people to repentance, to break away from the pattern of lording authority over others, of expecting might (political, religious, economic, professional) to make right and, in its place, embracing the pattern of Jesus' prophetic life of self-emptying (kenotic) service. For Jesus, these local, specific acts of God's deliverance of the forsaken amount to nothing less than the cosmic overthrow of the dominion of evil, of sin, of Satan. This worldview of Jesus is a paradoxical one, Minear argues, given to disclosure not by analytical argument but parabolic words and deeds, of which the definitive one was his crucifixion.[59]

The offense of the Gospel (to use Leander Keck's fine phrase[60]) lies, then, not in Jesus' performance of healings or exorcisms per se but rather in how those miracles help to reveal something far more world-shattering, namely, the origin and kind of authority Jesus was inaugurating and the decision it demanded: "[W]e will not grasp how healing meant revealing, and how revealing meant healing, without grasping the mystery of how weakness had become the channel of

---

[58] See Reiser, *Jesus in Solidarity with His People*, 26–29, 171–72.

[59] See Paul Minear, *To Heal and To Reveal: The Prophetic Vocation According to Luke* (New York: Seabury Press, 1976), 24. I am in Don Saliers's debt for introducing me to this profound study.

[60] See above, chap. 3, p. 69.

God's power."[61] Jesus' taking the latter all the way to his death makes the crucifixion, along with the resurrection, the definitive realization of this divine power exercised through humility in suffering service to the lowest, the revelation that the dominion of evil is not ultimately in charge. Jesus' death and glorification sealed with authority the prophetic implications of his miracles, table service, and teachings, which he clearly intended as applicable "to all types of human associations, whether political or economic or religious . . . constitut[ing] nothing less than the most revolutionary form of liberation from every kind of servitude."[62] Freedom resides in the awareness that in taking on this "from the bottom up" approach in whatever situations of urgent need, believers experience the invisible God's immanence in visible human actions. Belief in this fusion of the human and divine, the visible and invisible, is evident in Luke's disinclination to separate what modern readers would identify as the objective and subjective factors in the miracle accounts.[63]

The immense question remains, of course, as to whether and on what terms believers might embrace and practice the life of faith this gospel envisions. Minear's challenging yet inviting response:

> Any reentry into Luke's world presupposes and requires a world view the opposite of the 'flat-earthers,' those radical secularists whose earth is limited to one dimension; it requires a world view which gives absolute primacy to the reality of God and his governance of [human] affairs. Moreover, we will never reenter the world of the prophets unless we concede that God actually has available various means of communication with his people, means which explode the firmness and fixity of those patterns of thought by which we have domesticated the anarchies of history, making ourselves slaves of immanence in the process.[64]

The understanding of Christian sacraments and liturgy proposed in the first and present chapter, of their revelatory function for the practice of faith as a comprehensive way of life, of their engagement of the biblical word with the symbolic enactment of the paschal mystery,

[61] Minear, *To Heal and To Reveal*, 75.

[62] Ibid., 24.

[63] Here Minear's argument reminds us of John Pilch's treatment of blindness and faith in Luke. See above, chap. 3, pp. 91–93.

[64] Minear, *To Heal and To Reveal*, 100.

amounts to one such world-transforming means of communication between God and people. Sacramental liturgy, when understood and practiced not as quantified portions of grace dispensed inside sacred boundaries but as graced events disclosing God's active will among those hungering for it, has as its very purpose the making visible in and to human corporality the invisible mystery of salvation. Liturgy can only have such a healing and revealing force if members of the church, clergy and laity alike, give themselves over to the divine authority hidden in its unblinking openness to biblical proclamation, its tradition-based symbolism, its irreducible musicality of rhythmic sound and silence, its attentiveness to the real, live human stories in which it occurs—in a word, to its ritual promise of disclosing what could not otherwise be known. In the following three chapters, then, we turn to what the reformed sacramental rites make known, how they reveal merciful divine love transforming and healing the human experiences of sickness, alienation, dying, and grief with a hope borne of the shared faith that the God of Jesus can be trusted.

Part 3

Rites of Healing

Chapter 5

The Pastoral Care of the Sick:
Healing through Renegotiated Meaning in
Illness and Old Age

INTRODUCTION

The previous two chapters offered an interpretation of the scriptural and traditional grounds for the church's contemporary liturgical
ministry of healing. In these next three chapters I will investigate the
pastoral-theological details of the sacramental rites especially oriented
to healing, beginning with *Pastoral Care of the Sick: Rites of Anointing
and Viaticum.* As both that complete title and its General Introduction
indicate,[1] this liturgical complex is structured around the celebration
of two sacraments, anointing of the sick and Viaticum for the dying.
Theological commentators have repeatedly noted how the very title
and subtitle for this entire rite reflect the liturgical reform and renewal
envisioned by Vatican II coming to fruition.[2] The priority of the title
indicates that the fundamental purpose of the two sacramental foci,
anointing and Viaticum, is the pastoral care of the people for and with
whom they are celebrated. Put in the language of ancient tradition,
celebrations of these rites glorify God by sanctifying humans.[3] The two
sacraments named in the subtitle, as well as the organization of the
General Introduction, indicate the related but distinct situations each

[1] See International Committee on English in the Liturgy, *Pastoral Care of the
Sick: Rites of Anointing and Viaticum* (Washington, DC: National Conference of
Catholic Bishops, 1983), nos. 1–41. Hereafter, PCS.

[2] See Charles W. Gusmer, *And You Visited Me: Sacramental Ministry to the
Sick and the Dying*, rev. ed. (New York: Pueblo Publishing, 1989), 156; Lizette
Larson-Miller, *The Sacrament of Anointing of the Sick, Lex Orandi* Series, ed.
John Laurance (Collegeville, MN: Liturgical Press, 2005), xii; and Mary Col-
lins, "The Roman Ritual: Pastoral Care and Anointing of the Sick," *Concilium*
1991/2, ed. Mary Collins and David N. Power (London: SCM Press, 1991), 4.

[3] See above, chap. 1, pp. 7–8.

one serves: serious illness by "Anointing of the Sick,"[4] and immanent death by "Viaticum for the Dying."[5]

The two sacraments include several other pastoral rituals leading to and following from their celebration, supporting the potential pastoral efficacy of each sacrament and thus richly contributing to the liturgical ministry of these rites. "The rites in Part I of *Pastoral Care of the Sick: Rites of Anointing and Viaticum* are used by the church to comfort the sick in time of anxiety, to encourage them to fight against illness, and perhaps to restore them to health. These rites are distinct from those in the second part of this book, which are provided to comfort and strengthen a Christian in the passage from this life."[6] Following the logical order of the two, I will treat the anointing of the sick and its attendant rituals in this chapter and then turn to Viaticum and related services with the dying in chapter 6. The basic question governing the entire pastoral-theological investigation is: how does Christ, through the power of the Spirit, heal members of the church in these sacramental rites?

Before delving into each of the two distinct sacraments, however, a brief review comparing and contrasting other ways the church has served the sick can clarify the course for uncovering the treasures that still often remain hidden in the reformed rites for the sick and the dying.[7] Having thus distinguished the type of healing proper to the contemporary sacramental liturgies, the chapter will proceed by situating the rites for the sick in their historical development so as to, in subsequent sections, produce a commentary on their renewed form and practice.

THE RANGE OF THE CHURCH'S SERVICE: MEDICAL, CHARISMATIC, SACRAMENTAL

Given the anthropological, biblical, and theological ground we have covered in the preceding chapters, it should not be difficult to recognize that the efficacy of the sacraments of anointing and Viaticum, precisely as symbolic actions, resides in their bringing about healing in the midst of illness, not curing of biomedical disease. The rites of the

---

[4] PCS, nos. 5–25.

[5] Ibid., nos. 26–29.

[6] Ibid., no. 42.

[7] In this I take as my inspiration Gusmer's own schematization of the church's ministry to the sick and dying. See *And You Visited Me*, 154–66.

Pastoral Care of the Sick offer healing as part of larger efforts at caring for the seriously ill or dying by bringing to traumatic, chronic, or overwhelming situations a transforming sense of meaning as children of God, members of Christ's Body. Far from being believers' only response to the realities of illness and death, the rites must be practiced as part of a holistic approach to sickness, one recognizing the concurrence of disease and illness in the unique experience of each individual person. Christian tradition sees sickness and death as that against which we must always struggle, striving to sustain life as the good gift of the Creator within the perspective of serving God in a world that nonetheless is always passing away.[8] From its origins the church has acted on this belief, in imitative obedience to Christ, by caring for the sick in a number of ways, including personal care and charity, medical assistance, sacramental rites, and charismatic prayer.

As our study of the gospels taught us, in the world of the early church, families or fictive kin groups were an individual's sole source of support in illness. To be alienated from any such group, or for a family to have fallen so far into destitution as not to be able to help one another, was the concrete form that poverty took. What distinguished the followers of Jesus and successive generations of Christians was their outreach to the poor and sick, the practical love they demonstrated in openly forming fellowship groups (local churches) that actively reached out in service to the poor, the hungry, and the sick. In periods of persecution what impressed people about Christians included their resolute courage in arenas of torture and, less dramatically but no less effectively, their shunning of social boundaries in caring for the sick and needy.[9] In his effort to repress Christianity in the mid-fourth century, the emperor Julian realized the church's care for the poor was a key reason citizens were well disposed to Christianity. The empire would have to take up such philanthropic work as helping the sick if his suppression of the religion were to succeed.

Julian's agenda did not outlive him, of course. By the latter part of the fourth century bishops and holy people were constructing highly original social forms of charity by founding hospitals in Syria, Cappadocia, and Rome. As Christianity has grown over subsequent

---

[8] See PCS, nos. 3–4.

[9] See Peter Brown, *The Body and Society: Men, Women, and Sexual Renunciation in Early Christianity* (New York: Columbia University Press, 1988), 218–19, 289–90.

centuries, the care of the sick has comprised no small part of the time, talent, and treasure that dioceses, religious orders and congregations, and lay organizations have invested in hospitals, clinics, hospices, nursing homes, medical research and education, and so forth. What I want to note is that, while inspired by word and sacrament in service to the whole person, Christians who provide this type of care for the sick are engaged primarily in instrumental and technical, as opposed to ritually symbolic, practices. This work is a matter of using medicine, drugs, water, nutrition, shelter, hygiene, and therapeutic techniques to support, relieve, and at times even cure the sick and elderly. The work today primarily entails constant attention to the immediate needs (physical, psychological, emotional) of patients and seeking the best methods for instrumentally dealing with them. Insofar as Christians undertake all such work as service to fellow humans, these practices exemplify the ethical pole of Louis-Marie Chauvet's structure of Christian identity. This practical love in service to others both draws its strength from and brings verification to the symbolic exchange of divine and human love revealed in Scripture and experienced in sacrament. The worship of God in ethical service and the liturgical worship of believers gathered in Christ's name are distinct yet essentially related works of one and the same Spirit.[10]

Another Christian response to sickness, again from the very origins of the church, is what can be generally classified as charismatic ministry, thaumaturgy, or miraculous cures.[11] Such New Testament literature as the Pauline letters and Acts of the Apostles attest to certain believers receiving the charism, the empowering gift of the Holy Spirit, to heal and possibly cure people of sicknesses and afflictions. Numerous patristic authors likewise recount the presence of charismatic healers in their churches, a presence that nevertheless diminished in the wake of the Montanist crisis and growing official distrust of enthusiastic Spirit movements.[12] Such movements, nonetheless,

[10] See Louis-Marie Chauvet, *The Sacraments: The Word of God as the Mercy of the Body* (Collegeville, MN: Liturgical Press, 2001), 168–69.

[11] See Gusmer, *And You Visited Me*, 156–59.

[12] For treatment of numerous patristic texts describing charisms in the early church as well as the Montanist crisis, see the detailed index of Kilian McDonnell and George T. Montague, *Christian Initiation and Baptism in the Holy Spirit: Evidence from the First Eight Centuries* (Collegeville, MN: Liturgical Press, 1991), 344–46.

have recurred in Christian history,[13] with the Pentecostalism of contemporary times having found its own inroads in Roman Catholicism in the charismatic movement that peaked in the 1970s, while continuing strong in Protestant evangelical churches today.

The other major type of charismatic healing in Christianity has been the identification of the Spirit working through individual saints.[14] This popular recognition of charismatic healing came to take official form in the Vatican's requiring the confirmation of miraculous cures by beatified individuals as a condition for their being canonized saints of the church. The cult of the saints has likewise included the reverence of holy sites associated with certain saints as sources of healing, including miraculous cures. One of the more famous sites is Lourdes, France, where the Blessed Mother Mary appeared to St. Bernadette and others in the nineteenth century. Today the grotto at Lourdes attracts some six million pilgrims annually, including sixty thousand sick and handicapped people seeking healing in its waters. Over the past century and a half the International Medical Committee of Lourdes has certified a total of sixty-six miraculous cures.[15] Even though the vast majority of pilgrims at Lourdes are not seeking miraculous cures for themselves, those phenomena, associated with the initial apparitions of the Blessed Mother, are what distinguish the site as an exceptional place of prayer, devotion (e.g., the rosary, exposition of the Blessed Sacrament, and so forth), healing, and mysticism.

As with any typology, the two models I have outlined here, the medical and the charismatic, serve the function of breaking down the complex physical, social, and spiritual phenomena of health and illness by identifying and seeking to understand distinctive approaches to them. Such analysis should not imply that because medical treatment and charismatic-type ministries are oriented toward cures they exclude other dimensions of care. Biomedicine is practiced in the context of health care systems with a great deal of energy and resources being expended on the comfort, strengthening, and health-maintenance of

[13] See Yves Congar, *I Believe in the Holy Spirit,* trans. David Smith, Milestones in Catholic Theology, new ed. (New York: Herder & Herder, 1997), 126–66.

[14] See Peter Brown, *The Cult of the Saints: Its Rise and Function in Latin Christianity,* rev. ed. (Chicago: University of Chicago Press, 1982), 80, 113–20; and Elizabeth Johnson, *Friends of God and Prophets: A Feminist Theological Reading of the Communion of Saints* (New York: Continuum, 1999), 71–139.

[15] See "Pope 'will not seek healing in Lourdes,'" *The Tablet,* 7 August 2004, 26.

patients. Likewise, enduring charismatically centered practices such as the cult of Lourdes, while governed by narratives of the instrumental efficacy of prayer realized in miraculous cures, generate and sustain other forms of pastoral and medical care such as the founding of congregations or religious institutes dedicated to hospital work, various types of charities, and ministries that nurture faith amid life's burdens. Nonetheless, what distinguishes charismatic from sacramental ministry is the type of efficacy the former attributes to prayer—a mechanistic, instrumental approach with an overarching expectation of direct results, even miracles.

In the case of the rites of the Pastoral Care of the Sick, however, the symbolic—noninstrumental—goal of *healing illness* is operative. Here a quick review of what we've learned in chapters 2 and 3 about healing, as distinct from curing, is in order: The concept of *healing* does not ignore or isolate the person from the medical world, the use of mechanisms and techniques to relieve pain, give comfort, provide care, and possibly even cure the physical and/or psychological condition of the sick person.[16] But all that is incorporated into the larger picture of the meaning of the sick person's life in relation to God, self (one's bodily and psychological condition, the narrative history of one's life), friends and family, the church, society, and the natural/cosmic world. In the practice of these sacraments efficacy is a matter of overcoming the anomy and chaos wreaked by serious illness, relieving anxiety, and providing strength for the sick, those who care for them, and the wider community of the faithful.

The liturgical healing effected in the rites does not produce a once-for-all, permanent condition for the sick person (as opposed to modern imaginary expectations of possessing a total state of physical and psychological health). The healing Christ's Spirit mediates through sacramental rites is the affirmation of the sick person's inestimable value before God and people and the renegotiation of the person's mission in life. The foundation of that mission of following Christ was laid in baptism (the irreversible permanent condition of every Christian),

---

[16] "Doctors and all who are devoted in any way to caring for the sick should consider it their duty to use all the means which in their judgment may help the sick, both physically and spiritually. . . . Every scientific effort to prolong life and every act of care for the sick, on the part of any person, may be considered preparation for the Gospel and a sharing in Christ's healing ministry." PCS, nos. 4, 32.

but the details continuously emerge over the unique course of each individual's living and finally dying in that call. The sacraments of anointing and Viaticum, therefore, are necessarily repeatable, for the unfolding of a person's life story may involve any number of illnesses, afflictions, emergencies, or a worsening condition that place meaning once again in the balance, often putting faith to the test. In the Christian symbolic (sacramental) order, the meaning of life and death is revealed in Christ's paschal mystery. It is not surprising, therefore, to find the General Introduction to the Pastoral Care of the Sick opening with four paragraphs on "Human Sickness and Its Meaning in the Mystery of Salvation," before taking up successively the sacraments for the sick (anointing) and the dying (Viaticum).

Sickness, even in mild cases, let alone the more severe that are subject to sacramental anointing, can place lives in confusion. Thus in actual practice on the pastoral terrain what people ask for in sacramental rites covers a range of spiritual, psychological, physical, and social needs and inclinations.[17] That people ask is good, but the ministry of the church requires answering according to knowledge of the rites, which themselves are based on sound and ancient tradition. Still, this latter point is not obvious these days either. At various points in previous chapters I have noted people's resistance to the reform and renewal of the sacrament of anointing the sick, their clinging to extreme unction, last rites. This is humanly understandable in a modern context that, as I have tried to argue, seeks mechanistic and instrumental results.

But why look upon the sacraments this way? Such a view seems to be influenced by not only contemporary magical and consumerist thinking but also the burden of social memory, the theology and practice of anointing that has held sway in the Catholic Church for more than a millennium. This was the emergence of an instrumental, cause-and-effect understanding of liturgical rites. The collective memory of that theory and practice remains powerful.[18] I need, therefore, to outline that history directly, albeit briefly, lest its theology haunt the remaining pages of the present and next chapter. Having addressed what's wrong with that long-regnant theology of the sacrament, we will nevertheless

---

[17] See Larson-Miller, *The Sacrament of Anointing of the Sick*, 104–9.

[18] One of the more notable studies of social memory, including its ritual, psychological, and historical aspects, is Paul Connerton, *How Societies Remember*, Themes in the Social Sciences (New York: Cambridge University Press, 1989).

discover that there is no pristine primordial text or golden age to recover (as if that were possible). We can embrace the contemporary
reform and renewal confident of the Spirit's work as discerned in the
church (hierarchy and people), even as questions or problems concerning both history and the contemporary context persist.[19]

LEARNING FROM THE CHURCH'S HISTORY OF ANOINTING THE SICK

A Western Christian concept without parallel in Eastern Orthodoxy,
extreme unction was a development in medieval sacramental theology consolidating beliefs and customs about anointing, penance, sin,
death, and clerical ministry that emerged from the Carolingian period
(roughly, the mid-eighth to mid-ninth century).[20] The Greek rituals and
theology in the East, as well as the Ambrosian rites in the West, continued the ancient, traditional understanding of anointing as providing
spiritual and physical healing, the holistic notion of ritual care for all
sick persons that pervaded early Christianity. In contrast, the wider
Western church moved to an increasing, nearly exclusive emphasis
on the spiritual effects of anointing, even though the various rites in
this pivotal reform period conservatively preserved earlier words and
gestures symbolizing both spiritual and physical healing. The Carolingian sacramentary and various episcopal instructions came to identify
the subjects of anointing as only those whose sickness was unto death
and, thus, the spiritual benefits as the forgiveness of sins and purification of the soul for final passage from this life. Among the most important historical sources for this period are the hagiographies of saints,
which refer to anointing as "last rites," a ritual complex of anointing
the body with episcopally consecrated oil and administering Holy

---

[19] See also Gusmer, *And You Visited Me*, 67.

[20] For this historical section I draw from the respected and widely cited
work of John J. Ziegler, *Let Them Anoint the Sick* (Collegeville, MN: Liturgical
Press, 1987), 26–143, here 58–70. Other surveys of the history, including helpful
bibliographical references, may be found at Gusmer, *And You Visited Me*, 1–48;
James L. Emepereur, *Prophetic Anointing: God's Call to the Sick, the Elderly, and
the Dying*, Message of the Sacraments, ed. Monika K. Hellwig, no. 7 (Wilmington, DE: Michael Glazier, 1982), 15–78; and Walter Cuenin, "History of
Anointing and Healing in the Church," *Alternative Futures for Worship: Volume
7: Anointing of the Sick*, ed. Peter Fink (Collegeville, MN: Liturgical Press, 1987),
65–81.

Communion. While those and other sources portray significant variations in ritual, anointing was nonetheless always done in conjunction with penance or Communion or both, for which the order almost universally was penance-anointing-Viaticum. In further contrast from the earlier Christian centuries, the shift in the administering of anointing was from the laity's self-application of the clerically consecrated oil to the priest as the exclusive minister of the sacrament.

Explanations for these crucial changes in the Western understanding and rituals for anointing the sick situate them in the larger Carolingian agenda for correcting popular abuses and regulating the ministry of priests, but the strongest factor would seem to be the evolution of penance. The rigorous, lengthy public rites of penance that had evolved in the early Christian era, as well as the penalties, such as celibacy, that came to be imposed on penitents for the rest of their lives, had proven too demanding for most of the faithful. If people sought penance at all, it was at the time of death, and even this was further hindered by expensive stole fees the clergy widely demanded. With priestly remission of sins setting the eligibility for a person's receiving other sacraments, the anointing of the sick became tied to the deathbed. Priests likewise extracted stiff fees for anointing the dying, causing both sacraments to fall into desuetude.[21] Clerical abuses and misconceptions by the faithful would continue into the Middle Ages, while the theological and official trajectory of extreme unction would advance toward systematized uniformity.

Medieval scholastic theology's instrumentalist, cause-and-effect understanding of sacraments as signs of spiritual effects, contributed significantly to the solidification of the anointing of the sick as extreme unction. In the fourth book of his *Sentences* Peter Lombard advanced the name "extreme unction" not least by opening the subject as follows: "The anointing of the sick is done *in extremis* with oil consecrated by the bishop."[22] While he followed the influential Hugh of St. Victor in explaining the *sacramentum* of this rite to be the exterior anointing and the *res sacramenti* as the "interior" remission of sin and increase of virtue, he differed from Hugh by narrowing the subject of anointing to the terminally ill (*in extremis*). The Dominicans Albert the

[21] See Ziegler, *Let Them Anoint the Sick*, 69–70; and Gusmer, *And You Visited Me*, 27–28.

[22] Ziegler, *Let Them Anoint the Sick*, 72. See also, Empereur, *Prophetic Anointing*, 58.

Great and Thomas Aquinas were likewise influenced by Hugh's cause-effect view, whereby the remitting of sin was seen as the condition for the healing of the body. Thomas further argued that each sacrament has but one principal effect, with extreme unction's being the removal of the remnants of sin that would impede the soul's perception of divine glory after death. The sacrament forgave sins only insofar as any traces of sin lingered in a given person, requiring removal. Thus the sacrament of extreme unction's principal benefit was its power to dispose the soul for immediate glory. Albert and Thomas's understanding of the effect thereby led to their identifying the subject of anointing as the patient in danger of death. The Franciscans Alexander of Hales and Bonaventure likewise considered the sacrament as instrumentally serving those *in extremis*, but they differed from the Dominicans by explaining that the preparation for death entailed the removal of any venial sins diseasing the soul. The scholastics were all commenting on the rites as they knew them to be practiced, and yet their philosophical theories (sacramental theologies) would in turn shape the subsequent official doctrine and ritual practice of extreme unction.

As for disciplinary and conciliar documents in this period, these sought to correct clerical abuses and lay alienation from anointing the sick while also developing the doctrine of this sacrament as part of the move toward precisely defining the number, matter and form, proper ministers, and spiritual effects of the sacraments. The key council in this regard prior to Trent was Florence (1439), which defined the primary effect of anointing as healing the soul, with the possibility also of healing the body, but not explicitly mentioning the remission of sins. Many liturgical documents, on the other hand, while retaining the notion of a twofold effect, emphasized the spiritual as the remission of sins, with most also associating anointing the sick with penance and Holy Communion, along with various combinations of other symbols (blessing with ashes, imposition of hands, litanies, etc.). Most important for the eventual theology and polity that would emerge from the Reformation and Council of Trent, John Ziegler argues, were the numerous orders for anointing in the early sixteenth century, which articulated the sacrament's primary effect or purpose as the remission of sins in preparation for eternal life.[23] Consistent with the sacramental theology of the period, extreme unction was a means of grace whose primary effect was spiritual, in this case the preparation of the soul

---

[23] See Ziegler, *Let Them Anoint the Sick*, 83.

(and secondarily, the body) for death. The ritual order enacted the theology by placing the anointing rite after the administration of Communion, thereby significantly changing the highly symbolic language. Instead of the "last sacraments" including anointing as the middle movement between penance and Viaticum, "last rites" now solely referred to the anointing of the multiple body parts (eyes, ears, nostrils, mouth, hands, feet, loins) that had been instruments of the soul's degradation. Extreme unction thus became a sacrament with its proper supernatural effect, a forgiveness of sins distinct from that of baptism and penance: purification of the soul as final preparation for death.

The (evangelically disastrous) pastoral consequence of the medieval theology and polity of extreme unction, enduring into the twentieth century, was to make the priest's anointing action not just the preparation for but the very declaration of death. An instrumentalist sacramental theology had played itself out to its logical—and practical—conclusion. The spiritual and pastoral benefits of the ancient tradition of anointing the sick, the spiritual comfort and psychological support that Scripture and traditional symbolic gestures could provide to those seriously ill or in the *process* of dying, ceded to the priest mechanistically dispatching the person to die.

The Council of Trent, in its fourteenth session (1551), sought to reverse this practical theology of extreme unction, which the Protestant Reformers had duly excoriated (Calvin decried the "anointing of 'half-dead carcasses' as an abuse of the anointing encouraged by James"[24]). Reversing the scholastic theology governing the original draft, Trent's definitive text on extreme unction repeatedly named the subjects of this sacrament to be the sick, those so ill as to be in danger of death, as opposed to the dying, those who are all but dead. The pastoral difference is immense. The final decree does not identify a primary supernatural effect for the sacrament. Rather, it stresses the graceful work of the Holy Spirit removing sin and its remains, raising up the soul by instilling confidence in divine mercy (thereby strengthening against such diabolical temptations as despair), and possibly even curing the body, should that be in the divine plan for the person's salvation. The post-Tridentine catechism and sacramental *ordo*, as well as repeated papal declarations, all called for extreme unction to be administered as soon as sickness seemed mortally dangerous. In practice, however, both priests and people up to the present era clung to a mechanistic view of the rite. "A

[24] Gusmer, *And You Visited Me*, 33.

morbidity and fatalism became attached to 'extreme unction,'" Charles
Gusmer concludes. "In all truth, extreme unction became a pastoral failure . . . the most misunderstood, most uncommunal, and most unlitur-
gical of the seven sacraments of the Church."[25]

FREEING THE HEALING FORCE OF SACRAMENTAL LITURGY

The malaise into which the anointing of the sick had fallen was, of
course, the very type of pastoral-theological problem Vatican II's mandate for liturgical reform and renewal sought to overcome by recourse
to sound tradition.[26] For the anointing of the sick, as with all other rites,
liturgical theologians have probed the work of biblical scholars and
historians of the early church, finding in this case, as we have just reviewed, that the Carolingian period marked a key turning point in its
practice and theology. What had characterized ministry to the sick with
prayer and consecrated oil in the first eight centuries of Christianity was
the holistic, including symbolic, activity of what medical anthropologists call folk healing, about which we learned in our study of the New
Testament.[27] The summary of apostolic activity in Mark 6:13, for example, with its combined mentioning of expelling demons and anointing the sick with oil, clearly places the work in the folk sector of healing.

The text that would eventually provide the scriptural grounds for
the church's sacramental healing tradition, James 5:13-16, provides detailed instruction exuding the features of folk healing:

> Are any among you suffering? They should pray. Are any cheerful?
> They should sing songs of praise. Are any among you sick? They
> should call for the elders of the church and have them pray over them,
> anointing them with oil in the name of the Lord. The prayer of faith
> will save the sick, and the Lord will raise them up; and anyone who
> has committed sins will be forgiven. Therefore, confess your sins to
> one another, and pray for one another, so that you may be healed. The
> prayer of the righteous is powerful and effective.

While later biases, such as the scholastic limiting of sacramental
anointing to one spiritual effect, would lead to skewed instrumentalist

---

[25] Ibid., 36, 181.
[26] See above, introduction, pp. 15–21.
[27] See above, chap. 3, pp. 72–79.

146

interpretations isolating the various activities described in this text, medical and Mediterranean anthropology would encourage a more integrated view of the entire description. True to the folk sector, this passage does not isolate medical symptoms and outcomes from the broader, integral experience of suffering and encouragement within a community of faith. Prayer, touch, and anointing are together efficacious for the sick person, not in the sense of a biomedical cure but an attaining of relief that may or may not include the complete elimination of physical symptoms. Thus the outcome is described in terms of being saved and raised up, imprecise terminology by professional medical standards; yet, for those baptized into the paschal mystery, terms assuring meaning for their life struggles within the narrative of the crucified and resurrected Christ. Moreover, the efficacy assured here, the power of prayer, is not limited to results for autonomous sick individuals but rather encompasses a communally shared purpose for all, with some singing God's praises while others pray for comfort and forgiveness. Healing occurs among a community of faith, a faith being manifested in the full range of the members' personal and shared conditions of body and spirit.

The extant texts from the first several Christian centuries do not provide any liturgical rituals for anointing the sick with oil; rather, the evidence lies in several liturgical prayers for blessing oil, all of which point to the healing purpose of oil for the sick (not the dying) in the comprehensive practice of faith.[28] The most ancient is the *Apostolic Tradition* of Hippolytus, originally composed in Greek perhaps in the early third century and influential through translation into African and Arabic languages, as well as a Latin translation dating from the fifth century.[29] Variants in terminology exist among the translations, and in the case of the blessing of oil, which is an appendix to the eucharistic prayer offered by the bishop, these would seem to indicate a

---

[28] For the multiple, multivalent uses and meanings for oil in the ancient Mesopotamian and Mediterranean worlds, see chaps. by Stephanie Dalley, Angus Bowie, J. Roy Porter in *The Oil of Gladness: Anointing in the Christian Tradition*, ed. Martin Dudley and Geoffrey Rowell (London/Collegeville: SPCK/Liturgical Press, 1993), 19–45.

[29] For a review of current scholarship on this document, as well as cautionary conclusions about its authorship, location, and dating, see John F. Baldovin, "Hippolytus and the Apostolic Tradition: Recent Research and Commentary," *Theological Studies* 64, no. 3 (2003): 520–42.

range of understandings for the purpose (strength, health, sanctification) and administration of anointing.[30] The oil, like bread and wine, was brought forward by the people, and the bishop's anaphora rehearsed the memory of oil's use in salvation history, invoking divine power on the oil to be used by the people through either "taste" (presumably drinking) or external application. Both the situating of the oil within the cosmic and traditional belief system and its multipurpose use (along with bread, wine, and water) for both physical and spiritual sustenance and healing align the Christians' practice with the wider cultural folk medicine of their day. The unique difference, of course, was their specific belief in what God was accomplishing among the faithful through the power of the Spirit of the risen Christ, under the authorizing leadership of the bishop.

The *Euchologion* (anaphoric prayer) of the fourth-century North African bishop Serapion demonstrates all of this compellingly:

> We invoke Thee, who hast all power and might, Saviour of all men, Father of our Lord and Saviour Jesus Christ, and we pray Thee to send down from the heavens of Thy Only-begotten a curative power upon this oil, in order that to those who are anointed with these Thy creatures or who receive them, it may become a means of removing 'every disease and every sickness,' of warding off every demon, of putting to flight every unclean spirit, of keeping at a distance every evil spirit, of banishing all fever, all chill, and all weariness; a means of grace and goodness and the remission of sins; a medicament of life and salvation, unto health and soundness of soul and body and spirit, unto perfect well-being.[31]

The sort of sociocentric, bodily holistic, and cosmic sense of health that this prayer exudes is typical of premodern peoples as well as 80 percent of the contemporary global population.[32] The work of cultural

---

[30] See Ziegler, *Let Them Anoint the Sick*, 36–38; and Gusmer, *And You Visited Me*, 11–12.

[31] Cited in translation in Gusmer, *And You Visited Me*, 13. The reference to "every disease and every sickness" being removed is a biblical citation or paraphrase, a typical feature grounding traditional prayer in Scripture. In this case the reference clearly is to Matt 4:23; 9:35; and 10:1, the first two being summaries of Jesus' work of preaching, teaching, and "healing every disease and sickness," the latter, his sending the disciples to do the same.

[32] See above, chap. 3, pp. 77–79.

anthropologists and ritual and performance theorists can help us late-moderns to set aside both incredulity at the prayer's sizable list of physical symptoms alleviated and cynicism at its invocation of "perfect well-being." Participation in such ritual language is an engrossing performance of faith,[33] of confidence in a restored cosmic order that can engender health of body, mind, and spirit. The exuberant, confidence-instilling quality of this prayer points to the very nature of all blessing and intercession, faith that the God invoked can be trusted to provide what we genuinely need according to divine wisdom, as well as the rightness in our enjoying the good gifts of creation as shared among the people of God. This does not mean that people should or do expect a *permanent* state of perfect health, which of course is imaginary fantasy, but neither does this exclude compelling moments that touch us to the core with that sense of complete well-being, a consoling integrity of body and spirit experienced among the social body, the assembled community, the *communio* of the church.[34]

Other prayers from this early Christian period, including those found in the Gelasian and Gregorian sacramentaries, invoke the Holy Spirit upon the oil, similarly describing its use for the healing of body, mind, and spirit. The "healing virtue of the oil" resides not only in its physically soothing and fortifying qualities but in "its power in the hands of God or of the church to cleanse from sin and to restore strength of mind and body . . . one being hardly envisaged without the other."[35] These prayers, as well as the *Apostolic Tradition*, David Power notes, play on the word "anointing" in "relation to the prophets, priests, and kings of the Old Testament, to the baptism that the sick person has received earlier in life, and finally to the Anointed

[33] For a basic discussion of the concept of performance, see Catherine Bell, *Ritual: Perspectives and Dimensions* (New York: Oxford University Press, 1997), 159–64. See also, Connerton, *How Societies Remember*, 59.

[34] For expositions on the divine-human dynamics of Christian *communio*, synthesizing the best of modern ecclesiology and sacramental theology, see Bernard Cooke, *Sacraments and Sacramentaltiy*, rev. ed. (Mystic, CT: Twenty-Third Publications, 1994), 68–77, 123–33; and his "Body and Mystical Body: The Church as *Communio*," in *Bodies of Worship: Explorations in Theory and Practice*, ed. Bruce T. Morrill (Collegeville, MN: Liturgical Press, 1999), 39–50.

[35] David N. Power, "Let the Sick Call," in *Worship: Culture and Theology*, 248–49 (Washington, DC: The Pastoral Press, 1990). The essay originally appeared in *The Heythrop Journal* 17 (1978): 256–70.

in the Spirit, who is Jesus Christ."[36] Thus is the restoration of health (well-being) brought about through key symbols that construct and evoke meaning for believers, returning the afflicted person to the life of worship that is the mission of all in the community of faith, the church.

Those prayers imply what hagiographic and homiletic texts from the first several centuries indicate about the administration of the episcopally consecrated oil: it could be done by any of the faithful, most often by self-application or consumption, at times by charismatic figures,[37] and still in other cases by ordained clergy. The people's taking the oil with them from the Sunday assembly paralleled their carrying portions of the eucharistic bread home for daily self-communication during the week. Thus, the efficacy would seem to reside in the oil's having been blessed by the bishop, not in the person making the application, thereby accounting for the lack of ritual descriptions for those first centuries.[38] In what would prove to be a seminal document in the development of the sacraments of anointing and confirmation, Pope Innocent's letter in response to a Bishop Decentius in 416 affirms the necessity of the oil's being consecrated by the bishop, while affirming variety in administration, clerical and lay. Innocent's further concern was that the oil not be applied to penitents, since they were prohibited from sharing in the sacraments—evidence of the early association between sacramental participation and good standing in the church that would continue to the present, a concern for the health of the social body. Later medieval and Counter-Reformation concerns would lead to not only varied interpretations but actual modifications of Innocent's original letter to serve contested positions on the exclusive sacramental ministry of the priesthood. One other key feature of

[36] Ibid., 249.

[37] Ziegler notes hagiographic accounts of the Desert Fathers using oil in miraculous cures, explaining that in the better number of cases the illnesses were linked to demonic possession and, thus, the oil used in exorcising the evil spirit. "The maladies mentioned vary in nature from different forms of sickness, to paralysis, to loss of one or more of the senses, and to deformity." *Let Them Anoint the Sick*, 32. That summary strikingly exemplifies the types of imprecise health misfortunes, as well as the prevalence of afflictions in bodily zones (the individual person-body reflecting the condition of the social body) which, along with illness due to demonic possession, altogether characterize the healing accounts in the New Testament (see chap. 3, above).

[38] See ibid., 40.

the letter, however, gives earliest evidence of a doctrinal pattern that would become established tradition: Innocent's linking of anointing the sick to James 5:14-15.

The association of James with anointing the sick is found in other texts of the second half of the early Christian period, especially a commentary by the Venerable Bede in eighth-century England, who referred to Innocent and also distinguished the need to confess more serious sins to presbyters. Episcopal texts from this period in Gaul likewise refer to James for the tradition's apostolic origin. They consistently describe the care of the sick as including the administration of both the Eucharist and anointing as efficacious for both body and soul, asserting these as the proper recourse for ill Christians, as opposed to the services of sorcerers or pagan rites. None of the literature in this period, however, specifies the degree of sickness necessary for such sacramental ministration, let alone any stipulation about imminent death. What mattered in cultures that included strong folk medicine and pervasive spirits—evil and benign—was the priority of Christ's Spirit working through word and sacrament in the church, affecting "not simply bodily healing but a deeper wholeness: strength, forgiveness of sins, vivification, protection of body, mind, and spirit . . . the entire somatic realm of salvation for a sick person."[39]

For all the vast differences between the cultural worlds of early Christianity and the present, the approach to healing exemplified in those ancient texts is just the sort of holistic view of illness and well-being that, according to David Morris, contemporary people are increasingly seeking.[40] Ours is a postmodern society dominated by a biomedical, medicocentric, mechanistic approach to sickness that nonetheless is straining toward biocultural practice, treating illness as an event integrating emotion, memory, thought, body, and culture.[41] While

[39] See Gusmer, *And You Visited Me*, 21.

[40] "Illness in the postmodern age is understood as fragmentation, and what we seek from the process of healing is to be made whole." David B. Morris, *Illness and Culture in the Postmodern Age* (Berkeley: University of California Press, 1998), 67.

[41] "The ancient grounding of medicine in care and compassion is seriously challenged by a biomedical model that defines medicine simply as applied biology. In this approach, the primary function of medicine is to cure, and this requires that the physician be primarily a scientist. . . . In reaction to this narrow definition, some advocate a broader approach that adds the sociological

there is no question of late-modern Western society returning to spirit-animated sectors of folk medicine, comparative ethnomedical study does engender greater awareness of how people experience invisible (to them) germs, microbes, metastasizing cancer cells, and pathogens as assaulting a person's health and well-being. Although we reasonably turn to the modern medical profession for diagnosis of what, not who, is causing one's sickness, people are increasingly recognizing the multiple personal, interpersonal, environmental, and social forces impacting a patient's health, including the degree of dignity doctors and staff afford patients under their care.[42] Theologian and ritual theorist Thomas Driver argues that the comprehensive experience of health misfortune founds the need for symbolic healing activity: "The search for offending causes is a rational way of thinking and has led, as we know, to an enormous array of cures. But it compounds the problem of suffering. This is where ritual wants—needs—to come in."[43]

Such genuine human need for courage and strength, hope and companionship, dignity and purpose amid the personal and impersonal forces of illness encompasses the mission of the church's pastoral-liturgical service to the sick. Among the humanly powerful (research, clinical, economic) culture of modern medicine the Pastoral Care of the Sick functions as what postmodern theorists would identify as a *supplement*, a set of practices working not competitively against but complementarily with the modern medical system.[44] The rituals of the Pastoral Care of the Sick comprise part of the bioculture of Christian illness and health, a world shaped by baptism and Eucharist wherein meaning and decisions are discerned through a living sacramental

---

and psychological to the biological aspects of illness. Others would expand this further to a 'holistic' approach, adding religious and spiritual dimensions to the biopsychosocial model." Edmund D. Pellegrino and David C. Thomasma, *Helping and Healing: Religious Commitment in Health Care* (Washington, DC: Georgetown University Press, 1997), 75–76.

[42] See above, chap. 2, pp. 39–40. Franciscan friar and medical doctor Daniel P. Sulmasy, OFM, addresses physicians and other medical professionals' growing desire for a sense of transcendent meaning in a depersonalizing technologically and market-driven environment in *The Healer's Calling: A Spirituality for Physicians and Other Health Care Professionals* (New York: Paulist Press, 1997).

[43] Thomas F. Driver, "What Healthcare Professionals Need to Know about Ritual: A First Lesson," *The Park Ridge Center Bulletin* 5 (1998): 17.

[44] See Morris, *Illness and Culture in the Postmodern Age*, 70.

encounter with the person and story of Christ, that is, the paschal mystery, in the present conditions of people's lives. Practice of the Pastoral Care of the Sick, therefore, is not merely expressive of what already is known about the situation of the sick person but rather proclaims and effectively impacts the health of the person, affecting others committed to her or him as well.[45]

From the outset the Pastoral Care of the Sick, in its General Introduction, places suffering and illness in relation to both the comprehensive human condition and Christ's words and actions. Christ's words reveal "that sickness has meaning and value for [the sick persons'] salvation and for the salvation of the world," while the biblical stories of his healing of the sick reveal his "[love] for them in their illness." Faith in this Christ "helps them to grasp more deeply the mystery of suffering and to bear their pain with greater courage."[46] A vocational dimension to this sacrament is thus established from the start. The Introduction provides the substantive content for the ensuing rhetoric of strengthening and comfort, saving and "raising up," that pervades the instructional and ritual texts of the entire rite. Suffering believers are strengthened to persevere in illness and in so doing to contribute to the good of society and the church. They are, moreover, *in their very infirmity* to function as sacraments (living signs or witnesses) of the Gospel by joining their sufferings to Christ's "for the salvation of the world," reminding "others of the essential or higher things" of life, and "show[ing] that our mortal life must be redeemed through the mystery of Christ's death and resurrection."[47]

The effectiveness of the sacramental celebrations of the Pastoral Care of the Sick, then, or in the language of traditional Catholic sacramental theology, the grace they confer, has everything to do with identifying the people who are the proper subjects of their ministration. What the rites are able to accomplish, how they glorify God through healing people, is best grasped by considering for whom the various sacramental rituals are intended. Given the utterly pastoral nature of these rites, the most promising way in print to appreciate their healing

---

[45] For a discussion of pastoral care, including the ministry of word and sacrament, as essential to the "total health" of not only the sick person but all involved in his or her care, see Benedict M. Ashley and Kevin D. O'Rourke, *Health Care Ethics: A Theological Analysis*, 4th ed. (Washington, DC: Georgetown University Press, 1997), 435, 439–41.

[46] PCS, no. 1.

[47] Ibid., no. 3.

power is through some narrative description of their actual practice. Here I shall recount one story from my own pastoral work, the description of which can open into an analysis of the pastoral and liturgical theology of the rites.

PRACTICING THE PASTORAL CARE OF THE SICK TODAY: ONE NARRATIVE ACCOUNT

Since the year 2000 I have been occasionally serving Yup'ik Eskimo villages in the Hooper Bay region on the Bering Seacoast of Alaska, making the long trip from Boston either at Easter or Christmastime as my academic schedule allows. In the early 1980s, after finishing college, I had spent a year as a Jesuit Volunteer in a village farther north at the mouth of the Yukon River. Twenty years later I was surprised yet consoled to discern a call once again to be of pastoral service to those villages. I have made nine trips during this decade, most for about ten days, although I spent seven weeks in one village in the summer of 2001. I have come to forge close ties with folks of all ages in that village of about seven hundred. The settlement sits on a high spot of tundra, overlooking serpentine sloughs, whipped by Bering winds, the people practicing subsistence while constantly teetering on the edge of poverty, steeped in their native traditions yet caught between that primordial world and the relentlessly encroaching culture of media-driven consumption. One of the enduring Yup'ik values, nevertheless, is reverence and care for elders. This story is about one such elder, an eighty-year-old woman I shall call Mary.[48]

My most recent trip to that particular village, for Holy Week and Easter, was my first extended stay there in a few years, having made only a one-night visit during Christmastime two years before. I had, however, kept in touch with a couple of leading figures in the parish, one of whom had apprised me of a number of deaths that had occurred over the past year. The day before Palm Sunday I landed in the village, word of my arrival circulated, and I celebrated Mass with about a dozen people in the early evening. Before starting I inquired about the families of those who had died, as well as the condition of certain elders, especially Mary. I already knew that two of the recently deceased were Mary's brother and sister, but I was shocked to learn that another was one of her daughters, Sarah, a single parent in her

---

[48] Out of respect, I have changed her and all others' names in this story.

154

forties who had succumbed to cancer. Yes, advised the leader of the parish's eucharistic ministers who faithfully bring Holy Communion to the shut-ins, Mary was still in her home and able to receive guests and, yes, she would especially benefit from a pastoral visit. After Mass I took a pyx containing a few Hosts and a copy of the Pastoral Care of the Sick and walked the short distance to Mary's house.

Typical of homes in the Yup'ik villages, four generations live under Mary's roof, a crowded, hard-worn, prefabricated structure with a kitchen and living area in the center and pairs of small bedrooms on each end. That evening I entered a scene of all ages in the common room: Mary's fifty-something son Paul preparing dinner with his daughter, the daughter's toddler playing around the floor, Paul's niece and another teenaged girl eating at the table, a brother watching television, and finally, Mary occupying a minuscule portion of the couch. She had clearly aged over the past couple years, shortened by osteoporosis (Paul commented, "My Mom keeps shrinking!"), thinner, hearing and sight diminished, but still able to get around with a walker. I received greetings all around, but Mary did not recognize me at first (truth is, I had aged a fair amount over the past couple years as well), so Paul showed her a five-year-old photo of me on the wall, which sparked the connection. She smiled and clasped my hand in a still forceful grip, repeatedly saying "thank-you" in Yup'ik. Like many of the elders, including her late husband James, Mary had never learned English.

Mary made her way to the table and, very much the matriarch, instructed her son and granddaughter to serve me supper. As we all ate together, with Paul translating between his mother and myself, our conversation slowly shifted to the heavy stories of recent deaths. The story of Mary's sister's death included some remarkable occurrences in weather that served as signs of consolation to the family, contrasting with the account of her daughter's succumbing to cancer, remaining quietly at home, no doubt in much pain, to the end. During the conversation the younger people had all gradually drifted into other rooms. As I noticed the grief written on Mary's face Paul said his mother wanted to talk more about all this. Mary was pondering two things: how was she to pray during this coming Holy Week, and why was God keeping her on this earth while her daughter, brother, sister, and (three years earlier) husband had all been taken, leaving her behind? I knew it was not a moment for abstract explanations but rather a story. I was profoundly grateful to have a good one to share with Mary.

I asked Mary to remember the time we had first met during my initial pastoral stay in the village six and a half years earlier. The Jesuit who serves the region, in explaining his routine for the daily evening Mass, noted that after Mass each night he regularly brought Communion to one elderly couple who used to attend faithfully but now were housebound. I accompanied him to James and Mary's home my first night there, and after he departed the next day for other villages I made a point of doing so daily for the duration of my stay. Mary was frail (hobbled by an old, untreated foot and leg injury) but her mind was sharp, while James, some ten years her senior, lived with significant bodily and communicative debilitation due to a stroke. Their material poverty, the crowded quarters housing several generations, the elders' inability to speak English, the complete care the younger generations gave them (including as translators)—none of these things surprised me much, given my year's stay in a similar village nearly two decades before. What did impress me deeply from that start, however, was the profound reverence, the palpable joy, the consoling humility with which this aged couple celebrated the service of Holy Communion. They had long ago memorized the English responses to the parts of the Mass, many of which function in the Communion service as well.[49] After the brief reading from Scripture and my beginning the prayers of the faithful, Mary would offer in Yup'ik extended prayers of intercession, followed by the couple and as many family members as had gathered around reciting the Lord's Prayer in their native language. I would then administer Holy Communion to the couple and Sarah, who was primarily caring for them, and perhaps some others, after which followed silent prayer, the blessing, and then a greeting of peace shared by every person in the house, regardless of whether they had joined in the service.

My primary pastoral role was simply to lead them prayerfully in the rite as found in the Pastoral Care of the Sick, doing what the church does, a shared practice of the tradition that both served the faith of the elderly Yup'ik couple and quickly bonded us all. I was present in a posture of service to the elders, but the enacted ritual worship was affecting the family and also transforming me. At the center of the ritual were Mary and James, whose faces and bodies proclaimed such quietly joyful faith in receiving and sharing the Body of Christ,

---

[49] For the rite of Communion in Ordinary Circumstances, see PCS, nos. 81–91.

a sacramental action I came to realize was integral to the life they shared with each other and the entire family. I began to look forward to visiting them each evening. Their home was a short distance from the church, made long that year by relentless gale winds blowing horizontal sheets of snow and rain that glazed the surface of the terrain. With jolting gusts intermittently intensifying the headwinds, I repeatedly found myself temporarily immobilized, struggling to retain my balance on stretches of glare ice, even pushed backward at times. On successive evenings as I skidded, strained, or came to a complete halt alone in the darkness, the wind howling in my ears, I would find myself marveling: what in the world am I doing here? The answer became clear in the repetition: this is the life of the Gospel, and true to form, Christ is proving to be the one who has already gone ahead, waiting to meet me among people profoundly aware of their need for God. That need—their poverty in spirit, their trust—was eliciting a desire within me to be with Christ—and thus them—that I could never have come up with on my own.

A couple days before Christmas Paul called to say his mother wanted me to come for lunch with her, James, and a couple of their other sons. I arrived in the brief brightness of noontime to find one of the daughters-in-law preparing the meal, with Mary advising. The event, I slowly came to realize, was not only an act of hospitality on the cusp of Christmas but also a modeling of roles and practices from James and Mary to the generation succeeding them. At one point Paul recounted how his father James had patiently taught his sons through stories and the example of his own life. I decided to say something then to Mary and James, through Paul's translation, that had been building up in me: how over the past week they had become for me great teachers and examples of what it is to practice faith in the eucharistic Christ, how their celebration of Holy Communion challenged and inspired my faith. With tears in her eyes Mary replied that all her life, since her youth at the old regional mission school, she had always thought of the priests and sisters as the people she had to learn from. She never imagined she would hear one of them calling her his teacher. I just nodded and smiled.

That was the story, abridged and focused on the witness of her faith to me, that I told Mary in response to the directionless grief and loneliness she was now experiencing, years later, in the deep wake of her recent losses and the ebb tide of her own declining physical condition. I suggested that, while God's wisdom and timing are ultimately inscrutable, it seemed clear that Mary still had a role to play in this world, in her family, in the wider village and parish community who came to visit her and/or remembered her in their prayers. Mary's vocation, I told her, remains that of an elder to us, an example of practiced faith as an all-encompassing way of life, a source of encouragement and consolation to many through her embodiment of a world of memories and present affection. Her eyes registering acceptance, Mary responded through a serene smile with a repeated thank-you in Yup'ik.

After a quiet moment I noted how late the hour was and that we had not yet shared Holy Communion. Mary asked that I first celebrate with her the sacrament of penance, which we did in one of the back rooms, and then many of the family gathered around for the Communion service. In departing, I asked Paul how long it had been since Mary had received the sacrament of the anointing of the sick. He explained that she had twice been flown to the regional hospital for health crises during the past couple years and most likely had been anointed at some point. I averred that the present seemed like a beneficial moment for her to celebrate the sacrament again, if she were to understand it not as last rites but an anointing to strengthen and support her in her weakened condition and new spiritual challenges. Paul immediately nodded that he knew what I meant, saying they had been catechized in the reformed theology and practice of the sacrament. Paul later conferred with Mary, and we looked forward to celebrating the sacrament of anointing with her at some point in Holy Week.

FROM NARRATIVE TO ANALYSIS:
COMMENTARY ON THE PASTORAL CARE OF THE SICK

Mary's story gives abundant evidence for how the entire complex of activities entailed in the Pastoral Care of the Sick, with the sacrament of anointing functioning paradigmatically among them, comprise an ongoing, holistic work—a rite[50]—of healing through rich layers of affective symbolism. First, Mary's story shows how the sacrament of anointing is not about an isolated magic act or quick sacramental fix but rather a ritual that is part of a much larger pastoral and liturgical process engaging the elderly or sick person as an integral member of

---

[50] See Aidan Kavanagh, *On Liturgical Theology* (New York: Pueblo Publishing, 1984), 100.

a community of faith.[51] Healing here coincides with what we learned about it generally and in relation to illness specifically in chapters 2 and 3: It is a communal process addressing the suffering of individual members due to physical, psychological, social, or spiritual causes (or a combination thereof) against the horizon of meaning that their crisis or chronic health conditions put in question. Healing is a matter of reestablishing a sense of wholeness within a worldview, a transformation of the experience of misfortune by arriving at renewed or deepened meaning. Christians do this in terms of the person of Christ and the paschal mystery, but these as they become evident in the concrete conditions of their lives. The specific characteristics of old age or serious illness are what govern the shape of the communal (pastoral-liturgical) process—circumstances that create tensions of continuity and discontinuity in the lives of the elderly and sick but also the lives of those engaged with them.[52] I curtailed my pastoral narrative at the point at which we had discerned the tension in Mary's life as manifesting her need for the sacrament of anointing. Such discernment is central to the pastoral process of the sacrament. A consideration of discernment in Mary's case can open into a discussion of other pastoral, theological, and liturgical aspects of the process.

Discerning the Call to Anointing

The General Introduction of the Pastoral Care of the Sick specifies the sacrament of anointing as serving "those of the faithful whose

[51] The chapters in part 1 of the *Pastoral Care of the Sick* provide rituals for visiting the sick, visiting a sick child, communion of the sick, and anointing the sick. A further ritual resource for clergy and laity's ministry to the sick is "Orders for the Blessing of the Sick," chap. 2, nos. 376–450, in the *Book of Blessings*, the English version of the revised Roman Ritual approved for use in U.S. dioceses by the National Conference of Catholic Bishops and the Apostolic See. See International Commission on English in the Liturgy, *Book of Blessings* (Collegeville, MN: Liturgical Press, 1989), 121–47. This includes a selection of blessings for sick adults and children, as well as for people suffering from addictions or substance abuse.

[52] For another detailed description and argument for a holistic view of illness and healing as a process of reestablishing balance within a person's somatic and spiritual existence and as part of a larger communal and cosmic environment, see Jennifer Glen, "Rites of Healing: A Reflection in Pastoral Theology," *Alternative Futures for Worship: Volume 7: Anointing of the Sick*, ed. Peter Fink (Collegeville, MN: Liturgical Press, 1987), 33–63.

health is seriously [*periculose*] impaired by sickness or old age," explaining that "prudent or reasonably sure judgment, without scruple, is sufficient for deciding on the seriousness of an illness."[53] A footnote to this article explains the translation of the typical Latin edition's *periculose* as seeking to achieve a balance between the extremes of withholding the sacrament due to a highly restrictive view of what constitutes serious illness, on the one hand, and indiscriminately administering it (such as at large communal celebrations of the rite), on the other. The former is a retrenchment to extreme unction, an "abuse"[54] stripping the rite of its sacramental and pastoral force, while the latter falls into the trap of "trivializing serious sickness and reducing the anointing of the sick to the level of the blessing of throats on the feast of St. Blase."[55] Mary's health misfortune at the time of my visit was obviously a function not of overt sickness but rather old age. The rite likewise does not treat old age as a blanket cause for anointing but insists, rather, that the elderly person's condition be somehow "seriously impaired" or "notably weakened even though no serious illness is present."[56] The decision to anoint an elderly person including, as in Mary's case, someone who has received the sacrament before, is a pastoral judgment to be made with prudence but not undue scrupulosity. The rite's call for such discernment is wise. If the occasions for anointing become indiscriminate and the ritual action often repeated, then the sacrament risks losing its symbolic and therefore real force in relation to the other rites in the Pastoral Care of the Sick and thus the life of the church in its members.

The key to discernment here, as Gusmer has so well argued, is recognizing that health is not a narrowly biomedical matter.[57] Rather, the subjective condition of the given person, her or his personal experience of illness as opposed to the objective diagnosis of disease, is at issue: "[M]ost of all, it is not so much the person's medical condition that is determinative. It is rather the 'religious' condition, a spiritual powerlessness, the crisis that illness represents in the life of an ailing

[53] PCS, no. 8. See also, no. 97.

[54] Ibid., no. 99.

[55] Gusmer, *And You Visited Me*, 87.

[56] PCS, nos. 108 and 11. See also, no. 99.

[57] The rite does, nonetheless, advise a pastoral minister's consulting with doctors and other medical professionals caring for a sick or elderly person if that would seem helpful in discerning the need for anointing. See ibid., no. 8.

Christian as regards communication with self, others, and God. Recall the carefully chosen words of number 8: 'seriously impaired by sickness or old age.' Anointing addresses this crisis situation: life with Christ in the community of the Church, which is threatened by serious illness, in short, salvation."[58] While Mary had for many years been housebound and within the past two years hospitalized, her overall health, that is, her comprehensive well-being, was newly weakened if not seriously impaired by her grief over the loss of so many loved ones coupled with her awareness of her own frail condition. The transparency of her words conveyed the sense of alienation from God she was suffering through her questioning of why she was still alive while others had died, a questioning indicative of how death had come to figure in the lost sense of health or balance in her life. Death was lurking, but death not in the sense of imminent physical demise but rather a diminution in the desire to live. The spiritual and psychological suffering thereby certainly had the power to affect her physical condition as well.[59]

The sacrament of anointing of the sick serves this profound need for a renegotiation of one's life, the desire to know something of God's love and presence and one's own value and purpose in relation to others and the world around oneself. My pastoral discernment with Mary and her son Paul took into account her holistic condition not only in terms of Mary as an individual person but in light of her relationship to the family around her and the larger local community of faith in which she has so long played a part. Anointing Mary at that time would be a sacramental proclamation of God's faithful presence to her even in the absence of others who were now deceased, a renewal of her tested faith[60] in God's call and care for her, and a confirmation of her sacramental presence to those around her. Such discernment points to what God will offer the recipient through the ritual of the sacrament: a proclamation of Scripture leading to a threefold symbolic

[58] Gusmer, *And You Visited Me*, 87. Similarly, Ashley and O'Rourke: "Serious should be judged here not merely in physical terms, but also in psychological terms." Thus if the pastoral minister finds a sick or elderly person has anxiety so deep as to produce fear, despair, or anxiety over death, then that person needs the sacrament of anointing. *Health Care Ethics*, 448.

[59] See Glen, "Rites of Healing," 36–37. See also, Ashley and O'Rourke, *Health Care Ethics*, 435–36.

[60] See above, chap. 4, pp. 112–16.

action of prayer, hand-laying, and anointing with oil.[61] What readies the sick or elderly person, as well as those accompanying him or her, for participation in that sacramental ritual is a deepened sense of and desire for the grace the symbolic action promises for the recipient.

Symbolic Force in the Sacramental Gestures of Anointing

The revised sacramental rite of anointing couples the proclamation of the word with three symbolic gestures, drawn primarily from James 5:14, whereby the "rite signifies the grace of the sacrament and confers it": the presbyter's laying on of hands, the prayer of faith, and the anointing with oil.[62] Among the many theologians who have written on the anointing of the sick over the past few decades, James Empereur has made an important contribution by synthesizing much of his colleagues' thought into an argument for the prophetic dimension of this sacrament. David Power, as we saw above,[63] pointed out how sacramental anointing heals by drawing the sick person into the multivalent biblical symbolism of oil as not only palliative but empowering (of ancient priests, prophets, and kings, of Jesus as Messiah, of each believer in baptism). Empereur has brought further insight into the ritual and the salvation it affects by concentrating on the gesture of hand-laying:

> Laying on of hands points up very well the meaning of sickness and old age in a Christian context. Laying on of hands, because it is a commissioning in the Spirit, is concerned more with the restoration of the significance of life through invitation back into community, than it is with the restoration of one's former health and social role the person had prior to illness. Imposition of hands with its multivalent meanings becomes an appropriate symbol of the vocational aspect of the sick and elderly because rather than treating these people as dependent and recipients of the community's benefactions, it deals with them as adults, not as healthy or productive (according to the present culture's values) adults, but as peers who make a contribution to the community in terms of meaning. These liminal people are human acts of faith for the

---

[61] For a recent description and analysis of the threefold symbolism of this sacrament, see Larson-Miller, *The Sacrament of Anointing of the Sick*, 21–45.

[62] PCS, no. 5. See also, nos. 105–7, 121–26.

[63] See above, p. 149.

community regarding mortality and human limits. They are credal incarnations of Jesus' own passage into life.[64]

Just as gospel stories portray renewed or changed religious, and therefore social, status as integral to the healing Jesus brought about for the broad range of sick people he encountered,[65] so the church's sacramental service to the sick and elderly reorients and asserts their role in the community's life. The anointed person receives an empowering call to practice faith as trust in God, oneself, and others through the challenges of loneliness, feelings of abandonment or loss, stripping of self-sufficiency, or at times even dignity due to weakened bodily or mental functions, ceding of status or sense of worth on the basis of one's productivity, and more.[66]

The Introduction to the sacrament of anointing ascribes several symbolic meanings to the gesture of laying hands on the sick person. Situated there between the prayer of faith and anointing with oil, the laying on of hands is especially powerful insofar as it draws upon and integrates those other two aspects of the sacramental celebration. While primarily "the biblical gesture of healing and indeed Jesus' own usual manner of healing," the hand-laying "indicates that this particular person is the object of the Church's prayer of faith" while also functioning as "an invocation . . . for the coming of the Holy Spirit upon the sick person."[67] The healing power of the gesture is profound in both its basic human impact (the calming, steadying, centering, and/or commissioning that laying hands on the head or shoulders conveys) and its association with other sacramental rites: on catechumens and elect as they approach baptism, on those receiving the sacrament of confirmation, on men being ordained to holy orders, on or over the head of the penitent during the prayer of absolution, and not least, over the gifts of bread and wine in the eucharistic prayer. Those other sacraments are themselves multivalent in their empowering

---

[64] Empereur, *Prophetic Anointing*, 196.

[65] See above, chap. 3, pp. 83–86.

[66] See Empereur, *Prophetic Anointing*, 144–45, 170–71. Empereur cites a highly recommended earlier essay by M. Jennifer Glen, "Sickness and Symbol: The Promise of the Future," *Worship* 54, no. 5 (September 1980): 397–403.

[67] PCS, no. 106. Then, no. 107: "The prayer for blessing the oil of the sick reminds us . . . that the oil of anointing is the sacramental sign of the presence, power, and grace of the Holy Spirit."

symbolism, invoking the Holy Spirit as the transformer of subjects (people, but also the eucharistic elements) for evangelical service as well as the source of healing and strength for humans (and in the case of the eucharistic elements, making them healing agents for those partaking of them[68]). The power in the symbolism of laying hands on those to be anointed thus resides not only in the gesture's multi-layered significance within this particular sacramental rite but also in its eliciting people's broader experiences of hand-laying in interpersonal encounters and the entire sacramental economy of the church.

Such an appreciation for the symbolic, as opposed to merely instrumental, power of the key sacramental gestures in the rite of anointing points to how the sacrament functions not in mechanistic isolation but in concert with the sick or elderly person's entire practice of faith and the church's complete pastoral-liturgical life. In this regard Mary's case is exemplary as well. People experience health, as well as illness, through their participation in a practical worldview. Mary's decades-long practice of Christian faith in the Roman Catholic tradition had made her an integral part of the local church community (the same having been true for James). As she and James physically declined in old age, the integrity of their practiced faith, witnessed and emulated by many for decades, called others to share with them the practices of the Pastoral Care of the Sick and thereby further to encounter the crucified and risen Christ through them. I learned over the years that I am not the only one whose faith in the Eucharist has been strengthened through ministering Holy Communion to Mary and James in their home. I recall some years ago a minister of Holy Communion, with palpable eagerness, informing me after Sunday Mass that he and his wife would be bringing the sacrament to Mary and James and how

---

[68] The people's response to the invitation to Communion in the official English version of the Mass of Paul VI: "Lord, I am not worthy to receive you, but only say the word and I shall be healed." The invitation in the Latin *editio typica* text of the Mass of Paul VI draws more explicitly on Sacred Scripture, paraphrasing (no less!) from a story of Christ's healing the sick in the gospels: *Domine, non sum dignus, ut intres sub tectum meum, sed tantum dic verbo* . . . , "Lord, I am not worthy that you should enter under my roof, but only say the word . . ." (Matt 8:8//Luke 7:7). The dumbed-down English version eliminates the profound, ancient (ubiquitous in early church theological and liturgical texts) understanding and practice of the Eucharist as an experience of Christ the healer, a profound empowerment by Christ's Spirit in word and sacrament.

they looked forward to not only praying with them but also asking them to share with them some of their wisdom. Still, the eucharistic ministry of clergy and lay ministers clearly supported the faith of the elderly couple as well.

The ministry of the Eucharist maintains for the sick or elderly a powerful, tangible bond with the Body of Christ experienced both in the real symbolism of the bread and wine and the fellowship with the ministers who represent to the infirmed the entire assembly of Christ's Body.[69] The bodily gestures and repeated patterns of prayer echoing various movements of the Mass (penitential rite, a proclamation of the word, intercessions, the Lord's Prayer, and the climactic sharing in the sacrament of Holy Communion) connect the infirm with not only the contemporary community of faith but, through bodily memory in the ritual action, a wider communion of heaven and earth, images and stories of loved ones now distanced by time, space, or death. Faith is known in a lifetime of practicing such an array of relationships in all their consolations and conflicts, joys and sorrows, as interpreted and at times transformed by the word of God that speaks to the believer through the celebration of the Eucharist.

Healing Power in the Prayer of Faith

The entire economy of the Pastoral Care of the Sick, through its rites for visiting the sick[70] and celebrating Holy Communion with the sick, enacts healing by sharing and building up faith both in the lives of the infirm and those engaged with them. The sanctifying grace specific to the sacrament of anointing is the comfort, strength, and support of that faith precisely at moments when an elderly or sick person has reached a moment of crisis or fatigue, a difficult turn making one susceptible to anxiety, despair, guilt, or a wavering trust in God.[71] Thus it is in conjunction with hand-laying and applying oil that the prayer of faith not only comprises a key element of the sacrament of anointing but, according to the General Introduction, grounds the entire rite as healing action, a special moment of grace, an act of salvation: "In the anointing of the sick, which includes the prayer of faith (see James 5:15),

---

[69] For the pastoral theology of Communion of the Sick, see chapter 3 of the *Pastoral Care of the Sick*, here especially, no. 73.

[70] For the introductions and rituals for Visits to the Sick, see ibid., nos. 54–70.

[71] See PCS, nos. 5–6. See also, Ashley and O'Rourke, *Health Care Ethics*, 437.

faith itself is manifested. Above all this faith must be made actual both in the minister of the sacrament and, even more importantly, in the recipient. The sick person will be saved by personal faith and the faith of the Church, which looks back to the death and resurrection of Christ, the source of the sacrament's power (see James 5:15), and looks ahead to the future kingdom that is pledged in the sacraments."[72] The church's doctrine for this rite thus could not be clearer in its assertion that the divine grace of this sacrament becomes a reality not on some abstract plain of existence but through the ritual engagement—body and spirit, narrative and desire—of the recipient, ministers, and other participants. Christ comes "as physician and healer"[73] in the anointing of the sick through his Spirit's confirmation of the ill or elderly person's inestimable worth in the reality of his or her condition, the assurance of faith mediated through the church's ministry of word and sacrament.

Whether the sick person is calm or agitated, resolute or panicked, lonely or consoled is not the criterion for discerning the presence of faith. What matters is the person's honest presence to God, self, and others as one who needs God to be the trustworthy companion or sheltering parent or stronger sibling or Good Shepherd or all-powerful Lord who can accept our tears, bear our yearnings, withstand our anger—who only desires that we be real in our presence. How the proclaimed Scriptures and performed gestures of the sacrament might be "written on the body"[74] of the recipient is a function of the living narrative that each person is. The recipient may be so physically or mentally impaired that his or her act of faith completely resides in submitting to the action of the church, in its ministers and others gathered round, as not only bringing Christ to oneself but also oneself to God. Such a profound acknowledgment of faith's role in the grace of the sacrament gets at the heart of why the church condemns the delay of anointing the sick as an abuse and expects pastors to instruct the faithful in requesting the sacrament for self or others as soon as a person's

[72] PCS, no. 7.

[73] An explicit image in the model greeting with which the priest should receive the sick in the Introductory Rites of the Anointing Within Mass. Ibid., no. 135.

[74] See above, chap. 4, p. 118.

condition becomes serious.[75] The sacrament heals by bringing into powerful symbolic performance the faith of the person and the church as an action of the Spirit of Christ, an act of divine worship whose human consequences can then unfold in the immediate or long term, according to the person's unique condition, one's particular needs.

Ministers of the sacrament, whether priests or laypersons charged with the pastoral care of the sick, must have a profound faith in the paschal content and ritual performance of the rite, for they are the ones who help actualize "the faith of the church" through their service of the sacrament. The faith of the *pastoral* minister (as opposed to a mechanistic clerical dispenser of sacraments, a humanly disengaged instrument of rites) has a tangible impact upon the effectiveness of the sacramental celebration of anointing. The minister must have a thorough working knowledge of the rite as well as a profound belief in and expectation of God's acting through it in order to serve its purpose of saving, that is, healing, the recipient. Pastoral-liturgical competence must work in concert with personal-prayerful practice in the life of the minister, engaging one's own faith as desire for and resistance to God, experience of the presence and absence of the divine, strength in leadership and vulnerability in prayer, confidence and doubts in and out of season in one's life. If the minister's own ongoing desire is to know and trust the God revealed in the Gospel, then that faith will infuse the quality of the preparation and execution of the sacrament's celebration.

While it is undoubtedly preferable that the priest who will minister the sacrament have some pastoral contact and knowledge of the person to be anointed, as well as those in attendance, the efficacy of the sacramental celebration does not depend exclusively or even primarily on such interpersonal familiarity. What matters most of all is that he intend what the church intends in the liturgy, that he be open to the sick person and others in their need for the grace of the sacramental celebration, that he be steeped in Scripture and the tradition of the rite, expectant of encountering and contributing to Christ's presence therein. The priest, in collaboration with the other pastoral ministers, will thereby offer what the people need and ask of the church in this sacrament, creating the "space" for grace to be realized in whatever

---

[75] "In public and private catechesis, the faithful should be educated to ask for the sacrament of anointing and, as soon as the right time comes, to receive it with faith and devotion. They should not follow he wrongful practice of delaying the reception of the sacrament." PCS, no. 13. See also, no. 99.

ways God wills and people respond in the real situation and circumstances of the celebration.

While it must be infused with a love for God's people and the
church's liturgy, the minister's service also requires ritual competence, a thorough knowledge of how the "prayer of faith" is realized
in the rite of anointing. The "prayer of faith" in the reformed sacrament of anointing functionally encompasses the entire ritual celebration. Whether celebrated within or outside a Mass, the normal
ritual[76] entails introductory rites, the Liturgy of the Word, the liturgy
of anointing, and concluding rites. The liturgy of anointing's several movements include the laying on of hands and the anointing,
but there is no one part simply designated as "the prayer of faith."
Rather, the other elements include a litany (followed by the laying
on of hands), the prayer over the oil (followed by the anointing), the
prayer after anointing and, in the case of anointing outside Mass,
the Lord's Prayer. Every one of those elements of the rite, including
the hand-laying and anointing, entail the prayer of faith. The prayer of
faith suffuses the entire liturgy of anointing, taking different forms of
expression and thus actualizing faith—the human response to divine
grace—through a number of ritually related symbolic acts engaging a
range of human capacities for knowledge and emotion, a realization of
salvation in body and soul.

The litany entails brief invocations bespeaking the profound human
needs of the sick, to which the assembly responds, "Lord, have mercy,"
a highly familiar prayer, consoling in its repetition.[77] The priest performs the laying on of hands in silence, allowing the symbolic gesture
to bespeak prayer not only in the physical imagery but also the silent
thoughts he and all may have at that moment. The prayer over the oil,
whether a thanksgiving for already consecrated oil or an actual blessing thereof, includes the prayer forms of anamnesis and, in the case
of consecration, epiclesis; thus, the thanksgiving or blessing nurtures
faith by recounting the merciful works of God in Christ and proclaiming the Spirit's acting so again now. The sacramental matter of anointing the sick person's forehead and hands with the oil is accompanied

[76] See ibid., nos. 111–48. The rite treats the anointing of the sick in a hospital
or institution as an abbreviated rite necessitated "by the special circumstances
of hospital ministry" (no. 149).

[77] For the successive portions of the rite described in this paragraph, see
PCS, nos. 121–24.

by the prayer form: "Through this holy anointing may the Lord in his love and mercy help you with the grace of the Holy Spirit . . . May the Lord who frees you from sin save you and raise you up." The words of the prayer profoundly elicit the imagery and theology of healing revealed in the New Testament. As our biblical study in chapter 3 taught us, sin here is not narrowly a matter of individual immoral acts but the encompassing condition of guilt, failure, alienation, fear, loss, and death that serious illness or old age may entail.[78] The equation of salvation with being raised up not only paraphrases the letter of James but places the healing of this sick person within scope of Christ's entire saving work, namely, the power of the (paschal) mystery of his death and resurrection.[79] Therein lies the assurance of God's love and mercy not as a wish but as a realized promise, help for the sick coming as divine consolation in Christ's deliverance through life and death and the sure, empowering hope of sharing in his resurrection.

Finally, for the ritual prayer after anointing the priest selects from several options pertinent to the nature of the recipient's infirmity: a couple of general versions are followed by those for extreme or

---

[78] See above, chap. 3, pp. 91–93. Empereur's discussion of how anointing heals sin in the sick person builds upon the biblical tradition: "[S]ickness is that kind of marginal situation in which a person feels more deeply the existential guilt before God which is not the result of individual immoral actions. This guilt is concretized in the obvious alienation of being confined to one's room or bed, of being cut off from future planning or past enjoyments. . . . The rite of anointing deals with the kind of separation and fragmentation that results from this disorder of this imperfect world. People actively create this disorder when they sin and the sacrament of reconciliation addresses that kind of personal excommunication. But not all dehumanizing disorder is caused by individual immorality. It is anointing which takes the separation people experience in sickness and raises it to a meaningfulness which can be found in Christ. All humans are guilty before God; all people participate in the alienation of humanity. And what anointing can do is proclaim loudly in the Church that the heightened suffering of those who are sick carries a special meaning regarding Christ's triumph over the sin of the world not only for them but for the whole community. Anointing says that the partial and fragmented stories of the sick person and of the healthy community must be caught up into the larger incorporating story of Jesus Christ, a story, in short, which is entitled: the Paschal Mystery." *Prophetic Anointing*, 153–54. See also, 171–72, 179.

[79] See above, chap. 3, pp. 69–71, 94–96.

terminal illness, advanced age, before surgery, for a child, and for a young person. The content and variety of those prayers bespeak ways Christ heals in the celebration of this sacrament, as well as the concrete shape that the practice of faith takes in the lives of people suffering various health misfortunes. The selection of prayers after anointing thereby points to the range of human experiences of illness that the renewed sacrament of anointing seeks to heal. The contents of the prayers also provide guidance for the types of needs that various sick and elderly people undergo and thus present to pastoral ministers and others caring for them. Some consideration of these prayers can round out this commentary on the rite in terms of the key issues I have been identifying: appropriate subjects/recipients of anointing, what is meant by healing in the both the ecclesial and wider contemporary context, how the symbolic ritual action affects healing, as well as how the ritual prayer and gestures should inform preaching suitable to each particular celebration of the rite.

Disclosures of Healing in the Prayer after Anointing

The first two versions of the prayer after anointing are designated for general use, that is, for the broad range of serious health misfortunes that would make believers appropriate subjects of anointing. The first general version is addressed to God as Father in heaven and asks that the recipient be granted comfort in his or her suffering. The prayer continues with a series of descriptions of what suffering in illness can be like, each paired with a healing gift at once divine and human: fear–courage; affliction–patience; dejection–hope; loneliness–"the support of your holy people."[80] In any given case, one or more of the forms of comfort proclaimed in this prayer may have already been experienced by the sick person, such that the anointing and prayer are the ritual sealing of that gift (grace) in the sacramental power of the Holy Spirit. The celebration of anointing may, alternatively, be a ritual action motivating and empowering the sick person and those caring for her or him to work together for such spiritual growth in illness, confident in the grace (divine favor) conferred in the sacrament. Such spiritual growth is not instant but rather of a part with the entire physical and psychological process of the person's experience of illness and healing. The sacrament of anointing heals by assuring God's presence to the afflicted person and those surrounding him or her,

[80] PCS, no. 125-A.

revealing that the types of "absence" named in the prayer (fear, afflic-tion, etc.)[81] are the very sorts of realities in which God promises active presence as comfort, support, and personal growth.[82]

Among the myriad situations this first general prayer of anointing serves well is the moment when a chronically sick or elderly person's condition has deteriorated to the point that she or he must move per-manently into a nursing home or other such facility, thus having to relinquish a last measure of independent living and perhaps a home of many years. A group of students in one of my courses on liturgy and healing enacted the rite of anointing in a scenario, based on their own pastoral experiences, in which an early middle-aged woman had finally to arrange for her elderly mother, who was afflicted with Alzheimer's disease,[83] to be moved to a nursing home. Added to the daughter's anxiety over her mother's loss of her home and entry into a new environment was the fact that she lived in a city several hours away and could not visit her mother regularly. When the mother had settled in the nursing home the pastor celebrated the rite of anoint-ing along with both the daughter and the home-health aide who had cared for the elderly woman for a long time. While the mother was pleasant but unclear about what was happening in the rite, the cele-bration of the sacrament brought great consolation to the two younger women who, each in her own way, were deeply affected by the radical change in location and caregiving that had now come about, altering

---

[81] See above, chap. 4, pp. 116–17, 122–25.

[82] See Ashley and O'Rourke, *Health Care Ethics*, 445–48.

[83] Alzheimer's disease has emerged as an illness eliciting the characteristic postmodern social expectation that medical science must have some sort of drug already developed to provide a cure or significant relief, while special-ists predict any realistic pharmacological reduction in cases to be decades away. The felt need is urgent, with some 4.5 million Americans suffering from the disease, which one neurological research physician characterized as "a slow-motion disaster . . . It's very hard to sit by and watch. There is an overwhelming desire to do something, even if it's to give a useless pill." At a symposium hosted at Johns Hopkins University, doctors expressed frustration over patients' high expectations for drugs that are showing little benefit, as well as with experts' evasive answers over the drugs' efficacy. "The moderator summed up, saying: 'For us [researchers] to tell you [physicians] what to do, I think would be wrong. All you can do is look at your soul and do the best you can.'" Denise Grady, "Nominal Benefits Seen in Drugs for Alzheimer's Dis-ease," *New York Times*, 7 April 2004.

their own roles in her care. The sacramental gestures of hand-laying and anointing were tangibly consoling not only to the mother but to all involved. For the celebration's Liturgy of the Word the pastor chose John's account of the crucified Jesus giving his mother into the care of the beloved disciple (John 19:25-27), encouraging all three women to hear Christ's empathy with their own need to give and be given over into another's charge. As part of the entire ritual celebration, that word did not deny the pain and challenge of the moment, yet it empowered courage, patience, hope, and mutual support for the days ahead.

The second general prayer after anointing addresses Christ as Lord and Redeemer, asking for his Spirit to heal the sick person's weakness and forgive his or her sins, to "expel all afflictions of mind and body," restoring the person "to full health" so as to "resume his/her former duties."[84] It concludes by acclaiming Jesus "Lord for ever and ever," a christological title summarizing the entire prayer's confidence in God's hearing the expressed desire of the church assembled with the sick person, a faith based upon God's definitive revelation of our salvation in Jesus crucified and resurrected, the Lord. In contrast to the first general prayer's overall tone of endurance and well-being in infirmity, this second prayer speaks more to situations in which the health discerned as feasible and desirable is either recovery from sickness or, in the case of chronic disease, holistic adjustment to one's condition so as to move forward in life. Restoration to health is thereby a matter of successfully renegotiating the sick person's relationship with her or his own body and the wider social body, thereby benefiting both the individual's well-being and the common good.[85]

This second prayer collects the theological wisdom of the entire rite by articulating the impact that psychological and spiritual

[84] PCS, no. 125-B.

[85] In this way the prayer puts into ritual action the theology explained in the General Introduction, no. 6: "This sacrament gives the grace of the Holy Spirit to those who are sick: by this grace the whole person is helped and saved, sustained by trust in God, and strengthened against temptations of the Evil One and against anxiety over death. Thus the sick person is able not only to bear suffering bravely but also to fight against it. A return to physical health may follow the reception of this sacrament if it will be beneficial to the sick person's salvation." And elsewhere: "Part of the plan laid out by God's providence is that we should fight strenuously against all sickness and carefully seek the blessings of good health, so that we may fulfill our role in human society and in the Church." Ibid., no. 3.

172

stresses can have upon a person's sickness and recovery, not shying from the existential link between sickness and the felt need for
forgiveness from sin. In addition to touching on that crucial healing
dimension of the sacrament, the prayer's intercession for deliverance
from afflictions of mind and body indicates the sacrament's relevance to the types of illness David Morris describes as prevalent in
postmodern culture: cancer, chronic pain, arthritis, multiple sclerosis,
diabetes, depression and anxiety disorders. These are all medically
treatable conditions that nonetheless have strong historical, psychological, and cultural dimensions.[86] We are learning anew that mind
and body cannot be separated in the pursuit of health, as well as that
human corporality is not only a physical but also a social and traditional reality.

For believers afflicted with acute or chronic disease the sacrament
of anointing situates the quest for restored health in the healing assurance of Christ's desire for their wholeness and the church's support in
their striving for it. Preaching, counseling, and pastoral care in relation to anointing must also communicate to the sick person and all
concerned that, as in many other situations in life, God's grace is active in the honest expression of our desires and the concrete process of
our pursuing them. Faith is experienced as our confidently, or at least
honestly, letting God know what we want and trusting that God will
grant, in divine goodness and wisdom, what we truly need. In this
way, "full health" is not the modernly imagined state of perfect bodily
condition (which, of course, is always a socially influenced construct)
but rather an ongoing negotiation of the meaning of one's life, in its
concrete conditions, in relation to the message, vision, and promise of
the Gospel.

The types of (postmodern) health misfortunes listed two paragraphs
above press the question of what is meant by health and therefore
healing in relation to the rite of anointing and, indeed, within the
entire Pastoral Care of the Sick. The complete elimination of disease
symptoms does not necessarily define health, nor does the prevalence
of such symptoms necessarily constitute the need for sacramental
anointing. Each person's situation is truly unique. In the case of cancer,
the need for anointing would seem quite obvious given the seriousness of the disease and its always deadly possibilities. The sacrament

---

[86] See above, chap. 2, pp. 38–41, and Morris, *Illness and Culture in the Postmodern Age*, 17, 39, 51, 77, 115–28.

is best celebrated at the outset of diagnosis and treatment so as to place the person's well-being in the faithful embrace of Christ and the church. What is imagined (desired) and therefore sought in prayer will be a function of the diagnosis and prognosis, but the grace of the sacrament remains its manifestation of Christ's merciful and loving help through the grace of the Holy Spirit, empowering faith in this trying experience.

As one example, I recall anointing a woman in her forties, a wife and mother of several teenagers, who received a diagnosis of breast cancer requiring surgical removal followed by a regimen of radiation therapy—a genuine crisis for her, a person highly engaged in family, church, and professional work. In discussing her situation with me she spoke tenderly of her husband's great support and empathetically for her children, each coping in ways characteristic of their ages and personalities. We decided to celebrate the sacrament of anointing in their home on a Friday night, their weekly ritual evening for sharing dinner and extended conversation. That Friday evening, of course, introduced an unusual ritual addition, charged with tension yet supported by their regular practice of actively being together. Situating the sacrament within the ritual-time of the family set the woman's health struggle in the primary context of her life: the husband and children with and through whom she had for two decades known divine love and practiced faith in Christ as a shared human journey. The celebration of anointing was not only for this woman but also for all the members of the family with her.

That night and over the following months, indeed, the rite strengthened her psychologically and spiritually. As an affective and spiritual resource to which she returned often in memory and prayer, the anointing helped her integrate her bout with cancer (including subsequent radiation and chemical treatments) into her necessarily revised sense of what her health now looked and felt like physically, emotionally, socially, and interpersonally. As with any situation of cancer, the question of the future for this woman was open-ended, and she continuously had to seek peace in accepting the indefinite character of the disease in her life. She eventually faced further surgery for cancer elsewhere in her body. Gratefully, she has recovered again and returned to professional life and full activity in her family, which she continues to enjoy, while nonetheless, especially with her husband's companionship, keeping the reality of disease a significant part of her life and a subject of their prayer.

Other postmodern illnesses may require even greater attention to the person's total subjective health condition in discerning the need for the anointing of the sick: is the person suffering from illness to such a degree that he or she needs to renegotiate his or her life in relation to self, others, and God? In the case of many contemporary forms of sickness a primary dimension of the suffering experienced by individuals is shame or fear of stigmatization. Thus one person with a given chronic disease might be distraught and in need of anointing while another person with the same disease may not. One person with diabetes or multiple sclerosis may construct a sense of wholeness and well-being by minimizing the significance of the physical condition in the overall scheme of her or his life: "I don't consider myself sick, nor do I want others to see me as sick. The diabetes (or multiple sclerosis or obesity or depression or anorexia, etc.[87]) is simply a part of my life. It does not define who I am." For another person, however, the experience of the same diagnosed disease may pose a grave subjective challenge to the point of effectively taking possession of the person's life or well-being, indicating that for this person "the right time [has come] to receive [sacramental anointing] with faith and devotion."[88] The rite heals, again, not in the sense of completely eliminating the complex psychological, physiological, and

[87] Multiple sclerosis is a neurodegenerative disease characterized by the gradual destruction of neuron transmitters in the brain and spinal cord; thus, those afflicted with it usually experience stages of decline in physical health that may be well suited to repeated sacramental anointing. The classification of obesity as a disease is controversial in both scientific and civic circles due to the question of how much the unwillingness to change personal habits governs the condition—an issue fraught with stigma and shame. See Gina Kolata, "C.D.C. Team Investigates an Outbreak of Obesity," *New York Times*, 3 June 2005. The Center for Disease Control estimated obesity to be the cause of 112,000 deaths nationally in 2004, nearly three times the morbidity rates for drugs and alcohol. In 2004 the Department of Health and Human Services declared obesity a critical public health problem affecting millions of Americans and causing thousands of premature deaths. Such judgments indicate the seriousness of obesity as a postmodern illness and the possibility of individual sufferers' discerning the need for the anointing of the sick in their struggle with the condition. See Derrick Z. Jackson, "Why obesity is winning," *Boston Globe*, 19 August 2005; see also, Rob Stein and Ceci Connolly, "Medicare alters obesity language," *Boston Globe*, 16 August 2004, A1, A12.

[88] PCS, no. 13.

social conditions of the disease but rather by manifesting God's presence to and empowerment of the person's life, renegotiating the person's sense of self-worth and meaning. Celebration of the sacrament, whether in a private setting of just the pastoral minister(s), sick person, and perhaps a few others or in a larger communal liturgy, should also prophetically call the members of the church to adjust their own perceptions of the chronically ill person and his or her place in society and the faith community. Celebration of the sacrament heals by renegotiating the sick or elderly person's place within the Mystical Body of Christ, the fellowship of God's reign.

While cancer is no longer the taboo subject and cause for shame in American society that it was until the 1970s, suffering from depression or bipolar illnesses, conditions currently estimated to affect 20 percent of Americans during their lifetimes, continues to be stigmatized.[89] The Pastoral Care of the Sick explicitly mentions those suffering serious mental illness as potential recipients of the sacrament of anointing, noting that for such individuals "anointing may be repeated in accordance with the conditions for other kinds of serious illness (see no. 9)."[90] Again, discernment performed in conjunction with medical professionals is essential, as one person might cope well with a mental illness while another may experience it as an immobilizing affliction, thus calling for anointing. A person may feel shame over needing pharmaceutical and/or psychiatric treatment. The threat to holistic health and well-being becomes all the more obvious in the case of somebody needing to enter residential treatment. I once lived in a religious community in which one of the members had to resign from his job in order to seek residential mental health care. When the local superior asked me how we might pray for this man at the weekly community Mass, I responded that this was a perfect case for celebrating the rite for anointing of the sick within Mass.[91] After the

---

[89] "Depression is the leading cause of disability worldwide, according to the World Health Organization. It costs more in treatment and lost productivity than anything but heart disease. Suicide is the 11th most common cause of death in the united States, claiming 30,000 lives each year." Andrew Solomon, "Our Great Depression," New York Times, 17 November 2006. See also, Carey Goldberg, "Mental care found subpar as need grows," Boston Globe, 7 June 2005.

[90] PCS, no. 53.

[91] See ibid., nos. 131–48.

homily, I invited the superior to bring the afflicted man to a seat we had positioned in the open space in front of the altar. In order for the person receiving the sacrament in such a setting not to feel isolated or somehow made show of, it is important that someone accompany him or her, standing behind or beside the person as she or he sits to receive the laying of hands and anointing. In this case, all the community members came forward to lay hands briefly in silence. For the prayer after anointing I used Option C:

> Lord Jesus Christ,
> you chose to share our human nature,
> to redeem all people, and to heal the sick.
> Look with compassion upon your servant N.,
> whom we have anointed in your name with this holy oil
> for the healing of his/her body and spirit.
> Support him/her with your power,
> comfort him/her with your protection,
> and give him/her the strength to fight against evil.
> Since you have given him/her a share in your own passion,
> help him/her to find hope in suffering,
> for you are Lord for ever and ever.[92]

The wisdom in that prayer after anointing lies in the strong yet open-ended character of the words and syntax. Pastoral ministers need to trust the power in such texts as written, proclaiming them deliberately and with compassion so that all participating might hear in them whatever specific consolation the Spirit may give.

A further post-anointing prayer text worth noting is the option provided before surgery. Certainly any surgery requiring general anesthesia (categorically a serious matter) warrants anointing. Anointing, again, is not a magical insurance policy but rather assurance of God's presence and promise not only to the sick person but also in and through the "the skills of surgeons and nurses." The prayer does not hesitate to ask for a positive outcome, yet does so in an open-ended way: "May your servant respond to your healing will and be reunited with us at your altar of praise."[93] The wisdom in this prayer, true to all Christian petitioning, lies in its both honest expression of human

---

[92] Ibid., no. 125-C.
[93] Ibid., no. 125-E.

177

desire and confident trust in God's will, that is, faith in God as the one whose response is always for the good.

ANOINTING THE SICK AS SACRAMENT WITHIN
A LARGER PASTORAL PROCESS OF FAITH

The salvific efficacy of the anointing of the sick is enhanced by preparation of the recipient, along with loved ones or caregivers, for the celebration of the sacrament. The entire economy of the Pastoral Care of the Sick, in its rituals for visiting the sick and celebrating Holy Communion, enacts healing through the sharing and building up of faith both in the lives of the infirmed and those engaged with them.[94] Insofar as this sacrament builds on the conversion to life-in-Christ affected through baptism and sustained by the Eucharist, the conversion-vocational dimension of the anointing of the sick holds the key to unlocking ways pastorally to prepare for its celebration. Thus, I find in the stages and steps of the Rite of Christian Initiation of Adults (RCIA)—evangelization, liturgical catechesis, personal enlightenment, sacramental celebration, and mystagogy—resources for analogously ordering the pastoral-ritual process of bringing the sick or aged to the sacrament of anointing.

Just as with the RCIA, evangelization for the sacrament of anointing the sick entails a variety of activities, any number or combination of which may affect a person's considering oneself or a loved one as called to receive the sacrament. Given the extensive amount of material in the Synoptic Gospels involving Jesus' healing activities, the Sunday Lectionary cycles for all three years include no small number of occasions for homilies either touching on or entirely devoted to the sacrament of anointing. Such preaching can draw upon the best of current biblical exegesis to shed light on the social, religious, economic, familial, and other cultural factors that made healing in the world of the gospels something far more complex *and* humanly fulfilling than mere magic acts. People are hungry for homilies connecting that world to our own, where the struggles and crises of illness and aging are likewise not merely a matter of bodily functions and therefore need the sort of healing in Christ I described in the first major section of

---

[94] For overviews of the entire set of rituals comprising the Pastoral Care of the Sick, see Gusmer, *And You Visited Me*, 51–98, and Larson-Miller, *The Sacrament of the Anointing of the Sick*, 1–20.

this chapter.[95] Another way during the Sunday assembly to broaden believers' understanding of healing as both a divine and human phenomenon would be to have ministers of Holy Communion occasionally speak during the concluding rite of the Mass (that is, following the prayer after Communion) about their experiences of visiting the elderly and homebound. The testimony of the laity can be powerful. A further possibility for lay reflection on Sundays with pertinent Lectionary readings would be for parish nurses or other healthcare providers to speak about sickness and healing as holistic experiences within the life of faith.

In terms of catechesis and faith formation, many parishes today have Bible study groups popular with retirees. These can be venues for evangelizing and catechesis on the sacrament, relating the Word to the renewed liturgical tradition. As for personal growth and enlightenment through liturgical formation, the Pastoral Care of the Sick provides a variety of Scripture passages, intercessions, and prayers for visits and Holy Communion with the sick from which pastoral ministers can draw to serve the needs of particular individuals. Mary's story illustrates parish ministers, visitors, family, and clergy utilizing these resources in her home and at the church in ways that have supported her Christian vocation, enabled her sharing of faith with others, and contributed to her discerning when the sacrament of anointing would be beneficial.

While the sacrament of anointing the sick is an occasional rite, it nonetheless, like all liturgy, draws its source and shape from the paschal mystery, celebrated communally and through an annual cycle. Here can be drawn another analogy with the RCIA. I have had success in creating catechetical groups that meet several times in advance of a communal celebration of anointing the sick, modeling the sessions on the structure of those for the second stage of the RCIA.[96] These should not be "classes" but rather gatherings shaped around proclaiming Scripture, personal sharing, instruction, intercessions, prayer, pastoral

[95] See also, Bruce T. Morrill, "Challenges and Resources for a Liturgical Theology of Healing: Roman Catholic Practice and Postmodern Theory," *Liturgy* 22, no. 3 (2007): 13–20.

[96] See Bruce T. Morrill, "Practicing the Pastoral Care of the Sick: The Sacramental Body in Liturgical Motion," in *Practicing Catholic: Ritual, Body, and Contestation in Catholic Faith*, ed. Bruce Morrill and others, 99–114 (New York: Palgrave Macmillan, 2006).

music, and a variety of blessings.[97] As formation and discernment toward celebrating sacramental anointing of the sick, such sessions can draw upon the wealth of resources in the Pastoral Care of the Sick as well as the Book of Blessings and even the RCIA itself. Such a formation process creates solidarity among those experiencing sickness or old age as an affliction as well as those who love and care for them. It also can help prevent indiscriminate anointing of large numbers of people at communal celebrations of the sacrament. The celebration itself, especially if part of a Sunday Mass, serves as a form of evangelization to the local community, modeling faith in the Gospel as well as the reformed meaning and purpose of this sacrament.

Such a pastoral process for anointing might best be done through the Easter cycle, beginning with Ash Wednesday or early in Lent, when the pastoral team could invite people to reflect on whether the burden weighing down their baptismal faith at this time is that of sickness or elderly decline. The formation sessions could run through the Lenten season and include the opportunity for the sacrament of penance celebrated one evening communally. This would serve the rite's expectation that penance normally be celebrated on a separate occasion in advance of liturgy of anointing, since penance heals sin in a distinctly different way.[98] The communal celebration of anointing could then be celebrated during a major parish Mass on one of the Sundays in the Easter season, thereby proclaiming the vocation of the sick and elderly as a special share in the paschal mystery.

Such a communal celebration during Easter can teach the assembled parish—far better than lectures—that extreme unction is defunct, that the sacrament of anointing the sick is for the support of those experiencing hardship in illness or old age, who become signs of faith in the crucified and risen Christ. Situating the communal rite of anointing in Easter can also poignantly complement the other special sacramental rites typically celebrated during the season, all of which tend to focus on youth: infant baptisms, First Communions, and confirmations. The communal celebration of anointing during Easter counters the temptation, exacerbated by our media-driven society, of thinking that life is only really happening for and among the young, the physically

---

[97] See International Commission on English in the Liturgy, *Rite of Christian Initiation of Adults* (Washington, DC: National Conference of Catholic Bishops, 1988), nos. 81–97.

[98] See PCS, no. 101.

beautiful, and those full of promise according to worldly criteria. Easter is also the season of mystagogy, which for those anointed during a Sunday Mass would best take place on a day sometime after the actual celebration. Not only do the sick and elderly tire readily, but there also should be time for all to let the Spirit work its grace in the recipients as well as all the participants. During one or two more gatherings, set in the context of liturgical prayer, people could then share their reflections on the experience of the sacrament as well as their feelings as they face the future, whether in the short or long term.

As expressed in the rite's expectation that religious education, pastoral visitations, and a variety of rituals suited to individual and communal circumstances will be practiced,[99] the benefits of the sacrament of anointing are not instrumentally limited to the afflicted person but rather can extend to all the faithful involved. Through Christ's presence in word and sacrament, shared by ministers, the sick, and those gathered with them, the rite graces suffering believers with gifts that enable them to renegotiate (transform) their lives in relation to their illness. This renegotiation and personal transformation, the interpretation of the person's illness with a new meaning through the paschal mystery, is how the rite heals the sick and elderly. The rite, however, is also capable of gracing (transforming) the community with greater faith through their interaction with the sick and suffering, who become living witnesses for them of a crucial dimension of the Gospel, namely, that in the raising up of the lowly God's reign is known. In an overwhelmingly consumerist culture that glamorizes largely unattainable images of youthful beauty to the detriment of compassionate attention to the suffering, ill, and aged, the Pastoral Care of the Sick brings a much-needed vision and practical program for helping the faithful embrace the Gospel.

The rite's recurrent call for communal celebrations of the sacrament[100] makes pastoral sense not only for the strengthening of the sick and those who care for them but also for the ongoing conversion (transformation) of the entire community of faith. The symbolic and metaphoric (and thus performative and transformative) language of the rite's instructions and rituals consistently bespeaks healing and strengthening, comfort and pardon through the ministration of Christ as healer, Savior, Messiah, and physician—in a word, the sacrament of our salvation.

---

[99] See ibid., no. 13.
[100] See ibid., nos. 97, 99, 108.

Chapter 6

The Pastoral Care of the Dying:
Healing at the Hour of Death

INTRODUCTION

In the previous chapters we learned that healing comes through words and actions that retrieve a person or group from the margins of life to a renegotiated position within the social body (including its traditional and cosmic dimensions). This is no less the case when the ultimate threat to a person's life arises, namely, death.

Finding strength and peace to cope with the stages and finality of death, the definitive human experience of change, depends on the ability of those involved to draw from a repertoire of symbols and narratives fundamental to their corporately held worldview. The subtitle for the present chapter purposely serves to make this point. For Roman Catholics the phrase, "at the hour of death," draws upon the conclusion of one of the prayers most familiar and practiced in the tradition: "Holy Mary, Mother of God, pray for us sinners, now and at the hour of our death. Amen." In such a severe life crisis as death the Hail Mary for many Catholics is a source of solace and strength, ready to hand without need of explanation, hands often guiding repetition with a rosary prayed individually or in the company of fellow believers. That prayer constitutes but one example of popular piety complementing the reformed sacramental rites in service to the dying, a process of liturgical renewal challenged by the need to form the faithful in sound practices of a tradition weakened by the social and ecclesial conditions of late modernity.

Anchoring the church's pastoral care of the dying, and thus this chapter, is the solemn celebration of the Eucharist as Viaticum. A brief historical review can ground the doctrinal, liturgical, and canonical theology of this sacrament's primordial purpose of situating the dying person in Christ's saving passage through death in certain hope of resurrection. Articulation of that divine power will open into consideration of the needs for human healing characteristic at the hour of death—those both of the dying person and of the family, friends, and care providers—and how the entire ritual of the Pastoral Care of the Dying may serve them. I shall conclude by moving from elements of this rite at life's margins back to the church's central prayer and liturgy, arguing for practices the church needs to nurture in its members so as to grace them with a repertoire ready to serve at the hour of death.

VIATICUM, SACRAMENT OF THE DYING

Reclaiming a Lost Treasure

As noted at the outset of the previous chapter, the *General Introduction to Pastoral Care of the Sick: Rites of Anointing and Viaticum* explains the document's two-part structure according to the crisis each sacrament and its associated rites serve, anointing for the seriously ill or aged and Viaticum for the dying. The introduction to Part II reiterates accordingly that its rites "are used by the Church to comfort and strengthen a dying Christian in the passage from this life. The ministry to the dying places emphasis on trust in the Lord's promise of eternal life rather than on the struggle against illness which is characteristic of the pastoral care of the sick."[1] The reformed rite explains the healing power of Viaticum as twofold: the sacramental manifestation of the dying person's identification with "the mystery of the death of the Lord and his passage to the Father," and "the pledge of the resurrection that the Lord promised."[2] The theology recovers an ancient and universal treasure of the church.[3] In prescribing that every dying Christian be given this special form of Holy Communion, the ecumenical Council of Nicaea (325 CE), far from legislating something new, was seeing to it that the emergent penalties and limitations placed on penitents not exclude them from a long-standing custom,

---

[1] International Committee on English in the Liturgy, *Pastoral Care of the Sick: Rites of Anointing and Viaticum* (Washington, DC: National Conference of Catholic Bishops, 1983), no. 161. Hereafter, PCS.

[2] Ibid., no. 26.

[3] "The reception of communion as viaticum is a practice attested universally by the patristic, canonical, and hagiographical documents of the fourth, fifth, and sixth centuries." Damien Sicard, "Christian Death," *The Sacraments*, ed. Aimé George Martimort, trans. Matthew O'Connell, The Church at Prayer, rev. ed., vol. 3 (Collegeville, MN: Liturgical Press, 1988), 224.

"the ultimate and most necessary viaticum."[4] Pastors were to be solicitous in providing reconciliation and access to the Eucharist, manifestations of the boundless mercy of God, the key divine attribute consistently revealed in the early tradition's care for the dying. In citing John 6:54, Christ's promise to raise up on the last day those who eat his Body and drink his Blood, the council affirmed the biblical basis of the tradition—an association the current rite of Viaticum has recovered—and with it, a renewal of its solemn meaning and form.

The need for recovery, of course, points to a history of loss. Whereas the ancient orders for the celebration of Viaticum created an atmosphere of expectation around the hour of death, sharing in Christ's passage through death to resurrection, by the end of the first millennium Christians had developed a far more pessimistic theology of death, fearing God's judgment. The post-Tridentine ritual, published in 1614 and practiced until 1971, moved the reception of Communion prior to the anointing of the sick, stripping it of Viaticum's primordial paschal character as preparation for ultimate resurrection with Christ and thereby reducing it to a private devotion. Thus did the anointing of the sick usurp Viaticum as the sacrament celebrated *in extremis*. Holy Communion was not part of extreme unction; rather, an order for Communion of the sick functioned prior to and separately from the rite for the dying: "The manner in which the rites were organized had affected the understanding of the doctrine involved."[5] The ancient practice of Viaticum, including the profession of baptismal faith, fell out of practice for all but bishops and certain vowed religious.[6]

Today, post–Vatican II ritual and legislation oblige all to receive Viaticum, encouraging them to respond in faith to the "nourishment" the Eucharist affords for the journey from this life through death.[7] Both the rite's General Introduction and the 1983 Code of Canon Law require

---

[4] Ibid., 223. Here Sicard is directly quoting the council (in translation). See also, Robert Cabié, *The Eucharist*, trans. Matthew O'Connell, The Church at Prayer, rev. ed., vol. 2 (Collegeville, MN: Liturgical Press, 1986), 236.

[5] Sicard, "Christian Death," 227. See also Richard Rutherford, *The Death of a Christian: The Order of Christian Funerals*, rev. ed. (Collegeville, MN: Liturgical Press, 1990), 67.

[6] See Cabié, *The Eucharist*, 237.

[7] PCS, no. 27. See also canon 921, along with Frederick R. McManus's pastoral insights, in *The Code of Canon Law: A Text and Commentary*, study edition, ed. James A. Coriden and others (Mahwah, NJ: Paulist Press, 1985), 656.

pastors to be vigilant that Viaticum be celebrated as soon as death is clearly imminent so that the dying person may be cognizant and thus benefit personally and pastorally.[8] The regular expected form of the rite, furthermore, is that it take place within the celebration of a Mass, although provision is made for an alternate version "outside Mass . . . when the full Eucharistic celebration cannot take place" due to a hospital setting or other restrictive circumstances.[9] In either case, however, family, friends, and others of the faithful should participate.[10] This solemn sacrament, therefore, is meant to nourish the dying person with the eucharistic experience of grace as divine saving love through human participation with others as members of the Body of Christ, as opposed to a mere fideistic assertion that some "special grace" has been dispensed.

The full import of the church's renewed theology of the Eucharist, "the center of the entire Christian life,"[11] is thus operative in this situation at life's furthest edge. While the Council of Trent did not lose complete sight of the medicinal dimension pervading the patristic heritage of the Eucharist, still, its fragmentation of the mystery into decrees on Real Presence, sacrifice, and Communion[12] did little to recover and advance the ecclesial, communal, and eschatological dimensions of the eucharistic theology of the early church. All those aspects the Second Vatican Council's Constitution on the Sacred Liturgy highlights within its initial nine articles, making them the basis for its assertion of the liturgy's centrality to Christian life and the need to restore the full, conscious, and active participation of all the faithful therein. Still, one might ask, all to what end? A brief patristic lesson in the Eucharist is in order, for which I turn to Theodore of Mopsuestia, whose mystagogical catecheses comprise a rich compendium of the sacramental theology achieved in the fourth century.

---

[8] See canon 922, *The Code of Canon Law*, 656; and PCS, nos. 27, 176.

[9] PCS, no. 164.

[10] See ibid., nos. 164, 178.

[11] International Committee on English in the Liturgy, *Holy Communion and Worship of the Eucharist Outside Mass* (Washington, DC: National Conference of Catholic Bishops, 1974), no. 1.

[12] See David N. Power, *The Sacrifice We Offer: The Tridentine Dogma and Its Reinterpretation* (New York: Crossroad, 1987); and Joseph M. Powers, *Eucharistic Theology* (New York: Seabury Press, 1967).

The pastors of the early church instructed their people to practice and understand baptism and the Eucharist as the sources of their immortality and immutability, the ultimate healed condition for humanity. Theodore instructs his neophytes that communion in Christ's Body and Blood "strengthens the communion we received by the new birth of baptism." He then expounds on Communion in these mysteries as a "privilege . . . granted to us all without exception; for we all need it equally, as we believe that it confers the possession of eternal life."[13] This Communion is a participation in the divine nature of Christ (2 Pet 1:4) brought about by the twofold descent (epiclesis) of the Holy Spirit upon both the bread and wine and the assembly, members of Christ's Body by water and the Spirit. The Spirit transforms the eucharistic gifts into "the body and blood of Christ, free from death, corruption, suffering and change, like our Lord's body after the resurrection." The epiclesis on the assembled makes them subjects of "communion in the blessed mysteries . . . united among ourselves and joined to Christ our Lord, whose body we believe ourselves to be." Such partaking in the divine nature at the Eucharist compels among those sharing in it "harmony, peace and good works, and . . . purity of heart."[14]

This communion, moreover, is with not only the living but also the dead. Thus, the eucharistic prayer proceeds from epiclesis to commemorations of the living (especially those in need of prayer) and the deceased: "For this sacrifice obtains protection for us in this world, and on those who have died in the faith it confers after death the fulfillment of that transcendent hope which is the desire of the goal of all the children of Christ's mystery."[15] Participation in the Eucharist, Theodore concludes, affects our dispositions and actions in this life, forgives sins, and inspires us to live in light of the coming kingdom. By nourishing us with sacramental food the Holy Spirit makes us "immortal and imperishable in hope" and "leads us to share in the blessings that are to come, when we are fed by the grace of the Holy Spirit

[13] Theodore of Mopsuestia, Baptismal Homily V, translated in Edward Yarnold, *The Awe-Inspiring Rites of Initiation: The Origins of the R.C.I.A.*, rev. ed. (Collegeville, MN: Liturgical Press, 1994), 240. In linking baptism and Eucharist, Theodore draws from 1 Cor and Col.

[14] Ibid., 234.

[15] Ibid., 235.

in simple fact, without sacraments and signs, and so become by nature completely free from death, corruption and change."[16]

Theodore's teaching—representative of the best of early eucharistic doctrine, East and West—helps us to appreciate how every celebration of the Eucharist sanctifies participants by orienting the ethical virtues of their daily lives and their imaginations toward the horizon of death not as threat but rather promising fulfillment. And so the *Pastoral Care of the Sick*, in an outright reversal of the Tridentine ritual,[17] introduces its fifth chapter: "The celebration of the eucharist as viaticum, food for the passage through death to eternal life, is the sacrament proper to the dying Christian. It is the completion and crown of the Christian life on this earth, signifying that the Christian follows the Lord to eternal glory and the banquet of the heavenly kingdom."[18] The renewed rite of Viaticum heals the dying faithful, as well as those gathered around them, by allaying their fears of the unknown and dread of abandonment with the familiar symbols, words, and gestures of the Eucharist, along with special ritual additions that make it a solemn rite of passage. The church's labeling Viaticum as a solemn Communion indicates the special meaning of the Eucharist at this and all Christian life passages (e.g., confirmation, marriage, funerals) and thus its warranting ceremonial elements specific to the singular experience of dying.[19]

Safe Passage, Promised Destiny: Healing Elements of the Renewed Rite
Celebration within Mass is the preferable form of Viaticum, for it provides the dying person with the fullest symbolic identification with Christ's own passage through death to life. Still, the modern circumstances of dying (hospital and institutional locations) and the limited availability of priests make celebration outside Mass common. The rite, however, clearly guards against machanistic dispensing of the sacrament outside Mass by emphasizing the same criteria for good celebration as those for Viaticum within Mass: "[T]his rite should be a communal celebration. Every effort should be made to involve the dying person, family, friends, and members of the local community

---

[16] Ibid., 241.
[17] See Sicard, "Christian Death," 228.
[18] PCS, no. 175.
[19] See Cabié, *The Eucharist*, 236–37; and Sicard, "Christian Death," 228–31.

in the planning and celebration."[20] The importance of regular, full, conscious participation in the Sunday Eucharist as formation in a ritual repertoire of unequal worth for the life crisis of death becomes abundantly clear: "Appropriate readings, prayers, and songs will help to foster the full participation of all. Because of this concern for participation, the minister should ensure that viaticum is celebrated while the dying person is still able to take part and respond."[21] Both the dying and those with them can take consolation from the habit-memories elicited by the regular content and rhythms of the Mass, and thereby the promise of immortality it bears, when celebrated under such momentous circumstances.[22] Celebration of Viaticum outside Mass likewise includes numerous familiar elements from the Mass (just as does the rite of Communion of the sick), including the penitential rite, proclamation of the Word, recitation of the Lord's Prayer, sharing of the sign of peace, and the distribution of Communion to all eligible participants. Not to be underestimated in all this is the personal experience of the individual communicant's union with the Lord in the reception of the sacramental species.

Viaticum, whether celebrated within or outside Mass, also contains a number of unique ritual elements that contribute to its solemnity and, thus, to its power to strengthen and console the dying and those around them as death approaches. In addition to proclaiming the content of the collects, the priest presiding at the Mass or the minister leading the celebration outside Mass has special words of consolation and encouragement to offer throughout, drawing on the content and form of the sacrament. The minister is to begin with a brief instruction highlighting the timing of Christ's gift of the Eucharist—the night before he died—in relation to the moment the person for whom Viaticum is being celebrated has now reached. Communion in the Body and Blood of the Lord, this sharing in his very life, is "food for the journey" through death and the pledge of resurrection in him.[23] The climax of the celebration, the rite of Viaticum proper, offers options for

[20] PCS, no. 186; see also no. 178.

[21] Ibid., no. 178.

[22] On habit-memory and *habitus*, see Paul Connerton, *How Societies Remember*, Themes in the Social Sciences (Cambridge: Cambridge University Press, 1989), 22–29, 34–36, 84, 88; and Catherine Bell, *Ritual Theory, Ritual Practice* (New York: Oxford University Press, 1992), 79–88.

[23] PCS, no. 199.

inviting the dying person to Communion that reinforce this message, including references to Christ as food for the journey and the Bread of Life. After a priest administers the sacred Body and Blood he immediately adds, "May the Lord Jesus Christ protect you and lead you to eternal life."[24] The rite's preference for Communion under both species (a further reason for the preferred celebration within Mass) joins the table of the Word to the table of the Eucharist by enacting the Lord's promise that whoever eats his flesh and drinks his blood will be raised to eternal life (John 6:54). Participation in both the bread and the cup also enhances the meal imagery, strengthening the dying person's anticipation of joining in the heavenly banquet of the kingdom as revealed in numerous gospel parables.[25]

Baptismal symbolism likewise, and fittingly, features in the celebration of Viaticum, whether within or outside Mass. The liturgy may begin with a rite of sprinkling with holy water, accompanied by brief words recalling baptism as a participation in Christ's death, which has redeemed us for resurrection. Adding even greater solemnity is the baptismal profession of faith, which takes place after the homily in the Liturgy of the Word. This is the interrogative form of the Creed administered to adults and older children at the sacramental climax of the RCIA or to parents and godparents at the baptism of infants. Post–Vatican II renewal of the liturgy has sought to foster the baptismal identity and awareness of the faithful by inserting the solemn profession at such key passages in the Christian life as confirmation. Given most dioceses' separation of that sacrament from First Communion, some include the baptismal profession in the latter celebration as well. The paramount occasion for all to profess baptismal faith, nonetheless, is the annual Easter celebration, either after the assembly has witnessed the rites of initiation during the Easter Vigil or after the homily during Easter Sunday Mass. Executed in this dialogical form (presiding celebrant asking assembly whether they believe in each part of the Creed), this manner of profession provides a symbolic enactment of the real meaning of faith, namely, the human embrace of divine revelation that has come in the Word and through the Spirit. When enacted during Viaticum the profession of baptismal faith empowers an acceptance

[24] Ibid., 193. Lay ministers of the sacrament, however, are not authorized to offer these words.

[25] See Sicard, "Christian Death," 229, where the author quotes at length the 1967 Vatican instruction *Eucharisticum Mysterium* on this point.

of death as an act of trust in the God of the Jesus who himself trusted his Father unto death and so attained, in the words of the Creed, "the resurrection of the body and life everlasting" for all.

The litany immediately following upon the baptismal profession in Viaticum makes explicit the identification of the dying person with Christ and the eschatological hope of resurrection in its opening invocation: "You loved us to the very end and gave yourself over to death in order to give us life . . . Lord, hear our prayer."[26] The ensuing invocations shift from the recollection of baptism to anticipation of the Eucharist about to be shared, first quoting John 6:54 and then continuing: "You invite us to join the heavenly banquet where pain and sorrow, sadness and separation will be no more. For our brother/sister, Lord, we pray: Lord, hear our prayer." The beauty of this litany lies in its articulating the dynamics—for some, perhaps even struggle—of faith at the time of death by acknowledging what may be painful in the moment, and in that articulation placing the dying person in the welcoming embrace of Jesus, the banquet's host.

A final source of healing consolation available in Viaticum is the apostolic pardon, which in the Mass may be added to the blessing in the concluding rites, while in the celebration outside Mass, with a priest ministering, it is an option at the end of the penitential rite.[27] The apostolic pardon is a plenary indulgence that became customary in the fourteenth century and that Pope Benedict XIV included in the ritual for the dying in the eighteenth. French liturgical theologian Damien Sicard sees no reason "to lay special emphasis on this apostolic blessing *in articulo mortis*," as the current rite merely includes its possibility without further elaboration. The rite for extraordinary circumstances (penance-anointing-Viaticum) likewise mentions it only as an option.[28] Pastoral awareness and sensitivity to the age, customary practices, and piety of the dying person, as well as perhaps those of the attending family, would seem to be essential to making a wise decision about including the apostolic blessing in each case.

The text of the blessing for use at the end of Mass reads: "Through the holy mysteries of our redemption, may almighty God release you from all punishments in this life and in the life to come. May he open

---

[26] PCS, no. 191. See also, no. 205.

[27] See ibid., nos. 195, 201.

[28] Sicard, "Christian Death," 235–36. See PCS, no. 243.

to you the gates of paradise and welcome you to everlasting joy."[29] Classroom and pastoral experience lead me to believe that few, indeed precipitously diminishing numbers, of Catholics understand or are even aware of what a plenary indulgence entails. Many of the older faithful, notably among the baby boom generation, have set the notion aside as incompatible with their images of how God acts in justice and mercy. There are, on the other hand, some elderly and others who have been raised with and encouraged by the tradition and thus should definitely receive the benefit of the apostolic pardon at the time of death. The issue points to the utterly pastoral nature of this sacrament and the other rites for the dying. I turn then to brief consideration of the personal, psychological, and interpersonal needs of both the dying and the family, friends, and health care professionals attending to them.

MEETING THE NEEDS FOR HEALING IN THE DYING PROCESS

Surveying the Contemporary Pastoral and Clinical Context

Viaticum and the other rites in the Pastoral Care of the Dying, like all the sacraments of the church, are for the salvation of people, which specifically in these situations entails healing (salving) the fear and other sorts of psychological and spiritual pain that can arise in the dying process. Thus should the rite normally function as part of a larger pastoral ministry executed with attention to the needs of dying people and those around them. The complexity of this medical and pastoral service has generated a growing body of resources in such disciplines as pastoral care and counseling and medical ethics. Megory Anderson, an expert in the theory and practice of pastoral care to the dying, has gotten to the heart of the matter: "One of the challenges of the pastoral caregiver is that death is not as neat and clear-cut as one might expect."[30] Not only are the pattern and duration of every death

[29] PCS, no. 195. Viaticum outside Mass includes a second optional text: "By the authority which the Apostolic See has given me, I grant you a full pardon and the remission of all your sins in the name of the Father, and of the Son, + and of the Holy Spirit." Ibid., no. 201.

[30] Megory Anderson, "Spiritual Journey with the Dying, Liminality, and the Nature of Hope," *Liturgy* 22, no. 3 (July–September 2007): 46. Anderson, founder and executive director of the Sacred Dying Foundation in San Francisco, has authored numerous books and articles, including *Attending the Dying* (New York: Morehouse Publishing, 2005).

unique, often defying expectations based on general experience, but the open-ended ambiguity intrinsic to each death is augmented by practices and attitudes fostered in the death-denying culture of late modernity. Here I avail myself of only a representative sample of the literature to garner insights for the sacramental-liturgical ministry of Viaticum and its attendant rituals.

Some cultural critics are skeptical of the claim that ours is a death-denying society, given the endless production of movies, television programs, books—science fiction, romance, fantasy, horror—involving the topic of life after death.[31] That line of argument, nonetheless, only betrays the denial entailed in most of the plots' depicting the dead as living, active agents continuing to interact (for good or ill) in this present world. For pastoral caregivers, theologians, and ethicists, however, the denial in question concerns the painful process of dying, the agony of utter separation, and the wrenching event of death itself: "Suffering and death are facts of life," argues ethicist Peter Clark, "yet most aspects of American culture foster denial of this ultimate reality. Many Americans do not think about death, talk about death, or even want to see it. We have become a 'death-denying' society. As a result, American culture has created a 'conspiracy of silence' when confronted with suffering and death."[32] Sadly, both health care professionals and friends and relatives often perform according to this cultural mindset as they interact with the mortally ill, a pattern of behavior that exacerbates the fear and isolation patients tend to feel in the wake of learning they are dying.

As we saw in chapter 2, many doctors and much of the general population tend to have unreasonable expectations for professional medicine's ability to achieve cures in individual cases. The result, Benedict Ashley and Kevin O'Rourke observe, is that doctors tend to disengage from a patient once death is inevitable, a general pattern these two veteran ethicists compassionately contextualize in a highly pressured medical industry whose frontline care providers experience high rates of alcoholism, divorce, and suicide.[33] Fear is the problematic emotion here, not only fear

[31] This issue will also figure in chap. 7, below.

[32] Peter A. Clark, "The Transition between Ending Medical Treatment and Beginning Palliative Care: The Need for a Ritual Response," *Worship* 72, no. 4 (July 1998): 346.

[33] See Benedict M. Ashley and Kevin D. O'Rourke, *Health Care Ethics: A Theological Analysis*, 4th ed. (Washington, DC: Georgetown University Press, 1997), 397–98.

in the immediate situation, such as failure in one's task (a blow to self-esteem) or personally failing the patient, but also fear ultimately of death itself. "Because health care professionals are human, they tend to retreat from any phenomenon that causes fear or wonder. Death is such a phenomenon; it involves awe, fear, and mystery. For this reason health care professionals, just like other people, are tempted to avoid facing the evil of death."[34] Family and friends largely participate in this "conspiracy of silence," often resorting to avoidance, Clark observes, "[i]nstead of being sensitive to the needs of the terminally ill, talking about their condition and the time they may have left."[35]

Complicating reason and emotions, Anderson reports, is the growing phenomenon of "managed death," whereby physicians and technicians deliberate over each new symptom of the dying person, availing themselves of the impressive advances in treatment for specific diseases or symptoms as they arise in the patient. The result is a significant drawing out of the dying process, often devolving into a lengthy or even indefinite period of the patient's hovering near death. Not only the medical culture but also, in the case of Christians, religious emphasis on God's ability to "save" (here interpreted as "cure") and the obligation to "fight the good fight" aid and abet the denial of death such that: "As most hospice workers will tell you, the realization that death is imminent comes too late for most."[36] If medical professionals remain bound to the pattern of facing death only at the latest possible moment, Anderson argues, then ministers and members of faith communities need to provide the care of guiding the dying and their loved ones through a more integrative (healing) dying process.

With fear of abandonment, grieving major losses in one's life, the pain of separation, loneliness, and depression being chief among the afflictions the dying suffer, the key to pastorally ministering to them, their loved ones, and the professional caregivers is compassionate presence. The pastoral minister needs not only to establish and sustain an empathetic relationship with the dying person but also to foster and support mutual commitments of presence between the dying person and his or her family members and friends. For Christians,

[34] Ibid., 397. Here and throughout their text Ashley and O'Rourke cite peer-reviewed and scientific studies to support their statements.

[35] Clark, "The Transition between Ending Medical Treatment and Beginning Palliative Care," 347.

[36] Anderson, "Spiritual Journey of the Dying," 44.

such dependence upon one another sacramentalizes "that same dependence on God's love as Christ showed on the Cross. This dependence upon God manifests itself in our human dependence upon others. . . . When a person is experiencing pain and suffering, that person needs the help and presence of others. . . . Being present to another must occur in both words and actions. It is not enough to tell terminally ill patients to have courage because Christ is suffering with them. We [family members, friends, ministers] must be Christ for them by our loving presence."[37] The sacramentality of the relationship is mutual for, as veteran hospital chaplain Gerald Calhoun concludes, "For pastoral ministers the greatest satisfaction in accompanying the dying is not so much their growing in understanding what serious illness and death are all about, but rather their encountering the loving face of Christ in the fragility of their brothers and sisters."[38] Given the weighty challenges the dying process, augmented by the instrumental environment of modern medicine, poses to such mutual acts of presence, the healing pastoral mission of the church's sacramental-liturgical ministry, a powerful combination of words and actions, would seem to be all the more evident.

Sacramental-Liturgical Ministry through the Stages of Dying

Calhoun and Anderson both distinguish between the pastoral needs in the initial stages of ministry to the gravely ill person and those in the final stage (days or hours) when death becomes imminent. The optimal situation, Calhoun argues, is for the pastoral minister to establish a strong relationship with the person and his or her family as early as possible, namely, as soon as illness is diagnosed as serious. As we saw in the previous chapter, such is the very criterion the church now identifies for administering the sacrament of anointing the sick.[39] Calhoun explains, "most of the crises in a person's faith occur over a period of time when emotional and physical health is stable enough to concentrate on their relationship with God. . . . Often people encountering terminal illness experience a battle with God concerning the reason

[37] Clark, "The Transition between Ending Medical Treatment and Beginning Palliative Care," 349–50.
[38] Gerald J. Calhoun, "Ministry at the Time of Death," in *The New Dictionary of Sacramental Worship*, ed. Peter Fink (Collegeville, MN: Liturgical Press, 1990), 324.
[39] See PCS, nos. 8 and 97.

for their sickness and God's role in it. They also review their lives in an attempt to find meaning and purpose."[40] Again, as we saw in the previous chapter, these are the very types of issues the sacrament of anointing intends to heal as part of a comprehensive pastoral ministry to the seriously ill person and his or her family and loved ones. Indeed, Calhoun discusses how the sacraments of penance and anointing, as well as ongoing services of Holy Communion, are all apposite to this period in the person's seriously declining condition, even for those who have not been particularly active participants in the sacraments in their lives.

From her own extensive experience of ministry with the dying, Anderson articulates a cautionary observation about the reformed sacrament of anointing. She argues that the replacement of extreme unction with a sacrament for healing the sick has often caused the rite of anointing to aid and abet "the medical model of getting locked into an either/or situation. Either one heals or one dies."[41] Contributing to the problem, she says, is the way many churches regularly hold communal rites of anointing, offering the sacrament to anybody presenting oneself for it; such practices dilute the sacrament's symbolic and multivalent force of healing. Anderson's critique thereby lends support to the church's prohibition of indiscriminate administration of the sacrament.[42] When properly practiced, however, anointing ritualizes what Anderson calls for in these initial stages of dying, namely, fostering a sense of hope for recovery even as prayer for healing must be open to the possibility of death. This is a healthier both/and approach, serving the reality that the person is caught between dealing with serious illness (with its possibility of death) and certain death. "We must hold in our hands both realities: that all of us want to be made whole and well again; and that all of us must die, and to die we must be ready. Holding both of those realities begs for a way to be present in that liminal stage."[43] For these very reasons, I would argue, the wisdom in the church's prescription that pastors educate their people not to delay requesting the sacrament but rather call for anointing as soon as illness is evidently serious becomes powerfully clear. Pastorally informed celebration of the sacrament, as well as ongoing, pastorally sensitive

[40] Calhoun, "Ministry at the Time of Death," 320.
[41] Anderson, "Spiritual Journey of the Dying," 43.
[42] See PCS, no. 108, also no. 99.
[43] Anderson, "Spiritual Journey of the Dying," 46.

visits to the seriously sick and Communion of the sick, are vital treasures to be drawn from the reformed tradition in contemporary service to people struggling between serious illness, with the innate hope for recovery, and the probability of death.

When the seriously ill person's body begins to shut down he or she enters into what is clinically called "active dying," the penultimate stage to death itself. Anderson describes this period, which may last anywhere from hours to days, as a highly fluid space "where the soul wanders in and out of the body, with one part in the here and now, and the other part very clearly moving towards the afterlife. The dying often have visions, or conversations with people who are not tangibly present in the room."[44] These characteristics of this final period give evidence for the church's wisdom in prescribing Viaticum's celebration as soon as death becomes imminent so that the dying person can be as aware as possible of the words and symbolic gestures and thus benefit cognitively, spiritually, and corporeally from the sacrament.[45] We can only imagine, indeed trust, the extent to which elements of the Viaticum liturgy—eliciting both memories through baptismal and eucharistic symbolism and expectation of the heavenly banquet—may play a role in the imagination and thoughts of the altering state of mind for the dying person as he or she deteriorates. Should the dying process continue for some time, the provision of Viaticum "on successive days, frequently if not daily . . . simplified according to the condition of the one who is dying," offers further healing support to not only the dying person but also family, friends, and care providers.

In the less-than-ideal circumstances when serious illness is acknowledged only when active dying is already underway, the church's Continuous Rite of Penance, Anointing, and Viaticum (the first in the chapter of "Rites for Exceptional Circumstances"[46]) likewise offers healing not only to the dying person but also the attending family and friends. Pastoral care experts consistently observe the desire of Catholics of all ages that the dying person be sacramentally anointed.[47] The

---

[44] Ibid., 42–43.

[45] See above, n. 8.

[46] PCS, nos. 232–33.

[47] Anderson, "Spiritual Journey of the Dying," 42. Recall how individuals in their twenties and forties clung to the notion of extreme unction in my pastoral scenario in chap. 1, above. See p. 22.

problem may present itself when family members only come on the scene (usually in the hospital) without having witnessed earlier stages of pastoral-sacramental care and thus need to witness for themselves the comforting administration of anointing. For the pastoral minister in such cases to hold to explaining to loved ones that anointing is not the proper sacrament of the dying or that it has already been administered earlier would seem misguided by the assumption that people under such circumstances are responding to arguments rather than images. In such cases, if a priest is available, anointing would be not only pastorally appropriate but also justifiable by the rite's own instruction that anointing be repeated whenever a person's condition significantly worsens. The condition is not just a matter of the dying individual but also the entire body of people assembled around him or her. In cases where some or all of them are distraught over not having shared in the celebration of anointing with their loved one, the grave turn to active dying would seem to meet the criterion for repeating the sacrament.[48] In principle this surely is not ideal, but as Anderson cautioned above, no ideal situation of dying exists. Good total care is the issue.

Indeed, once active dying is underway the pastoral minister needs to attend more to the family and close friends, who often become more needy of assurance as their loved one becomes increasingly, even profoundly silent. Calhoun describes how even family members who have for a long time anticipated their loved one's death become overwhelmed with anxiety and confusion in the moment. "As the end draws near, a pastoral companion shows much compassion in gently urging the relatives to let their loved one die, to allow themselves and the dying person to let go." Encouraging them in such caring gestures as wetting parched lips or wiping a sweaty forehead or signing with the cross, along with leading them in simple prayers are, Calhoun argues, what the pastoral minister needs to provide.[49] Fittingly, chapter 6 of the *Pastoral Care of the Sick*, "Commendation of the Dying," provides

[48] The rite is clear on the proper order of the sacraments in such exceptional circumstances, which remains penance-anointing-Viaticum. That Viaticum is the sacrament of the dying is reinforced in the Introduction to the Continuous Rite, which prescribes for extreme emergencies shortening or even omitting anointing so as to administer Viaticum as quickly as possible, so that the dying person "may be strengthened by the body of Christ, the pledge of the resurrection." PCS, no. 237.

[49] Calhoun, "Ministry at the Time of Death," 322.

a variety of "prayers, litanies, aspirations, psalms, and readings," as well as encouragement to use any others that might prove beneficial: "These texts are intended to help the dying person, if still conscious, to face the natural human anxiety about death by imitating Christ in his patient suffering and dying. The Christian will be helped to surmount his or her fear in the hope of heavenly life and resurrection through the power of Christ, who destroyed the power of death by his own dying. Even if the dying person is not conscious, those who are present will draw consolation from these prayers and come to a better understanding of the paschal character of Christian death."[50] The chapter proceeds by providing numerous single-verse passages from Scripture, which might be repeated softly several times, fuller readings from certain biblical chapters, including such psalms as 23, 25, 91, and 121, the litany of saints, and other litanies or customary prayers.[51]

For the moment when death approaches, section 220 of the rite includes a half-dozen versions of the Prayer of Commendation, some of which are litanies, all of which enlist images of Christ as consoler and deliverer (e.g., shepherd), invocation of the angels and saints and especially Mary, including such prayers as "Hail, holy Queen, Mother of Mercy" (the *Salve Regina*). Once death has occurred, the chapter's last two sections provide fitting short prayers for not only the deceased but also the family and friends. At this point enters the ancient consoling prayer enlisting the saints of God coming to the deceased's aid, angels delivering him or her to Abraham's side, and God's bestowing eternal rest in perpetual light. Articulating these images at this point lays a foundation for hearing them again during the stages of the Order of Christian Funerals—comforting repetition promising further healing support for the loved ones. True to most sound tradition,[52] the rite's prayer after death, as well as chapter seven's "prayer for use by a minister who has been called to attend a person who is already dead,"[53] confidently petition forgiveness for the deceased's sins in light of God's boundless mercy. Confidence in God's love and mercy

---

[50] PCS, nos. 214 and 215.

[51] See ibid., nos. 217–19.

[52] See below, chap. 7, p. 232.

[53] PCS, no. 223, which adds: "A priest is not to administer the sacraments of penance or anointing. Instead, he should pray for the dead person using these or similar prayers." The priest should be sensitive to people's potential confusion, explaining that "sacraments are celebrated for the living, not for the

is reinforced when all join in praying the Our Father. The prayers may conclude with the minister signing the deceased's forehead with the cross, and in the case of an ordained minister, sprinkling the body with holy water. When performed competently and sensitively, allowing for silence and not fleeing in the face of tears, pastoral ministry of these rites can provide much solace and strength to all involved.

LIVING TRADITION:
A REPERTOIRE READY TO SERVE THE DYING

The effectiveness of the rites of the Pastoral Care of the Dying, of course, depends in no small part on people's experiential knowledge of (or at least familiarity with) the prayers, scriptural passages, litanies, gestures, symbols, and images its rites draw from the central liturgies and key seasons of the church year. To the extent these renewed practices of tradition are registered in the minds and inscribed on the bodies of the faithful they can provide a firm foundation when spirits are shaken and hearts broken in the crises of death. Herein lies the genuinely human and divinely redeeming value of the church's insistence on weekly participation in the Eucharist, annual renewal of baptismal promises and Communion at Easter (as well as penance, as necessary, in preparation thereof), communal (not private) celebrations of infant baptism, to mention just a few primary sacramental-liturgical practices of the Catholic faith. In late modernity, however, the resistance to the often unexciting practice of traditions is widespread, raising such dismissive plaints among Catholics as: "Why do I have to go to Mass on Sunday? It's not very well done, and I don't get anything out of it." Or, "Who needs to learn these prayers or go join in a church service when there are far more entertaining or interesting things to watch, do, or listen to online, over networks, and by downloads?" As Don Saliers has long argued, the problem for traditional practice in this "culture of hype" lies in a fundamental misrecognition of immediate feelings, instead of sustained formation in deep emotions, as the real substance of religious practice.[54]

---

dead, and that the dead are effectively helped by prayers of the living." Ibid., no. 166.

[54] See Don E. Saliers, *Worship as Theology: Foretaste of Glory Divine* (Nashville: Abingdon Press, 1994), 37–38, 146–48; and "Symbol in Liturgy, Liturgy as Symbol: The Domestication of Liturgical Experience," in *The Awakening Church: Twenty-five Years of Liturgical Renewal*, ed. Lawrence Madden, 71–78 (Collegeville, MN: Liturgical Press, 1992).

I conclude here with just a few examples of elements of the rites whose reformed and renewed practice promise resources at the time of death.

Turning first to the Mass: The post–Vatican II renewal of offering the cup to all who approach Holy Communion is no mere aesthetic nicety or lay power grab but rather a symbolic action that deepens not only the communal dimension of sharing in Christ's sacramental presence in a given celebration but also a formation for healing practice at the hour of death. The rite's preferred way to celebrate Viaticum is through offering both bread and cup to the dying person as a fuller symbolic realization of the person's oneness with Christ and foretaste of the heavenly banquet. But how can the symbol give rise to such healing thoughts in the dying person or family and friends if they have no comfortable familiarity with receiving under both species? The need for such formation in liturgically practiced faith becomes all the more urgent when the dying person is not able to consume solid food and thus can receive only from the cup, a scenario the rite carefully anticipates and pastorally accommodates.[55]

The regularly repeated language of the liturgy, of course, is another deeply formative symbol. Unfortunately, the priest-celebrant's invitation to Communion in the English text of the Mass of Paul VI is a weak echo of the eschatologically powerful biblical imagery in the original Latin. Rather than, "This is the Lamb of God who takes away the sins of the world. Happy are those who are called to his supper," a more accurate and pastorally formative translation would be, "Behold the Lamb of God, behold him who takes away the sins of the world. Happy are those called to the wedding feast of the Lamb." This is not a matter of liturgical fussiness but rather greater habitual, deeply owned knowledge of the biblical imagery[56] that can enhance the experience of hearing the minister's offer of Communion in the rite of Viaticum. Likewise, the people's response to the invitation in the English-language Missal, "Lord, I am not worthy to receive you, but only say the word and I shall be healed," falls short of a more accurate translation of the Latin, which would be, "Lord, I am not worthy that you should enter under my roof, but only say the word and my soul

---

[55] See PCS, nos. 175 and 181. Indeed, the rubrics for Communion in the Roman Missal encourage giving both species as an enhancement of the meal dimension and heavenly banquet imagery in the action.

[56] See John 1:29 and Rev 19:9.

will be healed."[57] While the former translation certainly forms the faithful in a habitually ingrained articulation of faith in the Eucharist as healing, the literal translation evokes the beautiful story of Jesus' encounter with the Roman centurion upon whose great faith Jesus remarked to those gathered round him. The evocation of that story each time reveals the biblical character of sacramental healing (faith in Christ, and by an "outsider," no less), a storeroom of treasure from which the faithful may draw as death approaches. To argue that such biblical allusions are beyond the common knowledge of the laity (as was the case at the time the English translation of the Missal was debated) only serves my point.

The invaluable, essential relationship of the proclaimed word to the celebrated sacraments, as we saw above in chapter 4, becomes clearly evident when one views the church's central liturgical acts, Eucharist and baptism, against the horizon of pastoral care to the dying. The wealth of the Lectionary cycle begs to be exploited by preachers who can better realize the fundamental characteristic of a genuine homily, namely, its relating integrally to the sacrament being celebrated, by occasionally yet regularly noting the healing content pervading the gospels and other Scriptures. Relating biblical narrative content to elements of the rites is an exercise experience has taught me people in the pews not only appreciate but enjoy. The key to bringing those connections to life, of course, is the use of narratives from the present context. When preachers share present-life stories in relation to biblical and sacramental revelation, homilies truly sing. The possibility, nonetheless, depends utterly on the close and constant contact of pastoral ministers with the people whom they have been charged to serve, a need certainly requiring greater efforts on the part of clergy but also laity as well. Another approach to homiletic preaching is an occasional relating of the content of the collects and other prayers of the Mass to their biblical sources so as to point out implications of our liturgical worship for the quotidian experiences and crisis moments of life—and death.

Along with the constant celebration of the paschal mystery, the other key to the renewed liturgy of the church is its keeping of time. Here I only note again the importance of the annual profession of baptismal faith at Easter, whether witnessed and repeated as neophytes approach the font at the Vigil or renewed in response to proclaimed

[57] See Matt 8:8//Luke 7:6.

word at Masses throughout the day. The personal connections dying individuals and those accompanying them might make through the habit-memory of the profession as well as memories of particular Easter celebrations, are as limitless as the unique experiences of each person involved. The church's occasional rites marking the seasons of life likewise offer beautiful occasions for ministers to help people make connections across the life cycle. The poured waters of infant baptism can occasion teaching about the use of holy water throughout Christian life and death. The proclamation of the litany of saints, part of both infant and adult baptism, is a practice that people consistently describe as the most touching to them not only at the Easter Vigil but also at priestly ordinations. Forming parishioners in the chanting of the litany likewise promises much consoling strength for the dying and their family and friends in the celebration of Viaticum. The Pastoral Care of the Dying, as noted in the previous section of this chapter, encourages the use of any number of other customary prayers and chants by the faithful. Thus does forming and encouraging one another in the daily praying of the Our Father, Hail Mary, Jesus Prayer, biblical canticles, as well as reciting blessings and signing of oneself and others with the cross in a variety of situations[58] shape lives of faith with something to offer the moment of death.

For all our advanced medical technology, we late-modern Christians are the nonetheless poorer at the time of death if we lack knowledge of the content and practices of faith that can bring meaning, and thus healing, once cures are no longer feasible and only palliative care is possible. Here is the poverty of a death-denying culture, one that does not want to practice traditions because they would keep the reality of death (*memoria mortis*) on the horizon. There is also the poverty of a church squandering the treasures the liturgical movement, post–Vatican II rites, and decades of theological-pastoral articles and books have made available. The clergy have responsibility for (because of so much control over) this pastoral material, and in this as in all matters, clericalism can and does do its harm. The laity, however, must also find the courage of their convictions in lamenting a lack of meaningful rituals for life passages today by taking up liturgical and other prayer

[58] See the wealth of prayers and symbolic gestures in *Catholic Household Blessings and Prayers* (Washington, DC: United States Catholic Conference, 1988); and International Commission on English in the Liturgy, *Book of Blessings* (Collegeville, MN: Liturgical Press, 1989).

practices of the faith to form habituated bodies of worship. The Gospel brings salvation to people, in whatever state of life, who acknowledge their profound need for God, embracing the challenging but life-generating truth that the God of Jesus is only known through humanly shared practices of word, sacrament, and ethics. Ongoing liturgical praxis forms people in the paschal mystery of death and life or, in the words of the beautiful Orthodox chant, in the joyous faith that Christ has trampled down death by death.[59]

---

[59] See Alexander Schmemann, *For the Life of the World: Sacraments and Ortho-doxy*, rev. ed. (Crestwood, NY: St Vladimir's Seminary Press, 1997), 95–106.

Chapter 7

The Order of Christian Funerals:
Healing through Hope in Bodily Resurrection

INTRODUCTION: FAITH'S ASSENT TO THE BODY

Christianity's healing response to death's bitter sting is faith in the bodily resurrection of Jesus. When we speak of human death as well as the resurrection of the body we are dealing with mystery, indeed two distinct, powerful, yet related mysteries in Christian life. For believers there is both the phenomenon common to all people, the definitive limit-situation that is death, and the call to shape one's entire vision for life around the belief that God raised the executed Jesus bodily from the dead, that is, faith in the paschal mystery: "In the face of death, the Church confidently proclaims that God has created each person for eternal life and that Jesus, the Son of God, by his death and resurrection, has broken the chains of sin and death that bound humanity. Christ 'achieved his task of redeeming humanity and giving perfect glory to God principally by the paschal mystery of his blessed passion, resurrection from the dead, and glorious ascension.'"[1] The confidence in God's redemptive will for all humanity proclaimed in the General Introduction of the current *Order of Christian Funerals* is a recovery of the evangelical faith native to the early centuries of Christianity yet often muted in the subsequent history of Western Christendom and beyond.[2] It is, as one might suspect, a complicated history, but my basic point here is that the content of biblical faith, divine revelation, comes only as an invitation within the social-cultural milieus of

<hr/>

[1] International Committee on English in the Liturgy, Inc., *Order of Christian Funerals*, 1989, no. 1. Hereafter, OCF. This passage quotes from Vatican Council II, Constitution on the Sacred Liturgy, *Sacrosanctum Concilium*, no. 5.

[2] For a fine survey of the history, see Richard Rutherford, with Tony Barr, *The Death of a Christian: The Order of Christian Funerals*, rev. ed. (Collegeville, MN: Liturgical Press, 1990), 3–112, especially 28, 59–60, and 86.

particular times and places.[3] The church's tradition has never healed the human fracture of death through a kind of textual positivism, as if one could assert propositions alone, everybody would comprehendingly assent, and the disconcerting challenges of death—variably sudden, protracted, tragic, violent, peaceful, yet always provoking loss, grief, and the like—would be simply settled. On the contrary, people wrestle with images, customs, traditions, and so forth, pulling them together at a given time to bring some meaning, some consolation, some hope, to the crisis of death.

Richard Rutherford sheds light on the promise and challenge the church always faces in service to the dead and bereaved: "The fact of death is the greatest human threat to faith in the paschal mystery. There is nothing in death that even hints at the viability of such a paschal faith."[4] In order to understand Christians' faith in the resurrection of the body, therefore, attention to theoretical arguments alone cannot prove an adequate theology. At the outset of her study of the doctrine of resurrection and its praxis from early through medieval Christianity, Carolyn Walker Bynum makes the following observation: "I assume that the technical arguments of philosophical and theological treatises frequently betray the problems they *cannot* solve— social and psychological as well as intellectual problems—in the limiting cases, examples, and metaphors they use and in the ways they distort or misread conventional tropes and images."[5] Philosophical argument and theological treatise cannot exhaust or even always recognize what Christians in a given time and place mean by resurrection of the body because the human body itself, as we learn from Louis-Marie Chauvet, is not reducible to simple description, concise explanation, ready comprehension. Chauvet's body theory, therefore, is crucial for the work of this chapter, providing a way to analyze the unruly reality of human subjects, communities, and institutions practicing the sacramental life of faith in time and space. A rehearsal of that theory is necessary at the outset, while elaboration on its rudiments will recur throughout this chapter's attempt to articulate and promote

[3] See Louis-Marie Chauvet, *The Sacraments: The Word of God at the Mercy of the Body* (Collegeville, MN: Liturgical Press, 2001), 3–9.

[4] Rutherford, *The Death of a Christian*, 122.

[5] Carolyn Walker Bynum, *The Resurrection of the Body in Western Christianity 200–1336* (New York: Columbia University Press, 1995), xvi (emphasis in original); see also 7.

the pastoral service of healing to suffering humanity available in the Order of Christian Funerals.

Chauvet, building on the work of Martin Heidegger, articulates the complex phenomenon of the human person as an "I-body," a subject whose corporality is a "triple body" comprised of culture, tradition, and nature.[6] Avoiding rhetoric of embodiment that might surreptitiously isolate spirit from body, making the latter a mere vehicle of the former, Chauvet wisely speaks of the person-body to indicate that each of us does not have a body but rather is a body, a body at once physical, sociocultural, and traditional. The body is *natural* in its physicality, sharing in the rhythms and forces of the cosmos. While there is a "givenness" to this participation in the physical universe, the way in which people develop meaning in relation to the cosmos comes nevertheless through the mediation of culture and tradition. Each human subject as body constructs meaning for one's life, uniquely according to one's own desires, through a myriad of socially shared symbols. Thus the body is the fundamental functioning symbol, the "arch-symbol," of human experience.[7] The *cultural* dimension of bodily subjectivity entails the customs, values, and symbols practiced by members of a social body, constantly changing, whether gradually or abruptly, due to various historical forces. In contrast, the *traditional* dimension of human corporality gives authority to seemingly change-less[8] symbols, narratives, rituals, and creedal beliefs connecting people with a more or less mythic past and the transcendent dimension of reality. In actual lived practice, the three bodily dimensions of human existence—natural, cultural, traditional—do not function, of course, independently but rather mutually influence each other, with one or the other often taking priority in certain circumstances.

---

[6] Louis-Marie Chauvet, *Symbol and Sacrament: A Sacramental Reinterpretation of Christian Existence*, trans. Patrick Madigan and Madeleine Beaumont (Collegeville, MN: Liturgical Press, 1995), 146–52.

[7] Ibid., 151.

[8] This perception of tradition as seemingly changeless by its practitioners (what anthropologists call the emic perspective) belies the fact that traditions are always subtly changing. Catherine Bell argues that the effectiveness of traditions depends on their ability to engage "collective images of the past," drawing on the authority of precedent and a perception of consensus that nonetheless allows for a "degree of latent conflict" in forms of "mere compliance, quiet evasion, or idiosyncratic rejection" (*Ritual Theory, Ritual Practice* [New York: Oxford University Press, 1992], 122–23).

Human experience is always a complex affair but never more poignantly than in times of life crises, among which death is particularly powerful. The traditional dimension for the Christian person-body's experiences of death is the paschal mystery. The narratives and symbols of Christ's death and resurrection, as well as their ritual enactment, however, are not passed on and appropriated by generations of believers independently of other cultural, natural, and traditional aspects of their lives. Thus how Christians ritualize healing for death is specific to time and place. The question becomes whether and how the saving (healing) force of the Gospel comes to life among a particular social and traditional body's real-symbolic engagement with death.

The reform of funeral liturgy that Vatican II mandated does seek to make the Gospel's healing grace effective in the lives of contemporary believers. With Rutherford I am convinced of the textual beauty, theological soundness, and pastoral effectiveness of the revised *Order of Christian Funerals.*[9] Still, like all ritual texts, this liturgical order can only function in a context. The text in motion, in the bodies of the participants, is never simply the body of the text in print. Context and text continuously play off one another as participants enact a rite's varied and numerous elements.[10] In order to argue for the distinctive power of the Order of Christian Funerals at the turn of the twenty-first century, I turn once again to narrative, a view of the ritual text in performed motion. A description and analysis of one enactment of the rite can disclose both the problems and promise of this rite's capacity to bring the healing of the crucified and risen Christ to situations of loss and bereavement.

DESCRIPTION AND ANALYSIS OF A CONTEMPORARY AMERICAN CATHOLIC FUNERAL

Description: Parallel Worlds of Symbolism

A few years ago I received a phone call from a professional colleague informing me that a mutual friend, a woman in her late

---

[9] Those seeking sound knowledge of the history, theory, and current form of the reformed *ordo* should study Rutherford's *The Death of a Christian* in its entirety.

[10] See Lawrence A. Hoffman, *Beyond the Text: A Holistic Approach to Liturgy* (Bloomington: Indiana University Press, 1987); and Kevin W. Irwin, *Context and Text: Method in Liturgical Theology* (Collegeville, MN: Liturgical Press, 1994).

twenties whom I will call Casey,[11] had died shortly after major surgery. This was a sudden, tragic death, traumatic not only for her family and many friends but also for the large youth population whom Casey had passionately and effectively served as a counselor in one of the most troubled lower-income neighborhoods of an old northeastern city. After a few minutes of consoling one another over the phone, this colleague Jackie and I got down to the business of initial plans for the funeral. Casey's family had asked that I prepare and preside over the funeral rites. At the time I was at some distance in another state, and the family of the deceased resided in yet another, so to Jackie fell the onus of coordinating the various concerned parties as well as much of the local arrangements. Several social bodies would be involved, including Casey's family, the youth and adults of the neighborhood in which she had worked, the staff of the local Catholic parish, and myself and others of her wider circle of friends and colleagues. What gradually became clear to me was that the worldviews, customs, imaginations, and thus symbolic fields[12] of these various groups were approaching the reality of Casey's death in significantly different ways, ways so different as to comprise parallel worlds of meaning at times only tangentially touching upon one another.

Casey's parents, devout practicing Catholics, entrusted me entirely with planning the rites. The first indication that my preparations would not be on the same page, so to speak, with others principally involved came when Jackie informed me a day later that she and a couple local parishioners had completed the program (her term) for the funeral, which would take place several days later. I asked how this could be the case since we had shared no conversation about the selection of biblical readings, responsorial psalm, hymns, and so forth, but I could instantly tell my question made no sense to Jackie. I asked her what the program entailed, and she said a photo of the deceased emblazoned with her name, dates, and the title "A Celebration of Life," the words to opening and closing hymns, the titles of two performance pieces the cantor would do at offertory and Communion,

[11] Out of respect for all parties, I have changed the names of the characters and limited some details in this story.

[12] Victor Turner contributed greatly to the development of the concepts of symbolic field and ritual drama in the young disciplines of ritual studies and performance theory. See, for example, his *The Anthropology of Performance* (New York: PAJ Publications, 1987), 21–32.

the names of the ministers and various volunteers, and a short written tribute to Casey. I had hoped to provide the assembly with an order of service that would aid their full, conscious, and active participation in the liturgy,[13] whereas what Jackie was calling a program seemed more like a commemorative pamphlet, a souvenir. I decided, nonetheless, to let that go. I could appreciate both the sincere, significant effort Jackie had already made and the evidently customary character of this program in the local community. I did, however, wonder about how the music had been selected. Jackie explained that the parish organist and cantor always used the same four selections. Jackie gave me the names and phone numbers of the associate pastor and music director (organist). While the latter never returned my calls, the young curate offered to meet me prior to the wake so as to show me around the church on the eve of the funeral Mass, which we eventually did.

The understanding (theology) operative in my mind as I prepared for Casey's funeral, coordinating and negotiating with the key players in this ritual drama, was what appears concisely in the *General Introduction to the Order of Christian Funerals*: "At the death of a Christian, whose life of faith was begun in the waters of baptism and strengthened at the Eucharistic table, the Church intercedes on behalf of the deceased because of its confident belief that death is not the end nor does it break the bonds forged in life. The Church also ministers to the sorrowing and consoles them in the funeral rites with the comforting word of God and the sacrament of the eucharist."[14] Pastoral-liturgical ministry at death, according to the church's biblically informed tradition, is a matter of at once offering a strong, loving message of confident hope and consolation while also not denying the reality that these are indeed needed. For indeed, the death of a loved one is the cause of sorrow, loss, and pain.

Study and pastoral practice have taught me that the Order of Christian Funerals offers consolation and hope precisely in its three-stepped structure—the vigil for the deceased, the funeral liturgy, and the rite of committal[15]—through a variety of prayer forms and texts, proclamations of the word, and sacramental symbols and gestures, especially in the funeral liturgy.[16] The funeral Mass is framed by unique introductory and concluding rites situating the deceased in the equipoise

---

[13] See OCF, no. 11.
[14] Ibid., no. 4.
[15] See ibid., no. 11.
[16] See ibid., nos. 5, 6.

between death's defeat at baptism and the final resurrection of the just in Christ (see 1 Cor 15), our joining as one in the communion of saints at the heavenly banquet. Such communion is at the heart of every eucharistic celebration. Thus between the special introductory rites and final commendation the funeral liturgy provides the familiar, comfortable rhythm of the table of the word and the table of the Eucharist, albeit with a heightened awareness of the eschatological dimension. That dimension is a key contribution the ecclesial practice of faith brings to this time of trial and sorrow, not by exclusively looking back (eulogizing) but by looking forward on the basis of remembering what God has done in the past in Christ and in the life of the believer, trusting that God will bring to fulfillment what God has begun. In this way the funeral liturgy is meant to function not merely as a vehicle for expressing what we (think we) already know about death, both generally and in this particular case. It brings rather an original word to the situation, what we could not know otherwise than by giving ourselves over to the ritual practice of Scripture and tradition.

Research and experience had also taught me that many Americans do have a tendency in some way to deny the reality of death. This is a controversial claim, both in terms of what such denial entails and whether it is prevalent in American culture (a point to which I will return further below). The shock of a sudden death, especially of a rather young person, might well trigger various forms of denial among family, friends, and associates, placing in question for them not only the fate of the deceased person but also the meaning of life in general, especially in its finitude. The Order of Christian Funerals provides means for both acknowledging loss and affirming continued union (communion) with the deceased. Prayers of intercession make real the memory of the deceased person, the good things but also difficulties experienced in life, as well as give the assembled a way to doing something for that person even now by joining their hearts and voices to those of the communion of saints.[17] Healing and consolation come then not by labored ruminations or didactic explanations but rather through symbolically rich words and imagery proclaiming "God's merciful love," pleading "for the forgiveness of their sins," recalling "God's mercy and judgment," and meeting "the human need to turn always to God in times of crisis."[18] The pastoral minister's

---

[17] See ibid., no. 6.
[18] Ibid., nos. 6, 7.

task is to prepare and lead the funeral so as to enable the people to connect their memories, hopes, fears, and grief with the Gospel message of salvation proclaimed and enacted in the rites, meeting their psychological and spiritual needs "to express grief and their sense of loss, to accept the reality of death, and to comfort one another."[19] Experience has consistently shown me that the Order of Christian Funerals is able to do this when provided by strong, loving, and wise ministerial leadership[20] attentive to the particular circumstances but also unwaveringly convinced of the way, truth, and life (John 14:6) just waiting to come as healing strength through the specific content of the rites.

Such was the mindset with which I approached the preparation and celebration of Casey's funeral. My earlier description of the "disconnect" between Jackie and me over the printed program, as well as the nonresponsiveness of the music director, indicated how I had started to become aware that, not surprisingly, other ideologies of funerals were operative in the planning and execution of the rites for Casey. This became abundantly clear in the case of the associate pastor, a recently ordained priest in his twenties, with whom I met at the parish church on the eve of the funeral Mass.

The church, a neo-Gothic structure typical of northeastern Catholic parishes around the turn of the twentieth century, was also typical in the post–Vatican II renovations it had undergone: removed altar rail, altar facing the people positioned in the sanctuary in front of the old high altar, defunct organ and choir loft in rear, electric organ positioned in one of the shallow transepts toward the front of the church, carpeting throughout the nave and sanctuary, pews (seating about four hundred) running from the very back of the church tightly up to the front, with one row removed about midway back (to allow for extra Communion stations). The baptistery, situated in one of the former side altars flanking the sanctuary, was replete with flowers, as it was still early in the Easter season.

As we began our conversation in the front of the church, my initial question for the associate pastor concerned how they normally positioned the coffin and paschal candle for their funeral liturgies. He said the funeral directors would take care of that, placing it there in the front,

[19] Ibid., no. 16.
[20] See Robert Hovda, *Strong, Loving, and Wise: Presiding in Worship*, 5th ed. (Collegeville, MN: Liturgical Press, 1983).

at the head of the main aisle. I wanted something more specific, needed to picture where the paschal candle would be positioned. He replied that placing the candle near the coffin was not their custom, and that in any event, the candle was currently part of the baptismal font display of Easter flowers and shouldn't be moved. Finding this priority of decoration over (pastoral) liturgical function disconcerting, I promised to be very careful about removing and replacing the candle the next day, but I simply could not imagine it not being by Casey's body.

The paschal candle, which within just the past few days had figured so powerfully in the Easter Vigil as the salutary symbol of the risen Christ, was not, in my estimation, expendable. Standing front and center with Casey's coffin,[21] it would offer those who regularly participate in the church's rites the symbolic opportunity to make connections between Casey, her body now contained in the coffin, and the rituals of baptism and Easter, two of the most joyful, encouraging, rejuvenating occasions in church life. Even for those unfamiliar with the Christian liturgical content of the symbolism, the candle's flame could serve as a symbol of life and promise, its flickering light eliciting a sense of vitality and warmth over against the oppression of the cold stillness of death.[22] To the young priest I explained that I always find the paschal candle a welcoming, beckoning light for the ministers and the family of the deceased as they bring the body from the church entrance up the nave to its position before the sanctuary. He crisply replied, "We don't do that here. The funeral directors have the coffin placed in front before the start of the Mass." I could barely believe what I was hearing from this clearly conservative cleric. How then did their funerals normally begin? "With the opening hymn," he answered, "like any Mass." Regretting having to sound so legalistic, I responded by asserting that I would follow the liturgical *ordo* of the church, as was not

---

[21] See OCF, no. 35.

[22] Flame and candlelight elicit in people across cultures feelings of security, consolation, and hope, as well as defiance of darkness and cold, both literal and metaphoric. Even in highly secularized contemporary societies the candlelight vigil is a widespread ritual form found in situations of protest or mourning, such as the massive nighttime demonstrations in Leipzig against communism in the former East Germany in 1989 (protest), evening ceremonies on college campuses across the U.S. after the shooting rampage at Virginia Tech in 2007 (mourning), and the worldwide public evening rituals after 9/11/2001 (mourning and protest).

merely my right but my duty.[23] I would explain to the funeral director that evening at the wake that we would meet the body and the family in the entryway of the church for the rite of reception, after which we would all process to the front of the church.[24] My young colleague graciously shrugged this off.

The last piece of information the associate pastor provided me in passing as he showed me around the sacristy came as nothing less than a shock: he would be doing another funeral the next morning, a small affair for an elderly woman with few loved ones, scheduled a half hour before Casey's. I stammered, "In the same . . . *here?*" He explained that this was no big deal, as he would be done in a half hour. Realizing this was not my responsibility and beyond my influence, I assumed a late start for our funeral, imagining people would arrive only to have to stand outside or in the back of the church. I said I hoped he wouldn't mind my being in the sacristy while he was in the sanctuary, and he said that would not be a problem. We parted cordially.

The wake took place at one of the neighborhood funeral homes, with Casey's family by the open casket receiving great numbers of visitors. Mutual friends of Casey's and mine, liturgical musicians and lectors in their parishes, helped with the celebration of the Vigil for the Deceased, leading all in the opening song and responsorial psalm, as well as proclaiming the first reading.[25] For the invitation to prayer at the climax of the introductory rites, I found the sample text bespoke

[23] See Vatican Council II, Constitution on the Sacred Liturgy (*Sacrosanctum Concilium*), no. 22.

[24] See OCF, nos. 158–62.

[25] "The vigil in the form of the liturgy of the word consists of the introductory rites, the liturgy of the word, the prayer of intercession, and a concluding rite. . . . Music is integral to any type of vigil, and so the vigil for the deceased. In the difficult circumstances following death, well-chosen music can touch the mourners and others present at levels of human need that words alone often fail to reach." OCF, nos. 57, 68. For a thorough argument for the nonverbal, bodily importance of music for liturgy, see Bruce T. Morrill, "Liturgical Music: Bodies Proclaiming and Responding to the Word of God," *Worship* 74, no. 1 (January 2000): 20–36; also in *Bodies of Worship: Explorations in Theory and Practice*, ed. Bruce Morrill (Collegeville, MN: Liturgical Press, 1999), 157–72. Kathleen Harmon's "Music Notes" column in *Liturgical Ministry* is a quarterly source of theological insight and information on the nature, content, and function of music in the reformed rites of the church.

sentiments and needs apposite to the situation of the untimely death of this much-loved friend and social servant: "My brothers and sisters, we believe that all the ties of friendship and affection which knit us as one throughout our lives do not unravel with death. Confident that God always remembers the good we have done and forgives our sins, let us pray [together in silence], asking God to gather Casey to himself."[26] The rite then calls for all to pause in silent prayer. As with all such opening prayers, the silence needs to be long enough to allow people to express their thoughts, that is, really to pray.[27] Such guided, purposeful silence draws each person into the action of prayer as well as bonds the entire assembly as opposed to leaving them spectators of some one minister who does the praying for them. This being unfortunately a crucial element of the reformed liturgy that priests largely ignore,[28] I find it helpful both to insert the directive "together in silence" into the invitation (see above) and then to close my eyes as I pray silently before I collect all the assembly's silent activity in the opening prayer. The rite then provides literally dozens of prayers for the dead and for the mourners suited to particular types of persons and circumstances, including for a young person or for one who has

[26] OCF, no. 71.

[27] Robert Cabié reports that the four-step pattern of Roman orations—*Oremus*, a period of silent prayer in the assembly, the priest's collect to the Father in the name of the people, and the people's *Amen*—appears in "the embryonic sacramentaries that go back to the end of the fifth century" (*The Eucharist*, trans. Matthew O'Connell, The Church at Prayer, ed. A. G. Martimort, vol. 2 [Collegeville, MN: Liturgical Press, 1986], 52–53).

[28] Sadly, all ages and ideological types of priests, rather than developing the practical mysticism of the reformed rites, tend to think that the way to foster the assembly's participation is through chatty greetings, personal musings, and so forth. Such is the prattle of television hosts and, thus, the mode for engaging individual, passive viewers. The fact that, generally in American Catholic liturgies, silences of any length tend actually to occur only when something has gone wrong or there is an awkward logistical break in the ritual exacerbates late-modern Catholics' (both priests' and people's) discomfort with silence, while a vocal minority bemoan the lack of "mystery" and prayerfulness in post–Vatican II rites. Silence, rather, needs to occur at key points that promise a fuller, deeper, more conscious participation by all. Thus, in the present case, the General Introduction devotes an entire article to the purpose and proper placement of silence in the funeral rites. See OCF, no. 34.

died suddenly.[29] I chose, however, the first option in the Introductory Rite for its articulating "the brevity of our lives on earth" and asserting "death is not the end, nor does it destroy the bonds that you [God] forge in our lives,"[30] words pertinent for a young woman leaving so many stunned friends and loved ones.

Scores of people were at the wake when we started celebrating the Vigil for the Deceased, people of all ages, educational levels, largely Roman Catholic. Given the cavalier approach to the ritual and symbolism of the funeral Mass the local associate pastor had demonstrated, I suspected that the Vigil may not normally be celebrated during wakes in that parish, and as we proceeded I got the impression most attending were not familiar with the rite. Still, one could sense the people's being drawn into the celebration through Scripture and song, prayer, and my brief homily, such that when we got to the prayers of intercession, for which the response is the classic *kyrie*, "Lord, have mercy," they became more vocal. Better yet was the subsequent recitation of the Lord's Prayer. The familiarity of those prayer forms is of great value at that and all the stages of the Order of Christian Funerals, for it offers people a comfortable and comforting means of participation. Notable to me that evening, however, were the dozens of teens who drifted in and out of the funeral home, many of them staying together in clusters on the sidewalk rather than in the ample space of the funeral home.

That adolescents would feel uncomfortable in such a situation was not surprising, nor was the fact that those who did join in the Vigil largely clung to the back. For them even the corporate recitation of *kyrie*s and the Lord's Prayer seemed unfamiliar. They struck me as not being at home not only in the space of the funeral parlor but also that of the church's rites. I realized at that point in the evening how much I would need to be mindful of not only the fragility of these young people's emotions over the loss of a trusted and loved mentor but also their minimal levels of catechesis and familiarity with the content of Scripture and liturgical tradition. With the pastoral theology of the rite my resolve was "to be mindful of those persons who are not members of the Catholic Church, or Catholics who are not involved in the life of the Church," and to "take into consideration the spiritual and

[29] See ibid., nos. 398–99, including for a young person (nos. 27 and 28) and for one who died suddenly (no. 42).
[30] Ibid., no. 72-A.

psychological needs of the family and friends of the deceased."[31] The rite identifies those needs to include expressing grief and loss, accepting the reality of this death, and comforting one another. While my introductions at various points in the funeral Mass and the homily would need to serve this delicate balance between sorrow and consolation, I believed the words and symbols of the rite itself, steeped in the paschal mystery, proclaimed simply, deliberately, and prayerfully, offered the best possibilities for healing during the funeral Mass. Healing in the Order of Christian Funerals comes not so much in explanations and ideas as in thoughts and images, sounds and sights, including the people themselves, corporately held in the church's ritual embrace.

The next morning I got to the church before the first funeral so as to meet the parish organist, whose not having returned my phone calls did seem to be due to her unwillingness to discuss music options for the Mass. She explained that she and the cantor would do a four-hymn Mass (the unfortunate pattern widely adopted in U.S. Catholic churches in the 1960s), for which the selections were invariable (e.g., the cantor always sings "Amazing Grace" as a solo during Communion), along with a setting of Psalm 23 after the first reading and a gospel acclamation. I explained that the funeral Mass would not begin with an "opening hymn," with the coffin already down front, but rather I would be greeting the body and family in the back of the church and that she should provide a processional hymn once we completed the introductory rites and moved forward from there. She, of course, was unfamiliar with the Roman Rite, but said she would follow my lead.

When I brought up the Song of Farewell for the Final Commendation, however, I met strong resistance. Similar to the associate pastor, the music director's reply was, "We don't do that here," and once again I was unwilling to concede an essential part of the rite,[32] especially since the traditional elements of the song contain such powerfully consoling images: the deceased not going into oblivion but rather the companionship of the saints, Christ's call, angels leading her to Abraham's bosom (drawing on the remarkable parable at Luke

---

[31] OCF, nos. 12, 16.

[32] "In the choice of music for the funeral Mass, preference should be given to the singing of . . . especially the song of farewell at the final commendation." Ibid., no. 157.

16:19-31), and the ancient symbols of eternal rest and perpetual light.[33] When her response was that she simply did not know it, I explained that there are a number of settings, the most accessible perhaps being to the tune of the Old Hundredth ("Praise God, from whom all blessings flow"), with which she must be familiar. She was adamant in her resistance, saying she did not have the music. At that point I picked up a copy of the hymnal lying on the bench and found the very setting in the index. She said she did not know when she should do it. I proposed that I announce the song as part of my introduction to the Final Commendation toward the end of the liturgy. She clearly was not happy but seemed finally resigned to tolerating this intrusive priest.

I took a walk under forbidding, overcast skies to clear my head, as well as to get out of the way of the first funeral, which was beginning at the top of the hour. I returned to the sacristy at about fifteen minutes past the hour, amazed to find the associate pastor already beginning the Liturgy of the Eucharist. The Liturgy of the Word, I surmised, must have entailed rapid readings and a perfunctory sermon, if any. So, I mused, this young cleric would indeed get that funeral done in less than thirty minutes. From the sacristy I observed him briskly read through the preface and into the eucharistic prayer. When he reached the institution narrative, however, he paused and entered into the same slow, deliberate recitation and elaborate, protracted elevations and genuflections I had observed the bishop do at that Vigil of Pentecost a couple years earlier. Here was the one place in what struck me as an otherwise rushed liturgy in which time no longer mattered, with every word deliberately articulated, every gesture meticulously executed.

When the time came for me to begin Casey's funeral, rain was falling steadily. Since the church, typical of those built in the early twentieth century, had no gathering area but only a narrow vestibule leading into the nave, and with the extended family accompanying the coffin being quite large, the rite of reception of the body (introductory rites) could not exactly take place in "the door of the church."[34] The funeral directors brought the coffin halfway down to the center crossing area, and Casey's parents, siblings, and the rest of family filled the aisle from there nearly back to the entry. As I walked from the sacristy into the broad, high, open space of the nave and down the upper half of

[33] See ibid., no. 174.
[34] Ibid., no. 159.

218

the aisle to greet the party, I was moved by a powerfully tangible sense of summit, feeling as if Casey's family and I were dignitaries meeting on a battlefield to negotiate the terms for surrendering her. They had fought their way through the previous days of shock, preparation, travel, and wake so as to reach the point of handing Casey over to God through the ministry of the church.[35] The configuration of family, coffin, assembly, and ministers in the space, meeting each other halfway and in a powerful silence, created that profound awareness.

I began by greeting the family and explaining to all assembled the baptismal symbolism of meeting by the entrance: When her parents and godparents had brought the infant Casey to be baptized, they were greeted in the entry of a church building, symbolically affecting what they desired of the church for her, a place in the life of faith.[36] In baptism, I continued, Casey had died and been born anew with Christ, joining the living company of all the saints, earthly and heavenly. Death's power was already in the past tense from the beginning of Casey's life through the power of water and the Holy Spirit.[37] For this reason, I proclaimed, we now sprinkle her body in this coffin with water from the Easter font and place a white pall over her coffin, replicating the white robe Casey received at her baptism.[38] Let us, I concluded, draw consolation and strength from this Easter season as we, with Casey's parents, godparents, and family, once again bring her bodily into the church, with the paschal candle from which she received the light of Christ at baptism guiding us forward, leading her home.[39] And consoling indeed was the strength with which the assembled sang the processional hymn, offering support to Casey's

---

[35] See Chauvet, *Symbol and Sacrament*, 185–89; and *The Sacraments*, 15–18, 37–38.

[36] See International Committee on English in the Liturgy, Inc., *Rite of Baptism for Children*, 1969, nos. 35–37. Hereafter, RBC.

[37] See OCF, no. 2.

[38] After the water rite, as the parents put the white garment on the baby, the celebrant exhorts: "See in this white garment the outward sign of our Christian dignity. With your family and friends to help you by word and example, bring that dignity unstained into the everlasting life of heaven." RBC, no. 99.

[39] In a further explanatory rite, as a parent or godparent lights the baby's candle from the Easter candle, the celebrant says, "This child of yours has been enlightened by Christ. He (she) is to walk always as a child of the light. . . . When the Lord comes, may he (she) go out to meet him with all the saints in the heavenly kingdom." Ibid., no. 100.

parents, family, and close loved ones as they processed through their midst behind her coffin.[40] Once in the sanctuary, I was, as usual, careful to allow ample silence after the invitation, "Let us pray," before concluding the introductory rites with the proper collect for funerals in the Easter season: "God of loving kindness, listen favorably to our prayers: strengthen our belief that your Son has risen from the dead and our hope that your servant [Casey] will also rise again . . ."[41]

The Liturgy of the Word began with Romans 6:3-9, which both echoed the words and symbols of the introductory rites and would provide the basis for the introduction to my homily, proclaiming hope that, despite our shock and grief over Casey's sudden death, her baptism into Christ's death was so that she "too might live a new life." The cantor and organist proved competent and inspiring in leading us through a responsorial setting of Psalm 23, the text and music unifying a corporate body of longing and hope.[42] For the gospel I chose[43] Matthew 25:1-13, the parable of the ten bridesmaids, the first of that chapter's three remarkable parables about Christ's final coming. After the homily friends of Casey announced the general intercessions (prayers of the faithful), adding to those from the ritual a few of their own.

On the eve of the funeral a fellow priest who had known Casey as a student balked when I told him, in response to his inquiry, the gospel passage I was preparing for the Mass. His problem concerned narrative about final judgment, for him a topic one should never broach at a funeral. I countered, however, that this parable offered the best news imaginable about judgment. Here was a young woman who dedicated her life to working tirelessly and effectively with at-risk youth. If ever

[40] "Processions, especially when accompanied with music and singing, can strengthen the bond of communion in the assembly. . . . During the various processions, it is preferable that the pallbearers carry the coffin as a sign of reverence and respect for the deceased." OCF, no. 41.

[41] Ibid., no. 164-D.

[42] "In the psalms the members of the assembly pray in the voice of Christ, who intercedes on their behalf before the Father. The Church, like Christ, turns again and again to the psalms as a genuine expression of grief and of praise and as a sure source of trust and hope in times of trial." Ibid., no. 25.

[43] Part III of the *Order of Christian Funerals* offers a wide range of Scriptural readings and psalms appropriate to funerals for adults, baptized children, and children who died before baptism. "In consultation with the family and close friends, the minister chooses the texts that most closely reflect the particular circumstances and the needs of the mourners." OCF, no. 344.

there were a bridesmaid who was ready to meet the bridegroom, lamp filled with oil, wick trimmed, I could not imagine who else it would be. I wondered to myself how that could not be even remotely evident to my colleague. The Lord had come for Casey at an unexpected hour indeed, and her dedication to career, friends, and family was the very embodiment of the way of life Christ teaches (just consider the "sheep and goats" parable that follows in Matthew 25). Casey had been a sacrament, a living symbol of that "newness of life" (Rom 6:4) that Paul instructs us all to practice in the wake of baptismal waters. Such was the basic content of my homily, not avoiding the tragedy of Casey's sudden death, nor with it our grief and loss, but also giving thanks at this Eucharist for our hope in sharing at the wedding feast of the Lamb (Rev 19:9) one day with her. Casey had shown us the way to live such that our Eucharist can be authentic, our lamps ready for whenever we might here the midnight cry, "Behold, the bridegroom! Come out to meet him!" (Matt 25:6). For each of us to live in imitation of her and thus of Christ (see 1 Cor 11:1) comprises our faithful keeping of memorial, both of Casey and of Christ's death, until he comes (see 1 Cor 11:26).

Those were the contours of my homily, which, as the rite proscribes, "is never to be a eulogy."[44] In the reformed rites, the homily is the specific type of preaching proper to liturgy: a "living explanation" of "the word of God proclaimed in the readings" leading the members of the assembly to a deeper participation in the paschal mystery present in the sacrament they are sharing and thereby toward its fuller realization in their own life stories.[45] The homily thus contrasts with a sermon, which is not liturgically based but rather treats a selected topic on faith or morals, as well as with a eulogy, which likewise has no organic relation to the liturgy but rather functions as a self-contained tribute to the dead.[46] Note, however, that the rite's prohibition of eulogizing in no way cuts the preaching off from the deceased person. Were that to be the case the homily could not achieve its purpose in the funeral Mass: "Attentive to the grief of those present, the homilist should . . . help the members of the assembly to understand that the mystery of God's love and the mystery of Jesus' victorious death and

---

[44] OCF, no. 27.

[45] *Lectionary for Mass: Introduction*, no. 24.

[46] See John Allyn Melloh, "Homily or Eulogy? The Dilemma of Funeral Preaching," *Worship* 67, no. 6 (1993): 502–18.

resurrection were present in the life and death of the deceased and that these mysteries are active in their own lives as well."[47] Consistent with the entire *Order of Christian Funerals*—its General Introduction and the content of its prayers, symbols, and gestures—the expectation is for an honest acknowledgment of grief and sorrow that nonetheless, in the words of the Prayer of Commendation, finds "sure and certain hope that, together with all who have died in Christ, he/she will rise with him on the last day."[48]

At the conclusion of the Liturgy of the Eucharist, following the prayer after Communion, the funeral Mass includes the option for a "member or a friend of the family" to "speak in remembrance of the dead before the final commendation begins."[49] During my phone conversations with Casey's family over the previous days I had asked them to consider this, and at the wake her brother told me that he would simply thank everyone for all their help and support. This he did, concluding with an invitation to the church basement where, he gratefully acknowledged, parishioners and neighbors had spread a great lunch. The invitation, however, was not exactly an open one, for the brother concluded with a vigorous warning: "Anyone who wants to mourn or be sad about Casey is not invited. The only people welcome are those who want to celebrate her life." I could not but hear that as a challenge to, if not contradiction of, my homily, wherein I had made a point not to deny the shock and sadness of Casey's sudden death.

Poignant in contrast to her brother's admonition as well was the invitation to prayer with which I immediately began the Final Commendation by Casey's coffin: "Before we go our separate ways, let us take leave of our sister. May our farewell express our affection for her, may it ease our sadness and strengthen our hope. One day we shall joyfully greet her again when the love of Christ, which conquers all things, destroys even death itself."[50] Upon allowing sufficient time for all to pray in silence, I invited the assembly to sing the Song of Farewell set to the familiar tune of the Old Hundredth in the parish hymnal. The text of the song has "a venerable history in Christian funeral

---

[47] OCF, no. 27.
[48] Ibid., no. 175-A.
[49] Ibid., no. 170.
[50] Ibid., no. 171-A.

rites" of the early church,[51] invoking images of the saints and angels coming to greet the deceased, bringing her to the bosom of Abraham, consoling the bereaved with the assurance that she goes not to wander fitfully in a dark netherworld but rather to rest peacefully in the perpetual light of Christ. As the assembly sang the hymn I incensed the paschal candle and Casey's body, bowing reverently to both in turn as I slowly circuited the coffin with the thurible wafting fragrant smoke. The power of this symbolic gesture to proclaim the sacramentality of the deceased person depends not only on the paschal candle's proximity to the coffin but also the presider's having likewise incensed the book of the gospels in the Liturgy of the Word, as well as the gifts and people during the preparatory rite of the Liturgy of the Eucharist.[52] The full evangelical impact of the symbolism as a revelation of the deceased person as sacrament, as a bodily encounter with the mystery of our creation and redemption in Christ, can only emerge at that concluding moment of the funeral Mass if the incensing of the body reflects the same honoring gesture given to the gospel and the sacred elements of the Eucharist. Otherwise, it risks being an arcane ritual gesture at best, a gimmick at worst.

The ordinary conclusion to the final commendation and thus the funeral Mass is the deacon or priest's invitation, "In peace let us take our brother/sister to his/her place of rest."[53] That simple direction launches the departure of the coffin, ministers, family, and friends to the burial site, where the third and final station of the Order of Christian Funerals, the Rite of Committal, takes place. Casey's parents, however, had decided on cremation, an option for which the U.S. Catholic bishops have provided a supplement to the *Order of Christian Funerals*. The family had adopted that appendix's stated preference that the cremation take place after the funeral Mass, allowing for "the

---

[51] Rutherford, *The Death of a Christian*, 194. The author provides insightful observations on why American Catholic parishes were slow to adopt the Song of Farewell in the 1970s, concluding: "Much work still needs to be done, however, for the song of farewell to characterize the rite of final commendation and thus allow it to express more fully the paschal faith and be a greater source of consoling hope through community song," 195.

[52] For a detailed discussion of the multivalent symbolism of incensing in the funeral mass, see my "Initial Consideration: Theory and Practice of the Body in Liturgy Today," in *Bodies of Worship*, 9–15.

[53] OCF, no. 176.

Vigil for the Deceased and related rites and prayers, as well as the Funeral Liturgy [to be] celebrated as they are provided" according to the normal rite.[54] For this purpose the funeral director had supplied a coffin resembling those made of grey metal but actually fabricated of highly durable cardboard, with which everybody seemed satisfied. I thus concluded the funeral Mass with the appendix's alternate form of dismissal, "In the sure hope of the resurrection, we take leave of our sister. Let us go in peace."[55]

Analysis: Different Approaches to the Body in Question

Three approaches to the person-body of the deceased emerge in the course of the preceding narrative and with them, three different theories and practices (theologies) of Christian death and the Catholic funeral. In the first, the person-body is *viewed, celebrated, and cremated.* Typical of Americans now for many decades, Casey's family engaged the services of a professional undertaker for the embalming and cosmetic preparation of her corpse for viewing in the Victorian-era parlors of his funeral home. The basic ritual in that context is the "last look" at the deceased, a forum for final direct contact with the person-body (understood by many to be an interpersonal exchange with the deceased, "saying goodbye"), paying respects to her family, and meeting common friends in her presence. Personal and retrospective dimensions characterize the overall ritual process, along with a dogged assertion of happiness as the prescribed tone for the memorializing: "celebrating a life."

From my initial conversations with Jackie it became clear that the fundamental purpose of the funeral rituals for her and the local friends and colleagues was to "celebrate" Casey, a way of memorializing that, while not necessarily at complete odds with the *Order of Christian Funerals,*[56] nonetheless asserted the cheerful retrospective

---

[54] *Order of Christian Funerals: Appendix—Cremation*, no. 418, cited here from: National Conference of Catholic Bishops, *Appendix—Cremation, with Reflections on the Body, Cremation, and Catholic Funeral Rites by the Committee on the Liturgy* (Chicago: Liturgy Training Publications, 1997), 2. Produced with an adhesive backing, this booklet can be affixed inside the back cover of the pastoral minister's copy of the OCF.

[55] Ibid., no. 437.

[56] "Christians celebrate the funeral rites to offer worship, praise, and thanksgiving to God for the gift of a life, which has now been returned to God,

focus. Recall how the program for the funeral Mass had little to do with the liturgy itself but rather was a souvenir leaflet emblazoned with Casey's name, dates, and "Celebration of a Life" framing her smiling photo. At the other end of the ritual process her brother instructed all at the funeral that the only acceptable attitude at the concluding lunch would be happy remembrance of Casey; the sorrowing he expressly excluded. Out of sight from all would be the unceremonious cremation of Casey's body, with the ashes then delivered to the privacy of her parent's home.

Still, despite all that consistent emphasis on happily remembering Casey—the expectation that each mind's eye should hold an image of her alive and laughing—I remain haunted by the sight of the young people, the preteens and teens Casey served, huddling on the sidewalk outside the funeral parlor and silently sitting at the back of the funeral Mass, making no attempt to wipe the shock and sadness from their faces. I wonder whether some of the words, symbols, and images from the Order of Christian Funerals served their honest emotions, their openly felt need. I would like to think so. The community center where Casey had worked made counseling available to the grieving youth, but that fact only points to the discontinuity between the public "celebrating" ritual and the private therapeutic services. One can only wonder what such an experience of ritual—as modeled, interpreted, and managed by the adults—teaches contemporary youth about what they can or cannot expect from Christian liturgy, whether it connects with or only parallels what is really going on.[57]

A second approach to the deceased unfolded before my eyes on the eve and morning of Casey's funeral, that of a person-body *before the*

---

the author of life and the hope of the just. The Mass, the memorial of Christ's death and resurrection, is the principal celebration of the Christian funeral" (OCF, no. 5).

[57] My reflections along these lines are highly influenced by Johann Baptist Metz's ongoing critique of the predominant practical, pastoral theology in North Atlantic parishes, his anxiousness over the church's ministry merely mouthing what society already knows and, thus, offering nothing substantial in the face of suffering. Metz, for example, argues that in our postmodern propensity for myths that are supposed to console us we have lost the "biblical meaning of consolation . . . a hope [that] resists the attempt to expel a sense for what is absent from our wisdom about ourselves" (*A Passion for God: The Mystical-Political Dimension of Christianity*, trans. J. Matthew Ashley [New York: Paulist Press, 1998], 160).

altar of priestly mediation. I refer to the efficient Mass the young associate pastor executed for the elderly parishioner, his normal practice of having the coffin (without paschal candle) parked in advance at the foot of the altar, his dispensing with both the official Roman funeral rite's introductory reception of the body and the entire final commendation. This altogether amounted to his replacing the Order of Christian Funerals with a simple Mass for the Dead, selecting from the funeral collects and prefaces for Christian Death available in the Roman Missal.[58]

Such an approach reeks of a clericalism contradictory to fundamental principles of the Second Vatican Council's doctrine of the liturgy, namely, the active participation of all in the paschal mystery and the multiple ways Christ is present in the rites (assembly, presider, word, and sacramental symbols).[59] Elimination of the reception of the body and final commendation effectively erases the deceased as a subject, as a person-body, as a sacramental sign to the assembled of her and their baptismal right and duty to share in the liturgical actualization of their membership in Christ's Body. With that erasure comes the discarding of the sacramental expression of the mission all baptized members are called to realize in their lives, the irrelevance of the content of Scripture as revealing God's word for this specific moment and people, the loss of a "sure and certain hope" shaped by faith in Christ's resurrection. In place of that celebration of the paschal mystery is the "default religion"[60] of the priest confecting the Body and Blood of Christ, an action apparently conferring dignity upon those present at the Holy Sacrifice, the deceased in the coffin, and the congregation in the pews.

In such a social division of ritual labor, the cleric's exclusive role in the real work of the Mass (the intensely choreographed consecration and his self-communication of the Sacred Species) to the neglect of his presiding over a liturgical assembly leaves everybody else to make of the event what they will. The music director provides one standard selection of four organ hymns performed with a solo vocalist. Those attending are most likely either consoled to witness the special Mass,

---

[58] See National Conference of Catholic Bishops, *The Sacramentary*, trans. International Commission on English in the Liturgy (New York: Catholic Book Publishing, 1985), 526–35, 951–55.

[59] See the Constitution on the Sacred Liturgy, nos. 7, 14.

[60] See Douglas J. Davies, *A Brief History of Death* (Malden, MA: Blackwell Publishing, 2005), 57–58.

226

satisfied that this death has been marked with proper seriousness and dignity, or put off by the religious content and official behavior, or left to infuse the ceremony with supplemental content, whether material (e.g., "celebrating a life" pamphlets) or only within the individual's thoughts.

British theologian and religious historian Douglas Davies observes that the complex contemporary "circumstances of death and funerals" (i.e., minimal knowledge of or interest in religious doctrines, life in pluralistic society, etc.) dispose people to "what might be called a cultural 'default position'" of following the standard path set by their religious and funerary professionals.[61] If those close to the deceased, such as the small family at the first funeral in the parish that morning, do not inject any parallel or additional ritual elements into the official service as provided (here, a simple Mass for the Dead), then the ceremony will indeed be brief. On the other hand, as Davies reports, while late-modern families of the deceased remain committed to the "default position" of the given religion's ritual, often only because it is the easier way "to ensure a satisfactory performance," they are increasingly assertive in their requests for personal readings or music "as markers of individuality set within the traditional framework."[62] Christian pastors in North Atlantic societies are, in turn, increasingly willing to shift from their traditions' symbolic framing of the deceased as a brother or sister becoming part of the communion of saints to "the individuality of each person—as individual in death as in life."[63] American Catholic bishops have recently been pushing back against this trend, even as many local priests find themselves incapable of providing solid theological and liturgical reasons for the official prohibition of eulogies at the funeral Mass, the inclusion of songs like "Danny Boy," and the insertion of nonbiblical readings.[64] The problem, I

[61] Ibid., 58.

[62] Ibid., 58–59.

[63] Ibid., 60.

[64] "The issue of what is decorous and what is not at Roman Catholic funerals flares up periodically around the country. A handful of . . . dioceses . . . forbid eulogies at funerals, said Sister Maryanne Walsh, a spokeswoman for the United States Conference of Catholic Bishops, and some others place limits on them. Bishops and pastors have occasionally discouraged the playing of popular songs like 'Danny Boy' or 'Wind Beneath My Wings.'" The laity's response has been widely negative: "Funeral directors in the archdiocese [of

would argue, is due in no small part to the clergy's ignorance of the practical, spiritual theology of the reformed rites of the church (in this case, the Order of Christian Funerals). Unable to form and guide their people in the biblically powerful, pastorally flexible scope of the rites, priests end up asserting their judgments concerning funeral practices on the basis of their clerical authority alone, even as that argument from power continues to lose force among baby boomer, millennial, and younger Catholics.[65]

The Order of Christian Funerals, then, comprises a third approach to the deceased person as a member of the Body of Christ *in communion with the assembly's celebration of the paschal mystery*. Citing 1 Corinthians 12:26, "If one member suffers in the body of Christ which is the Church, all the members suffer with that member," the General Introduction identifies the entire community, lay and ordained, as responsible for the "ministry of consolation to those who have suffered the loss of one

---

Newark, New Jersey] said that most funerals there include eulogies during the Mass, and that the decree had aroused widespread resentment . . . A funeral director who spoke on the condition of anonymity said that one group of mourners was heard cursing in the church parking lot last week after a eulogist was forbidden to speak" (Daniel J. Wakin, "Archbishop of Newark Bans Eulogies at Masses," *New York Times*, 23 January 2003). A couple years earlier the Archdiocese of Boston reasserted the policy of limiting the length and content of eulogies, only to stir controversy over the inconsistency of its application when it came to funerals for prominent politicians, not to mention clerics themselves. See "A Final Wish Unfulfilled" and "Eulogy Policy Isn't New," *Boston Globe*, 6 July 2001 and 18 July 2001, respectively.

[65] Since 1987 *National Catholic Reporter* has published extensive scientific polling data on adult American Catholic beliefs and practices every six years, tracking changes and generational differences each half-decade. Among the numerous categories and questions is that of Mass attendance. The 2005 poll found that only 15 percent of the youngest generation (18–25 years old) said they attend Mass weekly or more, whereas the 1987 poll found 30 percent of youngest reporting weekly or more Mass attendance. Tracking particular generations across time found that Mass attendance by baby boomers, for example, held steadily in the low-to-mid 40th percentile until 2005, when the number dropped to 35%. For further evidence of the declining importance of religious practices and authority of church leaders and teachings, including statistical data and narrative interpretations, see: "Survey of U.S. Catholics: American Catholics from John Paul II to Benedict XVI," *National Catholic Reporter*, 30 September 2005, at: http://www.ncronline.org/NCR_Online/archives2/2005c/093005/093005a.php (accessed October 3, 2005).

whom they love."[66] The theological heart of this approach, "rooted in that hope that comes from faith in the saving death and resurrection of the Lord Jesus Christ,"[67] I articulated at the outset of my description of Casey's funeral,[68] with the practical shape of that theology emerging throughout the ensuing narrative and its citations of the ritual text.

The point here is to recognize the rite's insistence—both in the theology of the General Introduction and the ritual's words and symbols—upon praising and thanking God for the life of the deceased while also ministering to the sorrow of the family and friends. "The responsibility for the ministry of consolation rests with the believing community," whose "faith . . . in the resurrection of the dead brings support and strength to those who suffer the loss of those whom they love."[69] This duty the faithful execute by both sharing their particular ministerial gifts throughout the three stages of the funeral rites and "assisting [the mourners] with some of the routine tasks of daily living," such as meal preparation, transportation, child or elder care, and so forth.[70] Thus the faith community's liturgical contributions and practical "acts of kindness" together effect a reintegration of both the deceased into the symbolic reality of Christ's Body—in death as in life[71]—and all the participants in the funeral process—family, friends, community, pastoral ministers—with the deceased into a singular celebration of the paschal mystery.

The integrated vision of the Order of Christian Funerals provides the members of the church with an ideal that, nonetheless, is only realized to varying degrees in practice, as my own narrative above attests. To use Chauvet's terminology, the three bodies of human subjectivity—natural/cosmic, social/cultural, and traditional—would appear to be vying with one another for the upper hand in people's efforts to construct meaning in the face of death. This pastoral reality, however, should be a cause for neither surprise nor alarm, for it is but one example of what Chauvet means by asserting that the Word of God's continual submission to the ambiguities of the body is the kenotic hallmark of our salvation in Christ. Chauvet argues for the patience and

---

[66] OCF, no. 8.
[67] Ibid.
[68] See above, pp. 210–12.
[69] OCF, no. 9.
[70] Ibid., no. 10.
[71] See Romans 14:8.

solicitude pastoral ministers should thereby practice in responding to frequent requests for liturgical rites of passage from people either ignorant of or resistant to the traditional content and practice of the faith.[72] Indeed, such a pastoral approach is a practical form that ministers' paschal faith as "the assent to a loss" takes.[73]

Such a complex reality warrants further analysis, which I will undertake by aligning Chauvet's theory of the triple body with a threefold typology of memorializing the dead that Davies has gleaned from the contemporary Northern Atlantic social landscape. Building on cultural anthropologist Bronislaw Malinowski's study of death, Davies proposes hope as always contextual, "related to lived architectural events and the allurement of place."[74] Places charged with social-traditional import allure people in their desire to flourish in the face of death. This recognition enables Davies to craft his typology of various burial practices: "When times change, through altered circumstance, dramatic events and the innovative creativity of individuals, new opportunities for allurement arise. In sociological terms new kinds of affinity develop between people and forms of memorial and hope."[75] Herein lies an affinity as well between Davies's typology and Chauvet's fundamental sacramental theology: faith's content is attained only through the "*triple body* of culture, tradition, and nature,"[76] mutually impacting conditions for how people attain meaning in life (and death). In the next section I will follow Davies's order for presenting three models of contemporary North Atlantic memorials to the dead, each of which has a particular way of locating hope that gives

---

[72] See Chauvet, *The Sacraments*, 51–54, 173–200.

[73] Ibid., 39. "In their significant materiality, the sacraments thus constitute an *unavoidable stumbling block* which forms a barrier to every imaginary claim to a direct connection, individual and interior, with Christ or to a gnostic-like, illuminist contact with him. . . . They tell us that the faith has a body, that it adheres to our body. More than that, they tell us that to *become a believer is to learn to consent, without resentment, to the corporality of the faith*" (Chauvet, *Symbol and Sacrament*, 153, emphasis in original).

[74] Davies, *A Brief History of Death*, 117.

[75] Ibid., 116.

[76] Chauvet, *Symbol and Sacrament*, 150 (emphasis in original). Elsewhere Chauvet proposes that "instead of being obstacles to the truth, sensible mediations of language, body, history, desire [are] the very milieu within which human beings attain their truth and thus correspond to the Truth which calls them" (*The Sacraments*, 6).

priority to one of Chauvet's three dimensions of human corporality. That analysis will lead, finally, to the healing power yet challenging content of faith in the resurrection of the body as the pivotal symbol at the juncture of culture and tradition in the current Christian (Roman Catholic) ritualizing of death.

LOCATING THE DECEASED: A TYPOLOGY OF CONTEMPORARY HOPE FOR THE DEAD

Communal, Eschatological Hope: The Traditional Body

Davies observes that peoples across times and cultures tend to integrate the dead into their worlds of meaning by reasserting the deceased's identity in relation to a new location in space and time: "Hope and place are inextricably aligned."[77] Traditional Christian hope lies in the eschatological fulfillment of "those . . . who have died in Christ" (1 Cor 15:18), whom Christ "will raise . . . up on the last day" (John 6:40). Beginning with the earliest generations, Christians buried their dead with reverence in expectation of their being raised "at the last trumpet," when Christ, "the first fruits of those who have died," will come "and the dead will be raised imperishable . . . changed" to immortal bodies like that of him in whose name they were baptized (1 Cor 15:20, 52, and see 29). That hope of immortality, while grounded in baptism, ancient Christians found assured through their sharing in the Eucharist, the "bread of life" (John 6:35), leading to their association of the bodies of their dead with the eucharistic body of the church.[78] The early believers came to celebrate the Eucharist on the graves or near the (symbolically decorated) sarcophagi of their beloved dead, with ensuing centuries bringing the building of churches on the burial sites of martyrs and saints. Vaults, tombs, and plots in the floors, altars, and graveyards of churches, as well as spaces in large cemeteries, eventually with sections consecrated by local churches, have comprised the traditional Christian locations of hope in the face of death.[79] Hope in this case, Davies summarizes, is eternal in nature and eschatological in form, shaping a vision not only for the afterlife

[77] Davies, *A Brief History of Death*, 117.

[78] See Cabié, *The Eucharist*, 38–39; and Rutherford, *The Death of a Christian*, 6–9.

[79] On the Carolingian origins and French linguistic roots of the cemetery, as well as the medieval development of the charnel house (ossuary), see Bynum, *The Resurrection of the Body*, 203–5, 212–13.

(eternal rest, perpetual light) but also for "the drive to survive and flourish in this life too."[80]

The Order of Christian Funerals carries out the Second Vatican Council's mandate that all rites be revised on the basis of sound tradition so that the church's liturgy might function as a renewed source for the faith lives of its members,[81] in this case as they confront the hard reality of death. Ancient Christian tradition, Rutherford summarizes, understood death as believers' hopeful, confident going to Christ, communicated through such symbols as sharing in the "rest" of Abraham, the model of life based on faith in God's promise, and such iconography as the Good Shepherd, loaves and fishes, vine and branches. Patristic treatises disqualified the despairing displays of mourning (wailing, physical mutilation) typical in their contemporary societies as incongruous with Christian faith in Jesus' resurrection, teaching instead that the humanly understandable grief of bereavement was to find expression through singing psalms and hymns, contemplating biblical images, and especially offering prayers. Augustine taught that the church passes no judgment on the deceased but rather trusting in God's mercy, offers prayers, alms, and the Eucharist for any and all the baptized who, except for the martyrs, surely die with some sin in need of forgiveness. Respect for the body of the deceased manifested faith in the redemption of human nature and hope in the resurrection of those justified in Christ.[82] In the sixth century Pseudo-Dionysius explained that bringing the body into the church "symbolized one's place in everlasting life as a follower of Christ," while prayer "over the faithful dead for the forgiveness of sins and the reward of a place in the company of patriarchs [proclaimed] the promise of unending life to those who love God."[83]

Beginning in the seventh century, however, confidence in God's mercy toward the faithful departed steadily ceded to fear of divine judgment; the hopeful going to sleep in Christ, to the dread of Christ the all-powerful judge. Gregory the Great and others took Augustine's teaching of prayer for the dead in an expiatory direction: "The

---

[80] Davies, *A Brief History of Death*, 118.

[81] See *Sacrosanctum Concilium*, nos. 3, 4.

[82] See Rutherford, *The Death of a Christian*, 15–19. For a discussion of the complexity of Augustine's teaching about body, resurrection, and judgment, see Bynum, *The Resurrection of the Body*, 94–104.

[83] Rutherford, *The Death of a Christian*, 21–22.

prayer of the Church, they taught, brought about the liberation of the faithful dead from the purifying fire of expiation for sin. Before long, this fire would become localized as 'purgatory' and the tradition of prayer for the release of the 'pour souls' its complement in popular piety."[84] The early eucharistic theology promising *koinonia* in the Body of Christ at the heavenly banquet diminished; in a medieval church preoccupied with fear of death, the offering of Mass functioned under an individualistic and atoning eschatology for languishing souls. The *Requiem* Mass, which began in the thirteenth-century papal court, made its way into the mainstream, becoming normative in the 1570 *ordo* of Pius V. While that liturgy retained measures of hope, such elements as its offertory prayers and *Dies irae* sequence would leave "a macabre mark on the expression of faith in the face of death."[85] While the post–Vatican II Order of Christian Funerals recovered the sound tradition of a paschal, ecclesial, eschatological hope, still it could not instantly erase the popular perception of the church's funeral rites as pessimistically focused on sin and fearful judgment. An often poor clerical comprehension and weak pastoral execution of the reformed Order of Christian Funerals, compounded by an individualistic and consumerist anthropology operative in society, leave open a ritual-symbolic void for other types of memorial to fill.

Internal, Retrospective Hope: The Social-Cultural Body

During the twentieth century a second type of meaning for death evolved in conjunction with "a consumerist outlook framed by a sense of personal freedom and individualism . . . the desire that life should be lived in as intelligible and authentic a way as possible but not necessarily in terms of established religious ideas."[86] In a veritable paradigm shift in death, modern people came to construct hope as "a retrospective fulfillment of identity of both the dead and of the bereaved" through narrative and symbolic exercises of "active memory" focusing on "their known and experienced past" of the deceased.[87] For Davies the key symbol of this internal, retrospective hope is the cremated remains of the dead, whose location began migrating significantly in the 1980s from the public, civic, and ecclesial spaces of

---

[84] Ibid., 24. See also Bynum, *The Resurrection of the Body*, 14, 113.

[85] Rutherford, *The Death of a Christian*, 60.

[86] Davies, *A Brief History of Death*, 85.

[87] Ibid., 122, 65.

cemeteries and columbaria to private places such as mantelpieces and backyards or locales personally associated with the deceased, such as a favorite recreational terrain or body of water.

The American neologism "cremains," Davies finds, signals the isolation of the bodily remains from the physical process and place of their production (crematoria, which tended to include chapel-like architecture), allowing an open-ended range of content and locations for funeral rites centered on memories of the deceased's commitments, passions, or pleasures. In 2006 the *New York Times* reported cremation rates at "close to 70 percent in some parts of the West." The *Times* article highlights the comments of a Mark Duffey, director of "the first nationwide funeral concierge service" in the United States: "'The body's a downer, especially for [baby] boomers,' Mr. Duffey said. 'If the body doesn't have to be there, it frees us up to do what we want. They may want to have [the service] in a country club or bar or their favorite restaurant. That's where consumers want to go.'"[88] Healing then comes internally by making "connections" with the deceased person's life story, a memorial process people increasingly seek to orchestrate for themselves, with ecclesial or civic traditions playing secondary, supportive roles, if any.[89]

American religious historian Gary Laderman arrives at analysis similar to Davies's retrospective interpretation of modern funerals—"the role of memory images in dealing with loss"[90]—by examining another location and disposition of the body in the twentieth century: the embalmed corpse on view in the funeral home. The modern practice of undertakers, originating in the wake of the Civil War, was by the 1920s a nationwide industry.

> The funeral home evolved into an American institution during a tumultuous period of social change: industrialization brought the 'machine age' to life; consumerism introduced new relations between

[88] John Leland, "It's My Funeral and I'll Serve Ice Cream if I Want To," *New York Times*, 20 July 2006.

[89] "'Baby boomers are all about being in control,' said Mr. Duffey, who started his company after running a chain of funeral homes. 'This generation wants to control everything, from the food to the words to the order of the service. And this is one area where consumers feel out of control'" (ibid).

[90] Gary Laderman, *Rest in Peace: A Cultural History of Death and the Funeral Home in Twentieth-Century America* (New York: Oxford University Press, 2003), 23.

people and objects; and faith in science and technology undercut even further the relevance of institutional religion to everyday life. The values beginning to energize the social body in the modern era contributed greatly to the shape and texture of the American funeral, and the final appearance of the embalmed body safely cared for in the funeral home. Nevertheless, the dramatic appearance of this new home for the dead in the first half of the century became a source for much public debate and led many individuals both inside and outside the industry to scrutinize the business of burial.[91]

Laderman's persuasive explanation for the successful establishment of the industry's practices includes the assessment that funeral directors were responding to what modern Americans wanted, namely, care for the deceased that was both consistent with scientific sanitary sensibilities and consonant with mourners' therapeutic need for bodily encounter with their dearly departed. That the departure (death) decreasingly took place among kin in one's home, due not only to medical technology but also to friends and family members living at significant distances, plus a "confusion around [grief's] value in the lives of busy, hard-working Americans,"[92] altogether contributed to people's need for the "last look." This ritual gesture, carried out in the funeral home, a space resembling both bedroom and front parlor, became for mourners an experience of confirming (accepting) that the deceased was indeed dead and a moment for a parting dialogue in one's imagination with the dead person. These aspects of the practice comprised what its supporters and propagators considered its therapeutic function. The "viewing," moreover, acquired the social dimension of winning honor and guarding shame. Popular culture came to judge the results of the mortician's work with the corpse, along with the extent of other amenities and services they purchased from the funeral director, as indicative of the family's care for their loved one.

Beginning in the 1930s and well into the second half of the century, however, viewing the embalmed corpse, along with other customs funeral directors had successfully established, came under repeated harsh religious, political, and class-oriented criticism. Socially concerned government and religious officials accused the funeral industry of taking financial advantage of the poorer class in their times of grief,

[91] Ibid., 47.
[92] Ibid., 102.

while certain Protestant and Catholic clergy also attacked morticians' efforts to achieve "that alive look" as valorizing the body to the detriment of the soul, a renewal of pagan idolatry. Congressional hearings, pastoral tracts, and exposés in news weeklies waged a power struggle with funeral directors over the bodies of the dead, with British commentator Jessica Mitford's *The American Way of Death* (1963) stirring up controversy and achieving big sales on the stands. Still, despite all the hype and eventual governmental regulatory actions during those decades, Laderman finds ongoing evidence for Jewish, Protestant, and Catholic clergy and local funeral directors largely building and sustaining positive working relationships.[93] In addition, patriotic association of the dignified display and disposition of the fallen soldiers' body with the glory and preservation of the American social body during and after World War II solidified popular acceptance of funeral directors as providing a service representing such cultural values as "individualism, democracy, freedom, and free enterprise."[94]

Granted the significant contested dimensions (economic, religious, political) of modern mortuary practice, still it seems that Americans largely adopted and have continued to utilize these services because they have suited the therapeutic approach to individual meaning making in modern society. Laderman summarizes the position espoused by funeral directors and supporters of the funeral industry: "This idiom framed the funeral as an instrument of psychological as well as spiritual healing for survivors, and the viewable body was defined as the active agent in the eventual triumph over the pain of losing a loved one. It was a moment to confront the reality of death, by looking in the face of the deceased without seeing the unsettling signs of decomposition, and thus begin the process of working through personal grief by creating a living memory."[95] The controversy within the professional medical, psychological, and popular debates about this "grief

---

[93] In the past decade the Roman Catholic Archdiocese of Los Angeles took such alliance with the funeral industry to a new level by entering into a leasing agreement with one of the largest funeral company chains in the country, allowing the corporation to build and operate mortuaries at six of its eleven cemeteries. See Leslie Wirpsa, "'Death care giants' team up with church: Relationship raises issues about church role in bereavement," *National Catholic Reporter*, 30 January 1998, 9–12.

[94] Laderman, *Rest in Peace*, 80.

[95] Ibid., 100–101.

mythology" basically concerned whether the embalmed, cosmetically altered corpse in comfortable repose at the funeral home signals a cultural denial of death. That rhetoric, however, does seem to be misleading, for the issue would seem often to reduce not to people's denial but rather interpretation of death, what images and symbols provide an adequate way to integrate the negative shock of death into "a sacred context for meaning and action in everyday life."[96] Observation through the twentieth century would seem to support the conclusion that most Christians, including Roman Catholics, have found the embalmed, displayed corpse symbolically consistent with, if not reinforcing of, their beliefs (however vague) about the continued personhood of the deceased as a subject of God's good creation and Christ's resurrection.[97] Whether theologians, pastors, and commentators are satisfied with popular (including Catholic) Christian understandings of the resurrection is a different question than an alleged American denial of death. To that question I will return in the concluding section of this chapter.

Meanwhile, the social landscape at the turn of the twenty-first century increasingly orients around a practical, comprehensive ideology of the individual, and with that, a continued struggle for control over the ritual body of death. Now, however, the contest is not between undertakers and some clergy, government, or other watchdogs but rather between the century-old funeral industry and new types of professionals—funeral planners (a subset of the generic event planner)—aligning with the individual consumer's assertion of authority over one's memorial rites. I have already introduced this new dynamic in noting the shifting location of cremated remains from the place of the coffin in traditional rites (churches, chapels, funeral homes, cemeteries) to complete absence from funeral services. Recall funeral concierge Duffey: "If the body doesn't have to be there, it frees us up to do what we want."[98] And what Americans want to do, increasingly, is memorialize themselves according to some activity or place that captures their

[96] Ibid., 110.

[97] See ibid., 130–31, 160–61. That the practices of American undertakers, nonetheless, remains a contested issue among some of the faithful is evident, for example, in a negative review of Laderman's work published by an American Catholic magazine of opinion. See John C. Cort, "Last Wrongs," *Commonweal*, 13 August 2004, 31–33.

[98] See above, n. 87.

personality and life story, whether that be along recreational lines (e.g., a service on a golf course, a concert at the local performing arts center) or a celebration of one's career. The *Times* relays the example of an ice-cream vendor who arranged for his old ice-cream truck to lead his funeral procession, concluding with the doling out of popsicles. A less idiosyncratic innovation well suited to digital image-based culture[99] is the "tribute video," which one funeral planner describes as a "spiritual biography" anchoring the funeral service as an "experience . . . where you get to really know a person."[100] Prepared and often narrated by the deceased at some point in her or his later life, the video would seem to function not so much as a memorial as a continued exercise of the person-subject expressing something further of oneself after death.

The emergence of funeral planners and individually tailored rituals is not only a development positively attuned to the late-modern social body but also a negative response to the keepers of the traditional body, pastoral ministers in local Christian churches. A *Washington Post* article describes baby boomers' dissatisfaction with the generally impersonal and "sometimes stale" quality of traditional, church-based funeral services—a sentiment this author can well appreciate given my encounters with the priest and music director at Casey's parish. Stepping into the void are "funeral celebrants," a concept originating in New Zealand and Australia now spreading in the United States, who testify to how "one size fits all" religious funerals are proving "less than fulfilling for many mourners and providing inadequate memorials for people who hadn't attended church regularly."[101] The desired alternative for many, just as I found among Casey's family and friends, is an upbeat celebration of life. The sister of a deceased auto-parts manager, for example, provided this assessment of the memorial rite a funeral celebrant created, accenting the woman's awards, nicknames, and sports proclivities: "I was really,

---

[99] For a philosophical analysis of the contemporary "universe of digitality" with its "simulations of the hyperreal," see Edith Wyschogrod, *An Ethics of Remembering: History, Heterology, and the Nameless Others* (Chicago: The University of Chicago Press, 1998), 178–200.

[100] Leland, "It's My Funeral and I'll Serve Ice Cream if I Want To."

[101] Ted Gregory, "Funeral Celebrants Say Goodbye, With a Twist," *The Washington Post*, 25 June 2005. Gregory, of the *Chicago Tribune*, reports the approximate number of professional funeral celebrants in the U.S. to be 550 at the time of his writing, with a former Baptist minister operating a training and certification program since 1999.

really happy that I went that route as opposed to a church service. . . . It really was a nice way to step back from the depression of losing my sister and smile a little bit and have some happy memories."[102] Laderman addresses these recent developments toward the end of his study, finding Oprah Winfrey's reported funeral plans, including Motown music and a self-prepared video eulogy, exemplary of "a widespread consumer interest in shaping funerals to embody and celebrate the life lived rather than conform to conventional traditions that suppress or limit expressive ceremonies."[103] Where does this leave the traditional Christian body? Before that concluding consideration, one further development in the social itinerary—a turn to the natural—warrants attention.

Earthy, Ecological Hope: The Natural Body

In Davies's third type, hope embraces the natural, cosmic body through new funerary practices variably known as green, woodland, or natural burial. Part of an ecological-environmental worldview, the concern over death is not simply for one's own person but for the planet. Green burial refers "to the process of burying a body not in any traditional form of churchyard or civic cemetery but in a variety of contexts such as a field in which trees can be planted above graves to develop into woodland. Similarly, a body may be buried in glades to develop into woodland."[104] With the objective—at once aesthetic and ethical—being the human body's natural decay and contribution to the earth, embalming, lined coffins, concrete vaults, tombstones and statues cede to cloth shrouds or biodegradable wood or wicker caskets, with shrubs, trees, or in some cases natural fieldstones as markers. Originating in the United Kingdom during the past couple decades and allied with the National Memorial Arboretum project, the woodland burial movement now accounts for over 10 percent of British interments. Since 1998 the United States has seen its first burial preserve in rural South Carolina usher in a small but growing number of green cemeteries dotting the land south and north, coast to coast.[105]

Davies analyzes woodland burial as countering both postmodernism and to some extent traditional Christianity. In contrast to the

---

[102] Ibid.

[103] Laderman, *Rest in Peace*, 184. See also, 139, 151, 180.

[104] Davies, *A Brief History of Death*, 81.

[105] William Kates, "'Green' burials usher in the ultimate recycling," *The Boston Globe*, 5 July 2006.

postmodern favoring of individuals' fragmented, idiosyncratic self-constructions over socially shared grand narratives, ecological consciousness is a comprehensive worldview. "Green" is proving a symbol powerful enough to encompass both life and death, with the corpse becoming one's final role in the "circle of life," nourishing the land and its creatures. While green burial need not necessarily entail rejection of Christian beliefs, Davies argues, still he finds belief in an "ecological immortality" driving this emergent practice, one that can in fact often function in place of conventional Christian understanding: "The key to the appeal of this outlook lies in a dynamic view of 'nature', of an ongoing system of which one is a part and not of some radical divide between mankind and nature . . . woodland burial furnishes an authentic basis for understanding both life and death for those for whom either 'heaven' or 'memory' is an unbelievable or inadequate means of making sense of life and of death."[106] A middle-aged woman, who with her family has adopted South Carolina's Ramsey Creek Preserve as their burial location, articulates the contrast: "I like that the land is wild and always changing with time . . . Whether we like it or not, death is about change. To pretend my [recently deceased] brother is just sleeping under a mowed and manicured lawn is to deny that death is about change."[107] The brilliance in this quote, for the purposes of our present study, lies not only in the speaker's enlightening what the so-called American denial of death often entails—the denial of change—but also in her implying that the traditional Christian images for death—rest, sleep, immortality—are likewise susceptible to interpretations that render them impotent for healing grief and fostering hope. To the content of the tradition then this chapter turns in conclusion.

FAITH IN THE RESURRECTION OF THE BODY: TRADITION IN PRACTICE

The Roman Sacramentary's first preface for Masses for the Dead (Christian Death I) proclaims, "Lord, for your faithful people life is changed, not ended." The power of these words to linger in thought and memory lies in their brevity and directness, and yet they belie

---

[106] Davies, *A Brief History of Death*, 87.

[107] Kates, "'Green' burials usher in the ultimate recycling." The newspaper article does not neglect the consumer angle, as well, noting the difference between average costs for a "traditional" (that is, American funeral industry) funeral and natural burials.

millennia-long variations in how Christians have interpreted the symbol of resurrection. The preceding paragraph of the preface duly situates this belief within the paschal mystery: "In him, who rose from the dead, our hope of resurrection dawned. The sadness of death gives way to the bright promise of immortality." The prayer clearly asserts faith as a human act of hope in a divinely given promise while leaving open questions about the character and timing of believers' immortality. Prayers, of course, are not theological arguments. Still the implications of how we understand our immortality in relation to Christ's resurrection are significant for how we face death—that of loved ones and ourselves—and carry out our lives accordingly.

The content of Christian hope is in question: Do the lines of the preface (Christian Death I) proclaim Jesus' resurrection as the source of all others, an unprecedented change in the human condition offered in hope to believers? Or might these words be heard to say that Jesus' resurrection gives hope by revealing to humans the sure destiny of their true nature? Put another way, does Christian hope in resurrection stand on God having done to Jesus something radically new for all humanity, namely, giving life after death? Or on the contrary, does Jesus' resurrection give hope by confirming humanity's innate capacity for immortality? And what of the timing in all this? Do the dead enter into the risen condition immediately? After asserting life's being changed, not ended, the preface continues: "When the body of our earthly dwelling lies in death we gain an everlasting dwelling place in heaven." While perhaps acceptable in the function of consoling the liturgically assembled faithful, who in the preface dialogue would have just lifted up their hearts to the Lord, the statement is biblically and theologically problematic. Biblical faith recognizes not the moment of one's bodily death but rather one's sacramental dying with Christ in baptism as establishing one's everlasting dwelling place. Baptism places all believers, living *and* dead, in the eschatological tension, waiting for Christ's coming again in glory *and* judgment. The words of the preface, on the other hand, could imply that death causes an immediate passage from earth (and the body) to heaven.

The sort of ambiguity about the resurrection the current preface for Masses for the dead betrays has riddled Christian belief since the earliest generations of the church.[108] Paul, whom Acts of the Apostles

---

[108] In the introduction to her book on early-through-medieval Christian beliefs about the resurrection of the dead Bynum asserts that our late-modern

depicts being laughed off the Areopagus in Athens for proclaiming the resurrection of the dead (see Acts 17:32), chose his words well in exclaiming at the outset of his discussion of the topic in First Corinthians: "Listen, I will tell you a mystery!" He proceeds to explain that the baptized will not all die but be changed, not immediately but only "at the last trumpet," when "the dead will be raised imperishable, and we will be changed" (1 Cor 15:51-52). Bynum reports that Paul's metaphor for the deceased Christian body as a "bare seed" that must die in order to become something else (e.g., wheat), sown in a perishable physical state so as eventually to be raised an imperishable "spiritual" body (1 Cor 15:36-37, 42-43), governed pastoral teaching in the earliest Christian centuries.

Irenaeus and Tertullian, each holding the whole person (body and soul) as the subject of salvation, asserted both continuity and change as paradoxically inherent to the radical transformation that will come in the final resurrection. For Tertullian, human identity resides in bodily particularity, so that "[e]verything intrinsic to what we are must reappear in the resurrected body," even if no longer useful as before. [109] Tertullian, Bynum argues, exploits the Pauline teaching about the corrupt becoming incorruptible to the maximum: God does not abandon the person in the repulsive demise of the flesh but rather makes it the fulcrum of salvation. Irenaeus likewise does not blink in the face of mortal decomposition but sees promise for the total human person who in this life has consumed Christ's Body, participation in a eucharistic mystery available to us only if kernels decompose in earth to yield something new, namely, grain for the sacred bread. [110]

While right through the High Middle Ages the Eucharist would prove crucial to Christian confidence in the resurrection of the body,

---

"considerations of self and survival take the body with impassioned seriousness," concluding: "[T]he deep anxiety we feel about artificial intelligence and organ transplants, about the proper care of cadavers, about the definition of death—an anxiety revealed in the images of bodily partition and reassemblage that proliferate in our movies and pulp fiction—connects us more closely than most of us are aware to a long Western tradition of abstruse discussion of bodily resurrection" (*The Resurrection of the Body*, 17).

[109] Ibid., 37.

[110] Ibid., 39. Bynum quotes Irenaeus's *Against Heresies*, bk. 5, chap. 2, par. 3. See also pertinent extracts of *Against Heresies* with commentary in Joanne E. McWilliam Dewart, *Death and Resurrection*, Message of the Fathers of the Church 22 (Wilmington, DE: Michael Glazier, 1986), 92–99.

popular imagination and doctrinal explanations of the connection between the material of the sacrament and the postmortem fate of believers reflected a major turn in theological anthropology. The understanding of salvation shifted from the reassembling of each person's unique bodily parts for their further (Pauline) transformation into a heavenly body to the (philosophical Greek) immortal soul's finally attaining in heaven the perfect, changeless body whose form it always bore in potency. Whereas earlier generations embraced Paul's seed metaphor in anticipating God's radical change of each believers' bodily condition in the final resurrection, the "extraordinary bodily discipline of the ascetic movement" in the fourth century led to identifying change itself as the problem.[111] Ascetics' mastery over basic needs of nutrition and procreation made their bodies symbols in this life (sacraments, we could now say) of the pure, unchanging, eternal state of the glorified bodies that Augustine would teach is the beatitude of those judged worthy of the resurrection of the dead. The Middle Ages brought a different twist to the iconic quality of saints. The faithful came to consider every part of the body as containing the sanctity of the whole person, just as every fragment of the Eucharist was believed to contain the total Christ. The identification took symbolic form in a proliferation of reliquaries containing fragments of saints' bodies similar in design to eucharistic monstrances.

Bynum mounts ample evidence for how the ascendancy of the language of soul through the Middle Ages was not a rejection of the body but rather a somatosizing of the soul. In the thirteenth century Aquinas's positing of the body's formal identity *in* the soul made possible an understanding of the self perduring independently of the physical body's rotting demise, such that at the final resurrection the soul can take up whatever matter provided and conform it to its changeless, perfected self. Unlike Augustine, therefore, Aquinas did not consider the deceased's soul detained from the vision of God until it united again with body at the last trumpet but, on the contrary, capable of the beatific vision immediately after death. Lest he contradict biblical faith in the resurrection of the *body*, Bynum argues, Thomas reasoned that the body the soul receives at the final resurrection is an expression of the glory the soul enjoys in its ongoing *visio Dei*.[112] The matter, however, remained a cause for much debate. The official ecclesial

---

[111] Bynum, *The Resurrection of the Body*, 112.
[112] See ibid., 265–71.

243

resolution of the beatific vision controversy in the 1330s defeated the claim that the individual cannot enjoy God until soul reunites with body; rather, Pope Benedict XII decreed, the souls of the just are able to do so separated from the bodies they will receive in the final resurrection. Belief in immediate judgment at death—resulting in beatific vision, eternal damnation, or temporal purgation—does not preclude all assembling at the trumpet call of Last Judgment, when the body will conform to the soul's final state. The papal bull of 1336 affirmed that souls can enter into the beatific vision whenever they attain full spiritual purification. Thus, "the doctrine of purgatory and the doctrine of resurrection were necessary to a theology in which death is decisive, prayers for the dead are effective, and self is a psychosomatic unity.[113]

One can see in that papal resolution, which holds doctrinal sway in the church to this day, content that both resonates with yet also challenges the imagination of modern and now postmodern Christians. The strong agency of individual selves, both that of the dead and that of the living whose prayers are efficacious toward them, would seem to be at home in contemporary society. Yet the notion of divine judgment implicit in the need for such prayers along with the full embrace of death's decisive character push back against an American culture largely in denial of the radical change that death so powerfully wields. To focus on the denial of change here is to recognize that ultimately the issue is, indeed, one of power. Denial of the radical change death entails is the denial of surrender, a persistence in asserting that one is and always will be in control over one's life and circumstances, a malaise in the contemporary social body in need of the healing ministrations nature and tradition afford.

To surrender one's body or that of a loved one to the earth's natural forces of change is to trust in a larger cosmic history that first and finally belongs to God. With the apostle Paul and the evangelist John, along with Irenaeus and Tertullian, who reflected upon those Scriptures, contemporary believers can perceive in the earthy decomposition of mortal bodies a powerfully kenotic "space" God has entered so as to heal every aspect of the human condition, even its seeming demise. Those earliest Christian authors can still teach us how the natural material comprising our eucharistic food reveals the goodness of all creation and the place of our bodies' waxing and waning therein, as well as God's promise to bring about in this created order an even

---

[113] Ibid., 282.

greater, unforeseen salvation. Christian tradition can discover a new saving, healing power in dialogue with such ecologically oriented movements as green burial by embracing the awareness that we are not strictly autonomous minds or souls merely using our bodies and this earth until no longer personally needed (or endured).[114] Christian faith, rather, can grow by considering how the union of the deceased body with the cyclical life processes of the natural environment invites us to a more cosmic Christology and pneumatology, salvific surrender to the Word and Spirit through whom God creates, sustains, and ultimately will redeem all.[115] Surrendering our bodies to the ecological environment that we received as a divine gift from the start, Christians can in faith embrace what Irenaeus so beautifully described as the two creative and redeeming hands of God—the Word and the Spirit—that have never let go of humanity, nor ever will.[116] That faith lies in the hands of the man nailed to a cross, whom the Father has made the firstborn of a new creation through the power of the Spirit (see Rom 8:10-11, 18-30; Col 1:15-20; Rev 1:5). Christian faith heals human spirits broken by the fearsome change inherent in death by proclaiming, through word and sacrament, a hope fulfilling, indeed, exceeding all natural and social expectations, the hope founded on the divine love that conquered human death in Jesus.

To surrender to the traditional body of the crucified and risen Christ is, in Chauvet's terms, to assent in faith to a salvation made possible by the Word's surrender to the mercy of the body. For those baptized into Christ, contemporary social denial of the radical change wrought by death entails squandering the true freedom that comes in

---

[114] Compatibility of green burial with Christian doctrine would seem to parallel the Catholic Church's endorsement of cremation as a viable option for the Christian corpse. The U.S. Bishops' cremation appendix for the OCF explains the viability of the practice as long as it is not undertaken as a rebuttal of Christian belief in the resurrection (as was the case for many in the fervor of post-Enlightenment Europe). The positive view of cremation, on the other hand, is the recognition that all bodies naturally decay to dust and that faith trusts in God's mysterious plan to create a new bodily existence for all in the resurrection on the last day.

[115] See Jürgen Moltmann, *The Spirit of Life: A Universal Affirmation*, trans. Margaret Kohl (Minneapolis: Ausgburg Fortress, 1992), 8–10, 230–36; and *God in Creation*, trans. Margaret Kohl (Minneapolis: Augsburg Fortress, 1993), 9–13, 98–103.

[116] See Irenaeus, *Against Heresies*, bk. 5, chap. 6, par. 1.

embracing the traditional body of the One who, in the astute terminology of N. T. Wright, has become the source of *life after life after death*. Wright underlines that phrase for its ability to convey the specific meaning of resurrection at the origins of Christianity. Since all the ancients, whether pagans, Jews, or Christians, could speak of some sort of enduring human condition directly following from bodily death, they recognized in the concept of *anastasis* (resurrection) a more provocative claim, namely, of a new life granted by God following the period of being dead. "Pagans denied this possibility; some Jews affirmed it as a long-term future hope; virtually all Christians claimed that it had happened to Jesus and would happen to them in the future. All of them were speaking of a new life *after* 'life after death' in the popular sense, a fresh living embodiment *following* a period of death-as-a-state (during which one might or might not be 'alive' in some other, non-bodily fashion). Nobody (except the Christians, in respect of Jesus) thought that this had already happened, even in isolated cases."[117] Wright argues for how biblical faith in the resurrection bears compelling content for believers' hope in what lies beyond death as well as the implications of that eschatological vision for the conduct of life in this present age.

Knowledge of the complete ancient Jewish context is essential for grasping the New Testament's message about Jesus' resurrection. "Resurrection was *never* simply a way of speaking about 'life after death.'"[118] For the classical prophets the concept had a metaphorical meaning bespeaking hope in God's bringing the nation of Israel back to life after destruction and exile through imagery eliding YHWH's powers of creation and redemption. In the face of mounting evidence in the third century BC that Israel could not withstand foreign political domination, Wisdom literature shifted hope to a new world, a new creation that the righteous, as newly embodied persons, would inhabit by the gracious favor of God. Such belief necessarily gave rise to varied conceptions of the intermediate state of the dead until the eschatological dawn of the new cosmic order.

The key to understanding the meaning of resurrection in second-temple Judaism, Wright argues, lies in its ranging between the metaphorical expression of the sociopolitical restoration of Israel and

---

[117] N. T. Wright, *The Resurrection of the Son of God*, Christian Origins and the Question of God, vol. 3 (Minneapolis: Fortress Press, 2003), 31.

[118] Ibid., 201.

the literal re-embodiment of the righteous, living and deceased, as the new people of God. The latter was the hope of those Jews who struggled against foreign contamination, collaboration, and corruption to the point of martyrdom, as well as all who by the first century CE yearned for YHWH's deliverance of a new order inhabited by a people recreated. While Herodians, Sadducees, and others collaborating with the Romans could not but be opposed to such rhetoric of resurrection, even scribes, Pharisees, or various revolutionaries committed to the concept could not imagine its happening bodily to just one person in advance of others. Thus, Wright argues, the resurrection of Jesus is both native to its second-temple Jewish milieu and startlingly original in its claim of his unique status as the risen one, source and promise of future resurrection for the people of the new covenant God has established in him.

Primordial Christian belief in the bodily resurrection of Jesus, far from focusing faith on a Christ merely removed to some distant heaven, was (and is for us now) a far more radical worldview committed to social orders and personal lives based on his lordship. Thus was the "*symbolic* world of early Christianity focused upon Jesus himself. The symbolic actions of baptism and eucharist, though of course having Jewish antecedents and pagan analogues, were consciously undertaken with reference to him."[119] For Christians, history, that most fundamental of human constructions, now orients itself to the risen Christ as a time of overlapping ages, the present order and the future "fresh act of creative grace when Jesus appears," when bodies, although "prone to suffering and decay," will be restored in the "full and final redemption of the creation, and ourselves within it."[120] The latter is what Wright means by life after life after death. In the interim the deceased continue existence in a state biblically and traditionally characterized as rest or sleep.

[119] Ibid., 580.

[120] Ibid., 581. Douglas B. Farrow argues convincingly for how the doctrine of Jesus' *bodily* ascension places the lives of the baptized in the ongoing course of "Jesus-history," utterly dependent upon the Spirit who makes the absent Christ present in ethical and liturgical lives patterned on his own. Recovery of the doctrine, Farrow also demonstrates, can help ward off the twin evils of clericalism and triumphalism that have so long plagued the church. See *Ascension and Ecclesia: On the Significance of the Doctrine of the Ascension for Ecclesiology and Christian Cosmology* (Grand Rapids, MI: Eerdmans Publishing, 1999), 7–14, 78–85, 222–29.

I return then, finally, to the metaphorical, symbolic language of the current *Order of Christian Funerals*, in which confident petitioning of rest, sleep, refreshment, and peace abounds, as in this typical conclusion that follows on the assembly's praying of the Our Father:

> Into your hands, O Lord, we humbly entrust our brother/sister N.
> In this life you embraced him/her with your tender love;
> deliver him/her now from every evil
> and bid him/her enter eternal rest. . . .[121]

The priest's introduction to the general intercessions in the funeral Mass proclaims the source of hope for mourners and elicits their faith in him: "Brothers and sisters, Jesus Christ is risen from the dead and sits at the right hand of the Father, where he intercedes for his Church. Confident that God hears the voices of those who trust in the Lord Jesus, we join our prayers to his . . ."[122] The ensuing petitions speak of the deceased's baptism that dispelled all darkness, participation in the Eucharist that leads toward the heavenly banquet, friends and family who have died and gone before, concern for those in this world now suffering injustice and death by violence, war, and famine, the family and loved ones of the deceased in need of healing from their pain and grief, and finally, all the assembled that they might live according to hope in the resurrection. Such are the words with which the faithful pray in the presence of their beloved dead, intercessions raising up not only the deceased and the assembly but all creation into the healing hands of God. Argument and explanation are not the order of the moment but rather bodily performance of ritual gestures that proclaim the content of a faith lived in between the times of this age and the new creation to come and phrases evoking a hope that heals when faith feels stuck in between. Consistently powerful in my pastoral-liturgical experience are those comprising the general intercessions at the Vigil: "Risen Lord, pattern of our life for ever . . . Promise and image of what we shall be . . . Son of God who came to destroy sin and death . . . Word of God who delivered us from fear of death . . . Crucified Lord, forsaken in death, raised in glory . . ."[123] To each invocation in that litany all respond, "Lord, have mercy," bespeaking at

[121] OCF, no. 117-B.
[122] Ibid., no. 167-A.
[123] Ibid., no. 78.

once the need of mourning hearts and confidence of faithful souls assembled as one body in the crucified and risen Christ, whom the presiding minister addresses in a concluding prayer, "You alone are the Holy One, you are mercy itself." [124]

The church's central liturgical action is at the font and the table, baptism and Eucharist, and both of these in conjunction with the proclaimed word.[125] These frame and animate the Order of Christian Funerals. Only by them can one make sense of what we do as a church, as well as what our hope is as a church in the face of death. Our not skirting the margins, allowing our faith to face the harsh reality of human death, not papering it over or whisking it aside, not shying from prophetic parables and sometimes stark symbols allows us to enter into and be consoled—if not in the moment then over time—in the paradox of the paschal mystery. For if we recover this belief in God's love for all creation unto death, recover it in a way that is practical for lives of faith, then we recover as well the patristic wisdom that the glory of God is the sanctification and salvation of people. God's graciousness answers the greatest of human need. God's powerful love is known in humans' living response to that grace. The paradox emerges in God's keeping of time, which is not ours, while the glory resides in an ethics, a way of life, practiced in eschatological hope that, in most sound tradition, characterize the entire Christian life, including death, as the worship of God.

[124] Ibid., no. 80-A.

[125] Gordon W. Lathrop has produced an eloquent ecumenical elucidation of the generative "juxtaposition" of word, water, and table in Christian liturgy. See his *Holy Things: A Liturgical Theology* (Minneapolis: Augsburg Fortress, 1993), 33–66, 100–103.

Part 4

Conclusion

Chapter 8

Recovering Ancient Treasure:
Tradition at the Service of Life's Margins

BETWEEN THE STONE AGE AND THE NEW AGE

In the windswept little seaside town of Plouharnel, France, boldly facing out into the vast Atlantic Ocean midway along the South Coast of Brittany, the oldest houses in the village are clustered around neither a fountain nor a well, let alone a cobblestone square with a church at one end. The classic whitewashed, black-roofed Breton homes, rather, sit around a remarkable prehistoric site: a mound of earth encompassing about an acre, bordered three-fourths of the way around by the wild, lush *ajonc* bushes characteristic of the region, with the northern side openly sloping up to immense slabs of stone resting atop partially protruding, tightly arranged vertical boulders. The Rondessec Dolmens (*dolmen* being the Breton term for "flat stone") are a set of three parallel, quasi-subterranean, low, narrow, stone-encased passageways, ranging from fifteen to thirty-seven feet in length, each opening out into wider, higher burial chambers.[1] A distinctive feature of the easternmost dolmen, or passage grave, is located at the southwest corner of the large trapezoidal burial room, where lies a much smaller, lower side chamber, accessible through an opening in the megaliths supporting the massive slabs overhead. There I found myself squatting on a dank mid-November morning, still and alone, occasionally noticing the chirping of birds in the wild shrubbery overhead or the passing of vehicles on the highway a short ways off, and thinking to myself: "My gosh! Two thousand BC! People were laying their dead, along with implements and pots and jewelry, as many centuries—millennia—before the life, death, and resurrection of Jesus as have since followed to our own day!"

---

[1] See Jacques Briard, *Carnac, Land of Megaliths*, trans. Angela Moyon (Paris, France: Editions Jean-Paul Gisserot, 2000), 14–18.

Caught up in that utterly somatic-conscious moment I was, quite literally, only half right. Archeologists actually date the gravesite back to four thousand BC, whereas the year two thousand concerns the dating of two gold collar-style necklaces discovered some decades ago in the westernmost of the three dolmens. An array of numbers—dates, dimensions, distances—was swirling in my head as I spent the daylight hours hiking from one Stone Age scene to another and, starving for information about what I had seen, reading whatever I could get my hands on in the evening. Over a forty-eight-hour period I had become quite enchanted by the megalithic sites in the town of Carnac and its environs, considered the most important prehistoric locale in Europe as well as the oldest place on the planet known to be continuously inhabited by humans, the home of complex, enigmatic *alignments* (parallel rows stretching over fifteen kilometers) of thousands of massive single upright stones and more than fifty extant dolmens, the oldest of which predate Knossos, the Pyramids, the Egyptian temples of Karnak, and Stonehenge.[2] Archeological evidence points to late Stone Age settlements on the South Breton coast by six thousand BC, while carbon-14 dating estimates the construction of the Kercado dolmen in Carnac at 4,600 to 4,700 BC. This impressive dolmen, its long stone passageways and burial chamber covered by a massive barrow of earth surmounted by a *menhir* (Breton for an erect standing stone) and completely encircled by stones standing a short distance from the mound's base, was in use for nearly three thousand years. In the eighteenth and nineteenth centuries the Kercado, Rondossec, and other dolmens yielded a trove of axes, flint arrowheads, pottery, beads, and other artifacts to scientists and then, not surprisingly, treasure hunters. Compromising damage to the sites inevitably ensued and, with the ever-increasing influx of tourists, increased in the twentieth century. After significant debate and vigorous local opposition, fences now protect the stones and terrain of the alignments, allowing only limited periods for walking among them in the winter off-season.

The notion of damage is, of course, perspectival. People today easily speak of "relative damage" as they argue from conflicting positions in relation to a contested proposal or event—a traffic accident, a risky medical operation, an earthquake, a military initiative—with the degree of injury, as well as culpability, ranging from epochal to nil. This is

[2] See ibid., 8–10, 27; and Greg Ward, *Brittany and Normandy*, 8th ed. (London: Rough Guides/Penguin, 2003), 380.

perhaps most readily evident in contemporary controversies, national and international, over ecological issues. Environmentalists struggle to raise popular awareness and influence governmental policies to counter deforestation in the Amazon basin, aggressive logging in the Pacific Northwest, oil drilling in the Alaskan Artic Wildlife Refuge, unrestricted snowmobiling in national parks, and so on, while nations strive to negotiate protocols for carbon monoxide and other chemical emissions with a wary view toward global warming and the ozone layer. Whereas some perceive devastation and the need to "heal" natural habitats, if not the entire Mother Earth, others scoff from their (to them) more realistic, reasonable perspective, one that bases human value on the expansion of economic capital and human peace of mind on the inevitable, unbroken trajectory of success in the physical sciences. There is no danger, at least not to "us" here and now.

Then come the voices from the margins ("them"), the peoples native to the specific environs in question (in the Americas or Australia, for example), often broken and struggling to retain or even recover their traditional ways that, to their estimation, hold the key to a better quality of life in a modern world whose economic and scientific progress has generally run them right over. Often today not only do they see all too clearly the evidence of damage—physical, psychological, social, and spiritual—among the scarred lives of their people, but they also perceive disrespect if not further exploitation by financially and socially comfortable Euro-Americans pursuing New Age holistic spiritualities, blissful states of mind and body through often romantic, selective appropriations of their indigenous beliefs and practices. History is indeed a question of *whose* history and, therefore, whose *future*, a present exercise of the human spirit—intelligence and values— forging meaning in circumstances physical and sociopolitical in their delineations, with death always constituting the limiting factor.[3]

[3] Political and liberation theologies have introduced and continued to press this issue for the church, with the leading contributions in each field including Johann Baptist Metz, *Faith in History and Society: Toward a Practical Fundamental Theology*, trans. J. Matthew Ashley, rev. ed. (New York: Crossroad, 2007), and Gustavo Gutiérrez, *A Theology of Liberation: History, Politics, and Salvation*, trans. Matthew J. O'Connell, rev. ed. (Maryknoll, NY: Orbis Books, 1988). In cultural anthropology a seminal work is Eric Wolf, *Europe and the People without History* (Berkeley: University of California Press, 1982).

And so I turn again to the ancient stone monuments of the Carnac area, those thousands of big rocks, humanly arranged millennia ago, some silently streaming along gently rolling meadows, others cut off and crammed by recent roadways, numb and speechless and, yet for all that, bespeaking an array of mystery and danger relative to both themselves and those who encounter them today. While the passage graves, long since ransacked for their artifacts and precious metals, bear a certain attraction not only to social and physical scientists but also a fair number of tourists, it is the utterly enigmatic alignments of standing stones (*menhirs*) that have so strongly captured modern human imaginations, attracting hundreds of thousands of tourists who, over many decades, managed to reduce the earth on which they stand to hideously eroded dirt, the land left in a drought-like desert condition. Add to this the problem of people knocking over the unstable stones, not to mention scribbling them with their own graffiti, and one gets a sense of why concerned scientists and other citizens came to argue that the megaliths of Carnac had become victims of their own modern success. Even this conventional statement, however, carries important unspoken assumptions about value and damage, beauty and danger, art and utility. For some, treasure lay beneath the dolmens in the form of objects that could be sold for monetary gain, while others saw a different sort of human value in the artifacts, treasure in terms of human history, a contemporary valuing of ancient ancestors by means of reverently preserving their handiwork so as to make it available for generations to come. In either case, nonetheless, the fundamental operative question concerns judgment about what brings value to human living, what makes people feel fulfilled, whole, significant. In this case, the answers would seem to be immediate financial gain or wealth, on the one hand, and a greater, larger sense of historical human lineage and one's place therein, on the other.

With the prospect of extracting direct financial gain from the sites long gone (the tourist industry being another topic), people have been combing over Carnac's colossal alignments for another century and a half with other sorts of value questions in mind. The perspectives modern people bring to the stones say as much if not more about themselves as they do about the primitive yet undeniably elegant, powerful alignments. These stones sit there as an immense puzzle concerning both prehistoric social (symbolic, religious, economic, familial) behavior and the endless and thus *contemporary* quest to understand the ultimate relationship of humanity to the earth, the vast physical cosmos, and whatever might exist "beyond." There is, I am wagering, no small lesson here about how we late-modern people, including the millions who self-identify as Christians, go about constructing our worldviews, especially in the face of those limit situations—including sickness, interpersonal or social alienation, and death—that, no matter how much we might want to believe in scientific and technological capabilities, defy our explicit and tacit claims to total control over life.

Theories about the purpose of the large and complex stone alignments of Carnac range from legendary to naturalist, from military to agricultural, from funerary to astrological.[4] While some in the eighteenth century embraced a naturalist perspective, proposing that earthquakes, floods, fires, and other cataclysmic storms had caused the alignments, such reversion to raw natural forces could scarcely stand up to the precisely ordered rows of megaliths. The rest of that century, therefore, yielded interpretations focusing on that orderliness, a combination of the military, funerary, and legendary. The rows of great stones had been erected to honor those fallen on a great battlefield, or they were the product of Roman soldiers' systematic construction of campsites, or they were Roman soldiers themselves, murderous pursuers whom St. Cornely had turned to stone. The turn of the nineteenth century brought theories of religious monuments, a notion, granted certain qualifications and nuances, still favored by some contemporary scholars: Carnac was the site of general assemblies of Druids. The stones were aligned to represent the stars, the sun, and moon, curved in a serpentine manner symbolizing the annual cycle of seasons or the signs of the zodiac, or positioned for the worship of heavenly bodies.

Astronomical theories for the alignments of not only Carnac but its relation to other megalithic sites in the region reached new sophistication in the twentieth century, especially through the publications of a Scots scientist, Alexander Thom, who claimed to have discovered a standard of measure (the "megalithic yard") operative within and among the alignments.[5] While popular opinion has favored

[4] See Aubrey Burl, *From Carnac to Callanish: The Prehistoric Stone Rows and Avenues of Britain, Ireland, and Brittany* (New Haven, CT: Yale University Press, 1993), 1–25; see also, Briard, *Carnac, Land of Megaliths*, 3, 23–30; Ward, *Brittany and Normandy*, 382–83.

[5] See Burl, *From Carnac to Callanish*, 16–17, 131–46.

his theory that the stones amount to a vast system for charting and predicting lunar and other celestial movements, other scientists have been able to point out no small amount of lacunae within and counterevidence against his otherwise attractive theory, as well as conjectures about prehistoric humans methodically lighting fires in position with the huge stones and recording findings over nine- or eighteen-year cycles. A very different sort of response to the megaliths were popular perceptions of them as phallic symbols and fertility sites, leading nineteenth-century church officials to place crosses atop many, to destroy others, and to condemn the practices of young couples sliding down the Grand Menhir on May Day.[6]

MOTIVATION FOR A TREASURE HUNT: PLACING TRADITIONAL RITES IN PERSPECTIVE

My point in describing the megaliths of Carnac and reporting the range of theories about them in the conclusion to a book on contemporary Roman Catholic liturgical practices of healing is basically about perspective, and this in two senses. First, by even briefly considering the theories about the alignments generated over the last two centuries we can take stock of several fundamental biases from which modern people might tend to approach enigmatic questions—in this case, the phenomenal rows of standing stones and scores of prehistoric passage graves. But we might also keep in mind the puzzles of body and spirit, time and space, unity and alienation, life and death, to which the stones point. The second sense of perspective is that of the Christian in the midst of postmodernity.

First, several modern perspectives are evident in response to the mysterious megaliths: To argue that the alignments constituted a center for religious beliefs and practices would seem to point to a certain confidence in humans—even prehistoric ones—to construct monumental objects and execute rituals affirming human corporality in relation to cosmic processes. Such interpretations, whether scientific or popular, can carry with them an implicit criticism of a Christianity perceived as condemnatory of the body and the natural. Eclectic practices or all-out pursuits of pre-Christian spiritualities often seek a wisdom inherent in aligning human bodies and spirits with the waxing and waning of physical and even supernatural forces in the universe. On

[6] See Ward, *Brittany and Normandy*, 410.

the other hand, the more recent, highly elaborate astronomical theories about the Carnac alignments would seem to indicate a reliance on humanity's scientific ability, when faced with such vastly complex bodies as stars and galaxies and the question of our relationship to them, to go about attacking the problem systematically, setting out timetables and distance measurements and graphs (whose well-aligned points would seem to be multi-ton boulders!). Repeated experimentation, time, and trial and error can eventually discover the physical processes at work in the universe and perhaps something about the place of our bodies therein. There is, finally, also the ecclesial authorities' need to place the prehistoric (yet still powerful) rocks under the sign of the cross, an affirmation of the ultimate source of power, cosmic and traditional, as well as the power of its vicars here on earth to define what is and is not permissible for those in their realm. Modern people's responses in these cases have demonstrated: fascination with, if not practice of, ancient animistic, astrological, or other pre-Christian European religions; the propensity to see scientific enterprise at work, even among prehistoric peoples; and the anxiousness of ecclesial hierarchs to exert control over what would seem to rival the authoritative claims of the Christian faith or lead the faithful to abuse of their own and others' bodies.

The second sense of perspective returns to this closing chapter's opening paragraph, written in the first person singular by a well-educated, North American, middle-class Catholic liturgical theologian. Although it is the sort of experience that defies cogent analysis (and thus is usually ignored in academic books of theology), I want to note the sheer bodiliness of my unexpectedly captivating two days among the megaliths in Carnac. The visual wonder I experienced looking down, along, and across the alignments set me on a sense of mission in relation to the dolmens. To bend low and scoot through the tunnel of the eastern Rondessec dolmen, feeling an unsolicited sense of danger and the unknown for those few seconds before standing upright inside the rather spacious, somehow comforting and enfolding burial chamber: this sort of bodily awareness draws on the primordial human experience of birth but also the uncertain passage toward death. Human societies to this very day, by means of ritual traditions, have exploited this sort of bodily knowledge in a wide array of rites of passage that are always touching on the great limit questions of life and death, placing meaning in question, mystery at the center, time in the balance, bringing reason to its knees. Rudolph Otto coined the contemporary classic language of the "holy" or sacred to analyze this type of human experience that is at once terrible and inviting.[7] More recently, as we have seen in chapter 7, Louis-Marie Chauvet has emphasized the irreducibly bodily nature of such human experience of the transcendent, arguing that each person-subject's thoughts and desires are constructed as a person-body at once physical, cultural, and traditional.[8]

My own construction of experience in that moment included an array of *physical* awareness: smelling the fragrances of shrubs above and dank earth below, hearing the birds sing, feeling the dampness of the cold humid air in my shoulders, and touching the closeness of the boulders just overhead and all around, sensing a sort of secure bodily containment. At the same time, my awareness also turned *cultural* as I noticed the sound of cars speeding along the nearby road, creating thoughts about the dissonance between the world of automobiles, car stereos, and cell phones and whatever prehistoric people might have looked like and been thinking, walking along that coastal plane millennia ago. The most important factor shaping my awareness in that moment, however, was my religious faith *tradition*, as I found myself calibrating the date of those prehistoric passage graves in relation to the life, death, and resurrection of Jesus of Nazareth.

The questions over which I began to puzzle were by no means original to me; indeed, they were conditioned by the often challenging conversations I have shared with students, parishioners, fellow pastoral ministers (Roman Catholic and otherwise), friends and family, religiously practicing and nonpracticing alike: What can it mean to say that Jesus of Nazareth, a first-century Palestinian Jew, was bodily raised from the dead? How is his death and resurrection the defining moment for the life and death of all peoples around the globe and down the ages, across past millennia and for seemingly countless centuries still to come? What does faith in this Jesus "say" to me or to my loved one or to us together when physical disability from an auto accident is permanent, or he or she has been called up for active duty

---

[7] See Rudolph Otto, *The Idea of the Holy: An Inquiry into the Non-Rational Factor in the Idea of the Divine and Its Relation to the Rational*, trans. John W. Harvey (New York: Oxford University Press, 1958).

[8] Louis-Marie Chauvet, *Symbol and Sacrament: A Sacramental Reinterpretation of Christian Existence*, trans. Patrick Madigan and Madeleine Beaumont (Collegeville, MN: Liturgical Press, 1995), 147–51.

in a war zone, or the only remaining medical option is palliative care? How does the content of the gospel stories of Jesus' work of teaching and healing, as well as the witness of the first generation of believers, affect people's experiences of sickness and health, life and death, here and now, let alone against the vast expanse of time and space? Is not faith in the Gospel incredibly scandalous in its utterly particular claims about this Jesus of Nazareth? Do we not do better, really, by filling in the blanks of life's enigmatic events and passages—its interpersonal and social alienations, illnesses, and deaths—with whatever consoling forms of art and science, philosophy and folk wisdom we have the luxury of collecting and conveying through the vast communications capabilities of our postmodern age? Are we not at this point in human history—at least those of us with the luxurious availability of modern medicine—more realistic in placing our faith in science and technology, using our religious ceremonies (liturgies, rites, and sacraments) as vehicles for an aura of dignity and ultimacy, or perhaps final authority, when life crises have finally broken down all those economic and technological defenses?

SETTING OUT ON A NEW TRADITIONAL QUEST

The rites studied in part 3 of this book grew out of the programmatic mandate of the Second Vatican Council's Constitution on the Sacred Liturgy: ". . . the sacred Council judges that the following principles concerning the promotion and reform of the liturgy should be called to mind, and that practical norms should be established."[9] That document, as is well known in academic theological circles, was the liturgical movement's many decades of historical research and ritual experimentation come to official fruition in the church. Setting aside theologies and practices of the rites as clerical duties canonically executed before largely passive and varyingly receptive laity, the council from the start proclaimed the liturgy the privileged means whereby all the faithful actively participate in expressing the divine and human mission of the church in Christ.[10] In order for such a drastic change in perception and practice to occur, the council ordered "that, where necessary, the rites be revised carefully in the light of sound tradition, and

[9] *Sacrosanctum Concilium* (The Constitution on the Sacred Liturgy), in *Vatican Council II: The Conciliar and Post Conciliar Documents*, ed. Austin Flannery, rev. ed. (Grand Rapids, MI: Eerdmans, 1992), no. 3.
[10] See ibid., no. 14.

that they be given new vigor to meet present-day circumstances and needs."[11] While this recourse to ancient sources predating the medieval and Tridentine synthesis is, again, well known to scholars of the liturgy, the immediate history after Vatican II was one in which the vast majority of the faithful received the "new Mass" and other revised sacramental rituals under the mistaken impression that the principle of reform was a matter of modernization. People, including many of the clergy, got the point that the liturgy should achieve a "new vigor" in the contemporary context, but the tone was often one of "updating" and adjusting on the surface, rather than a fundamental renewal from depths of "sound tradition."

This brief assessment of the popular reception of the liturgical renewal in these initial decades after the council is by no means intended to be comprehensive but rather seeks to make one basic point. It would seem that the liturgical, and thus ecclesiological, renewal mandated by the council did in its first few decades witness an abandonment of many pious customs formerly practiced by the faithful in relation to the rituals and symbols of the church, as well as realize a general reception of the reformed rites. What seems to have evaded many of the faithful, clergy and laity alike, however, is a practical awareness of the entire enterprise as a recovery and advancement of tradition. That may have proven too great a stretch, if not countercultural, for modern thinking. At least that would seem to be true for the generations who were already adults or who grew up from the time of the council. Vatican II took place in the waning moments of modernity, with its concluding Pastoral Constitution on the Church contextualizing its mission precisely in the "Modern World." The ironies of that historical moment abound and are perhaps captured in all that is symbolized by the year 1968, an era radically questioning authority, tradition, and social conventions.[12]

---

[11] Ibid., no. 4.

[12] Some fifteen years ago David Power argued that the church now practices its liturgy amid "ruins," both the ruins of pre–Vatican II cultural Catholicism and the ruins of a modernity that in the twentieth century realized unprecedented global warfare, economic marginalization of entire peoples, and an increasing threat to the planet as a habitable environment. Noting the increasing disparity between the liturgical vision of Vatican documents and the local dispositions of the faithful, Power argued at the outset of a major book on the Eucharist that the current practice of the church's liturgy is done amid those

At the dawn of the twenty-first century, more than forty years after the conclusion of the council, a further generation of young people has grown up and begun to assume its place in a world taking a rapidly postmodern turn. Traditions are not so much eschewed as eclectically taken up and put aside by young women and men inundated with an endless stream of multimedia sounds and images and accustomed to approaching a broad range of decisions and actions according to the consumerist mentality of the free market.[13] This is a postmodern world of pastiche—of continuously selecting and deciding and rejecting and moving on in all areas of life—not much accounted for in the documents of Vatican II or, for that matter, the subsequent strategies for promoting and reforming the liturgy. And so the church's charge to seek a way forward for the salvific tradition entrusted to us must ask anew: What now are the "present-day circumstances and needs" of the people called to the Gospel? And how can the church's liturgy, with recourse to sound tradition, serve them?

Much of the *modern* reform and renewal of the church and its liturgy has focused on the Mass and, to a secondary extent, the Christian Initiation of Adults, the primary or central sacraments of Eucharist and baptism. The postmodern era, on the other hand, may call for a different locus for promoting and reforming the liturgy for the benefit not only of the faithful but also of the wider world. In a time characterized by fragmentation and non-foundational flux, totalizing corporate systems and marginally functioning supplements to them, ongoing threats of terrorism and far-reaching military industrial complexes, the sacramental rites that may well "speak" to the needs of people and thus promise renewal for the church are those that most explicitly offer healing. The present book is an invitation into how the rites that serve the sick, aging, dying, the dead, as well as those who accompany them, might lead the way in a new quest for tradition, a renewed undertaking and practice of liturgy in postmodern life. It may be that a new traditional ministry of word and sacrament at life's margins promises a strengthening of the church's center, its mission of glorifying God through prophetic and pastoral service to the healing needs of humanity.

---

ruins. See David N. Power, *The Eucharistic Mystery: Revitalizing the Tradition* (New York: Crossroad, 1992), vii–viii, 9–13.

[13] See Vincent J. Miller, *Consuming Religion: Christian Faith and Practice in a Consumer Culture* (New York: Continuum, 2004), 66–72, 154–57.

Index of Names and Subjects

Calhoun, Gerald, 195–96, 198
Calvin, John, 145
cancer, 23, 39n34, 152, 155, 173, 174, 176
Canon Law, 1983 Code of, 185–86
Center for Disease Control, 175
Chauvet, Louis-Marie, 13n22, 17, 20, 111, 116–26, 138, 206–8, 229–31, 245, 260
Chicago Tribune, 238n101
church
    ancient, early, 69, 113, 137–38, 143, 146–50, 241–43, 246–47
    assembled in liturgy, 6, 13, 15, 23, 56, 62–64, 68, 94, 104, 105, 120, 126, 149, 172, 177, 180, 187–89, 215, 226, 228, 241
    hierarchy, leadership, 26–29, 33–35, 127–28, 137, 148, 150, 227
    laity, 25–26, 29–30, 34, 42, 54, 145, 150, 202, 226, 228
    medieval, 19, 143, 242–43
    as sacrament, body of Christ, 15, 31–32, 62, 111, 128, 137, 149, 153, 165, 176, 186
    sexual abuse scandal, 25–30, 33, 42
Clark, Peter, 193, 194
commodification, consumerism, 52–53, 54–55, 77, 118–19, 141, 233–34, 237
communion (*see under* participation)
community, 12, 46, 54–55, 85–87, 95, 97, 121, 140, 147, 159, 177, 181, 188, 229
compassion, solidarity, 36, 70, 113–15, 123, 151n41, 177, 181, 193–94, 198
confirmation, sacrament of, 16n30, 150, 163, 188, 190
Connerton, Paul, 141n38, 189n22
Cooke, Bernard, 11n19, 16n29, 18n34, 30n12, 115, 117n41, 149n35
Cort, John, 237n98

covenant
    in Christ Jesus, 9–10
    God and Israel, 8–9, 103, 247
creation, 4, 7, 14, 104, 149, 234, 237, 244, 246–49
Crossan, John Dominic, 74, 81n50, 82, 87n67, 90
culture, 30, 52–53, 118, 151–52, 203, 211, 225n57, 227
cure, curing (*see also under* healing), 50

Dalmais, Iréné H., 7, 10
Davies, Douglas, 227, 230–40
Davies, Stevan, 80n47
death, 14, 15, 30, 33, 55, 70, 76, 94–95, 104, 144–45, 183, 188–89, 202–6, 216, 232
    deceased person, 200, 210–11, 223, 226, 228, 236–37, 247
    denial, marginalization of, 37, 69, 193, 203, 211, 237, 240, 244
    extreme unction, last rites, 22, 24, 42, 126, 141–46, 151, 185, 196
    hospice, palliative care, 138, 193–95, 203
    meaning, meaningful, 82, 210, 248–49
    mortality, awareness of, 162–63
    process, stages of, 191–200
    reformed rite, Pastoral Care of the Dying, 183–204
        apostolic pardon, plenary indulgence, 191–92
        Viaticum, 135–37, 141, 142, 183–93, 197–98, 201
depression, 28n7, 173, 175, 176, 194, 239
diabetes, 175
disciples, discipleship, 84, 115
disease (*see under* illness)
doctrine, dogma, 52, 109, 112, 124, 144, 151, 166, 185, 206, 244

266

rationality, reason, 37, 66, 67
scientific, technological worldview,
45–48, 73, 75, 82, 108, 130
therapeutic mindset, 74, 81, 235–36
Morrill, Bruce, 16n30, 214n25
Morris, David, 37–44, 67, 74–75, 82,
93–94n77, 151–52, 173
multiple sclerosis, 175
mystery, 7, 10, 11, 12, 50, 113–14, 121,
153, 205, 242

narrative, 55–56, 64, 82, 94–96, 102,
108, 109, 118, 154–58, 183, 202
nature, natural (*see under* body)
New York Times, 26–27, 39n34, 44,
175n87, 234, 238
Newsweek, 44, 48
Nicaea, Council of, 184

obesity, 94n77, 175
O'Malley, Sean, 27, 36
O'Rourke, Kevin, 153n45, 193

pain, 4, 10, 27, 31, 38, 40–41, 55, 66,
117, 172, 192
participation, *koinonia*
communio, Christian community,
12, 98–99, 121, 149, 165
liturgical, 6, 11, 20, 101, 109, 122,
165, 187, 189–90, 228
in the paschal mystery, 21, 185, 187
sharing in God's life, 6, 7, 11, 12,
13–15, 86, 121, 125, 201
paschal mystery
celebration in word and sacrament, 10–11, 13–15, 17, 18, 21,
56, 62–63, 102, 110, 130, 141,
169, 184, 187, 190, 202, 204,
228–29
Christ's death and resurrection, 7,
9, 11, 14, 17, 36–37, 64, 94, 96,
99, 104, 109, 130, 163, 172, 180,
195–96, 221–22, 245

paradox, scandal of cross, 9, 15, 17,
34, 69–71, 116, 125, 249
Passover, 9, 111
source of Christian faith, 9, 17,
36–37, 70, 94, 96, 99, 101, 110,
112, 120, 125, 159, 205, 208
pastoral care (*see* ministry)
Pastoral Care of the Sick (*see under*
anointing, sacrament of the sick)
Paul, apostle, 11–12, 104, 112, 117,
138, 221, 241–44
Pellegrino, Edmund, 151n41
penance, 142–43, 145, 150, 180, 184,
197–98
Peter Lombard, 143
philosophy, 68, 206
Enlightenment, 67, 118, 245n116
hermeneutics, 57n75, 115–20
metaphysics, 18–20, 119, 144
phenomenology, 116–17, 207
Pilch, John, 73–74, 83, 86, 93n77, 95, 97
Pius V, *ordo*, 233
poor, poverty, 11, 64, 78–80, 86n63,
89, 107, 113, 137, 235, 262n12
postmodern, post-modernity, 37–44,
94, 118–19, 149, 152, 173–76, 183,
227, 244, 261–63
power, 30, 34, 35, 39, 49, 52, 55, 64,
71–72, 77, 79–82, 86–90, 95, 98,
112, 124, 147, 165, 169, 244
Power, David, 149–50, 162, 262n12
prayer (*see also under* healing *and* liturgy), 50, 89, 115, 140, 199, 203,
232–33
priest, priesthood
Christian community as, 12–13
clergy, 30, 34, 42, 145, 202, 203, 228,
236
clericalism, 4, 18, 34–36, 56,
127–28, 226
as sacramental celebrant, 4, 16, 20,
108, 124, 143, 150, 162, 167,
190, 191–92, 215n28, 226

purgatory, 244
purity, 78, 85
    holiness, cleanness, 78, 83–84
    impurity, contagion, pollution, 83, 98

Rausch, Thomas, 108n10
Reiser, William, 64n9, 88–89, 95, 112–17
religion, religious
    popular, 46, 48–52, 54–55, 89, 139, 183, 235
    practice, 32, 33, 46, 52–54, 122–23, 200
    and science, 45–48, 108
Remus, Harold, 80, 97, 115
resurrection
    of believers, of the just, 211, 242–43
    bodily, 9–10, 102, 111, 205, 231, 241–49
    Christ's, 9–10, 64, 94, 105, 112–13, 120, 129, 241, 245–46
    doctrine, 206, 237, 241–42
    eternal life, life after death (*see also* immortality), 144, 187, 205, 218, 232, 243–47
    new creation, first fruits, 10, 95, 109, 112, 114, 204, 244
revelation, 9, 11, 17, 20, 69, 70, 94–95, 120–21, 125–31, 190, 202, 205
rite, rites (*see also* liturgy), 4, 110, 151, 158, 180, 202–3
Rite of Christian Initiation of Adults, 23, 178–80
Rodgers, Susan, 50–51
Roman Empire
    Julian, emperor, 137
    occupation of Palestine, 77–79, 90, 113
Rutherford, Richard, 205n2, 206, 208, 223n51

sacrament, sacramental
    character of believers, 16–17, 125, 126, 164–65
    efficacy, power of, 140–41, 144, 162–67, 169, 174, 177, 197
    instrumental, mechanistic approach to, 21, 36, 42, 44, 56, 66, 119, 124, 125, 141, 145, 158, 167, 186, 188, 226
    nature of, 4, 15, 17, 18, 20, 36, 52, 56, 66, 111, 136, 152–53, 187–88, 201
sacred, sacral, 4, 10, 13, 37, 56, 107, 124, 260
sacrifice, 49–51, 54–55
    cultic, liturgical, 9–10, 13, 186–87, 226
    ethical, spiritual, 12–13
saints, 48, 139, 211, 217, 231, 243
Saliers, Don, 200
salvation, 4, 66, 85, 94, 96, 141, 169, 194, 242–43
    history as medium of, 7–8, 10, 15, 17, 20, 71, 80, 96, 106, 108, 111, 115, 122, 148, 247
    redemption, 7, 15, 79, 172
    salus, healing, health, 5, 153, 165, 192
    sanctification, 7, 21, 135, 249
Santos, Audrey, 49–55, 67
Schillebeeckx, Edward, 15–16, 122n48, 123n50
Schmalz, Julia, 55n70
Schmalz, Matthew, 54–55
Schmalzbauer, John, 51n61
Schmemann, Alexander, 101n3
Schneiders, Sandra, 57n75
Scripture
    canon, 64, 121
    lectionary cycle, 65, 179, 202
    proclamation in liturgy, 6, 56, 62, 65, 94, 104, 120, 161, 166, 172, 190, 220–21

worship
  as cultic, ritual action (*see also* liturgy), 8, 35, 56, 79, 85, 108, 122, 202
  as entire Christian life, 6, 8, 13, 202, 249

Wright, N. T., 9n12, 35n20, 67, 70, 90, 98, 111n22, 124n51, 246–47
Wyschogrod, Edith, 238n99

Ziegler, John, 144, 150n37

(specify about bodily brokeness)

Paper ① ~ add'l verbs
② something about grace being bestowed
  ↳ we talk about actual grace (given to move one to God)
  ↳ the individual by means of grace becomes a site of healing.
      ↳ may include a physical ~~cure~~ cure but this isn't polic
  observing
③ the hardening of ↳ we do not determine the effects of God's grace
                other sacraments is imparted
④ connected to many other sacraments is imparted
central
  "saved from one's isolation" is important